DATE DUE	

THE BOOK
of
OUR HERITAGE

Second Volume

ADAR — NISAN

ELIYAHU KITOV *The Book of our Heritage*

The Jewish year
and its days of significance

Translated from the Hebrew
SEFER HA-TODA'AH
by NATHAN BULMAN

REVISED EDITION **

FELDHEIM PUBLISHERS
Jerusalem • New York 1978 / 5738

Revised Edition

ISBN 0 87306 153 5
(3-volume set: 0 87306 151 9)

PHILIPP FELDHEIM, Inc.
96 East Broadway
New York, NY 10002

FELDHEIM PUBLISHERS Ltd.
POB 6525
Jerusalem, Israel

Printed in Israel

CONTENTS

A GUIDE TO OBSERVANCE

INSIGHTS, REASONS, MEANINGS AND ALLUSIONS

Adar

ADAR ❖ MIXED-SEEDS ❖ WHEN ADAR COMES JOY IS IN-
CREASED ❖ THE SEVENTH OF ADAR ❖ LOOKING FORWARD TO
SALVATION ❖ FEAR OF DIVINE JUDGMENT ❖ MIDRASHIC
COMMENTS ON THE BIRTH OF MOSHE ❖ MIDRASHIC COMMENTS
ON THE DAY OF MOSHE RABENU'S DEATH ❖ THE CUSTOMS
OF THE SEVENTH OF ADAR ❖ THE EXTENT OF DIVINE JUDGMENT.

CHAPTER ONE

נֵר לְרַגְלִי דְבָרֶךָ וְאוֹר לִנְתִיבָתִי (תהלים קיט, קה)

ADAR

The month of Adar is the last month of the year counting from Nisan, and is thus referred to in Scripture. Even in the event of a leap year, when a second Adar is added to the regular twelve months, the second Adar is also called the twelfth month. Thus, it is written in Megilat Esther: 'And in the twelfth month, which is the month of Adar;' which, according to Tradition, was the second Adar of a leap year.

Rosh Chodesh Adar always consists of two days. In a year which contains two Adars, Rosh Chodesh of the second Adar also consists of two days; the first Rosh Chodesh day being counted also as the 30th day of the first Adar. In an ordinary year containing only one Adar, the month contains only 29 days, with the subsequent Rosh Chodesh (that of Nisan) consisting always of one day.

WHEN ADAR COMES JOY IS INCREASED

The Sages have said: 'Just as joy is reduced when the month of Av comes, likewise, is joy increased upon the advent of Adar.

'Rav Papa said: Therefore, an Israelite engaged in litigation with a non-Jew, should avoid him during Av, which is a time of ill omen for him; and should make himself available during Adar, which is a fortunate time for him' (Ta'anit 29). For, 'Heaven revolves merit towards a day of merit,' and joy towards a day of joy. And no month is as joyous as Adar; it being so replete with unseen blessing, that the evil of no antisemitic eye can affect its blessing.

When *Haman Harasha* (the evil Haman) wanted to discover through astrology which month would be the most 'vulnerable' one for Israel, he cast lots in order to arrive at his

11

choice of months. The lot fell upon the month of Adar. Therefore, Adar was transformed for the Jews from a month of grief and mourning to one of rejoicing and festivity; their happiness was all the greater. And the month of Adar became the very symbol of joy to them.

THE SEVENTH OF ADAR

The 7th of Adar was the day on which Moshe Rabenu was born, and the day on which he died after a life of 120 years. For God completes the years of the righteous to the day and month. As it is said: 'The number of your days I shall complete' (Shmot 23).

The pious abide by the custom of fasting this day and of saying the special 'Tikun for the seventh of Adar' that is found in the sidur. For the death of the righteous is an atonement, and fasting, repentance and prayer likewise atone for Israel. When both types of atonement occur together, total forgiveness is achieved for the people of Israel.

In a leap year which contains two Adars, this fast is generally observed the second Adar, with some observing the fast the first Adar also.

LOOKING FORWARD TO SALVATION

On the seventh of Adar, everyone should take to heart two concerns, and should resolve to make them part of his constant awareness: Waiting for salvation, and the fear of Divine judgment.

The importance of 'waiting for salvation' is to be learned from the birth of Moshe Rabenu.

The circumstances of Moshe Rabenu's birth were attended by great sorrow. Pharaoh had decreed: 'Every son that is born, you shall cast him into the river.' For three and a third years Pharaoh's officers and all his people lurked in ambush for every pregnant Jewish woman. When her time came to give birth and a son was born, they immediately seized the child and cast him into the river. Every Jewish child emerged from his mother's womb, marked for immediate death, and all Israel, young and old, lived in anguish and despair. When Amram, the greatest of the generation saw his people in such great anguish, he said: 'We strive for naught !' He rose and divorced his wife, so that they might bring no further children into the world. At the time, his wife was already three months pregnant with Moshe. All Israel then also divorced their wives. At that hour, a Holy Spirit rested upon Miriam — who was five years old — and she said: My mother is destined to bear a son who will save Israel ! Her words infused new courage and faith in her father and mother and they remarried, whereupon all the others did likewise. And then the saviour of Israel was born.

And how much anxiety and anguish there were after Moshe's birth! Pharaoh's entire people, men, women, and children, all lurked to capture and destroy him, and behold ! he was cast defenseless into the river.

After he was saved from the river, he faced even greater danger. While he was yet a suckling infant, he fell into the mouths of lions, having been brought to the house of Pharaoh; a house from which relentless anger and destruction emerged against Israel. And Moshe was after all only an infant, who had never known his father, nor recognized his mother, nor saw his people. The wicked could now even raise him to become an enemy of Israel, and to join our earlier enemies. Amram's despair still remained justified: 'We strive for naught !'

Come and see how mighty is the faith of those who look forward to salvation ! Had it not been for Miriam's faith, and the faith of all those others; had Moshe not been born, what would have been the lot of all the world ? For it would have reverted to formlessness and emptiness. Now that he was born — though he was placed between the teeth of lions — he was destined to emerge, to save his people and to illuminate the whole world unto all generations. The wicked themselves would soon be forced to say, because of him, 'The Lord is righteous.'

FEAR OF DIVINE JUDGMENT

Moshe Rabenu was the master of all the prophets. From birth the prophetic spirit rested on him. He brought salvation to Israel, and performed miraculous signs and wonders in Egypt. He split the sea, and paved a road in the Heavens above. He wrestled with angels and received the fiery Torah. He spoke with God face to face and taught Torah to all Israel. He provided them with sustenance for forty years in the wildernss. He waged war with Sichon and Og, and stopped the sun and the moon in their behalf.

But when he committed a minor misdeed at the time of the 'waters-of-dispute,' and the sanctification of God's Name was thereby unintentionally diminished, death was decreed against him, and he was denied entry into the Land of Israel. Neither his own merit, nor all his achievements in behalf of Israel, could protect him against the severity of Divine justice — which is the attribute-of-truth of the Creator.

How great then is the depth of Divine judgment, and how fearful of sin ought a man to be !

MIDRASHIC COMMENTS ON THE BIRTH OF MOSHE

'And a man went from the house of Levi' (Shmot 2): Where did he go ? Rav Yehudah Bar Ravina said: He went by his daughter's advice. We have learned: Amram was the greatest of the generation. When he saw that *Pharaoh Harasha* (the evil Pharaoh) had decreed: 'Every son that is born you shall cast him into the river,' he said: We strive for naught. He rose and divorced his wife. They all rose thereupon, and divorced their wives. His daughter then said to him: Father, your decree is harsher than that of Pharaoh. For Pharaoh has decreed only against the males, while you have decreed against the males and the females. Pharaoh has decreed only in this world. While you have decreed in this world as well as in the world to come. Pharaoh is wicked — it is doubtful whether his decree will endure. You however, are righteous — your decree will certainly endure... He then rose and remarried his wife. Whereupon they all remarried their wives' (Tr. Sotah 12).

'And he took a daughter of Levi:' It is not written, 'And-he-remarried,' but rather, 'And-he-took.' Rav Yehudah Bar Zevina said: He accorded her the treatment of a bride. He set her in a palace, with Miriam and Aharon dancing before them, and the ministering angels saying: 'The mother of the daughters rejoices' (Shmot Raba 1).

'And the woman conceived and bore a son:' Had she not been pregnant with him for three months earlier? Rav Yehudah Bar Zevina said: Her giving birth is compared to her conception. Just as her conceiving was without pain, so was her giving birth' (Tr. Sotah 12).

'And she saw him that he was good.' Rabi Meir said: His name was 'Tov' ('good'). Rabi Yehudah said: He was worthy of prophecy... Others said: He was born circumcised. The Sages said: When Moshe was born, the whole world was filled with light. It is written here, 'and she saw him that he was good.' And elsewhere it is written: 'And God saw the light that it was good' (Bereishit 1. Yalkut Shmot 166).

'Why did she cast him into the river? So that the astrologers might think that he had already been thrown into the water, and would no longer search for him...

'When Moshe was cast into the water it was said: Their saviour has been cast into the water. Immediately the decree was suspended.

'Rav Acha Bar Chanina said: That day was the sixth of Sivan. The ministering angels said before God: Lord of the Universe, shall one who is destined to receive the Torah from Mt. Sinai be smitten by water on this day?

'Shall I go and call for you a nursing woman from among the Hebrews?' Why did Miriam say, 'from-among-the-Hebrews?' Was it then prohibited for Moshe to nurse milk from a non-Jewess ? ... She had brought Moshe to all the Egyptian women for nursing, and he rejected them all. And why did he reject them ? God said: Shall the mouth which is destined to speak with Me, draw nourishment from defilement ?

'Another interpretation: God said: This one is destined to speak with Me. Tomorrow the Egyptian women will say: I am the one who nursed this one, who speaks with the *Shechinah*' (Shmot Raba 1).

MIDRASHIC COMMENTS ON THE DAY OF MOSHE RABENU'S DEATH

'And the Lord said to Moshe, your days have drawn near to death' (Dvarim 31). The Rabis said: It is hard for God to decree death upon the righteous. As it is said: 'The death of his pious ones, is dear in the eyes of the Lord' (Tehilim 116). You may know that this is so, because God should have said to Moshe: 'Behold *you* are to die.' He did not however do so, but rather referred to Moshe's impending death by saying: 'Your days have drawn near to death.'

'And the Lord said to Moshe: Your days have drawn near to death.' Of this it was said: 'If his height shall rise to the heavens, and his head shall reach the clouds ... he shall perish. Those who see, shall say: Where is he ?' (Job 20). Of whom was this verse said ? Of the day of death — to teach us that even if a person makes for himself wings like a bird and rises up to the Heavens — when his time of death arrives, his wings are broken and he falls.

'If his height rises to the heavens:' This refers to Moshe, who rose to the heavens; whose feet trod the clouds; who was like a ministering angel; who spoke to God face to face, and received the Torah from His Hand — when his end arrived, God said to him: 'Behold your days have drawn near to death.'

'When Moshe saw that the decree against him was sealed, he formed a small circle, and stood within it, saying: Lord of the Universe: I will not move from here, till you revoke the decree. He then clad himself in sackcloth and ashes, and stood in prayer and supplication before God, till Heaven and Earth and the order-of-creation trembled. Whereupon they all said: Has it become the will of God to renew His world? A *bat kol* (an echo of a Divine voice) issued and said: It is not yet become the will of God to renew His world ... but, 'In His hand the soul of every living being rests.'

'What did God do then? He proclaimed in every gate of every firmament, that Moshe's prayer was not to be accepted, to be brought before Him, since the decree against him was sealed. When the voice of prayer rose upwards in ever growing strength, God called to the ministering angels: Descend quickly and close the gate of every firmament. For the prayer of Moshe was like a sword which severs and pierces every obstacle. Moshe then said before God: Lord of the Universe, You know how I strove, and how much anguish I knew in behalf of Israel, till they came to have faith in Your Name. how much anguish I knew till I established Torah and mitzvot for them. I thought: Just as I saw their trouble, likewise will I see their good. Now that the good of Israel has arrived, You say to me: You shall not cross over this Jordan river. You then make your Torah untruthful, for it is said there: 'On his day you shall give his wages.' Is this payment for my forty years of labor and toil, till they became a holy and faithful people? God said to him: It is a decree before Me! Said Moshe before God: Lord of the Universe, if I am not to enter alive enable me to enter dead, just as the bones of Yosef were brought in. God answered: Moshe, when Yosef came to Egypt, he did not pretend to be an alien, but said that he was a Hebrew. When you however, came to Midian, you pretended to be a stranger. (The daughters of Yitro said to their father about Moshe: An Egyptian man saved us. Moshe knew and remained silent.)

'Lord of the Universe, if You will not bring me into the Land of Israel, let me remain like the beasts of the field who eat grass, drink water and see the world; let my soul too be like one of them.'

'It is much unto you.'

'Said Moshe: Lord of the Universe ! If not, leave me in this world like a bird who flies in all four directions, gathers its food every day, and at the time of evening returns to its nest. Let my soul too be like one of them.'

'It is much unto you.'

'When Moshe saw that he was not regarded, he went to Heaven and Earth and said to them: Seek mercy for me ! They answered: Instead of seeking mercy in your behalf, we need to seek mercy for ourselves. As it is said: 'For the heavens will decay like smoke, and the earth will wilt like a garment' (Yeshayahu 51).

'He went to the sun and the moon and said to them: Seek mercy in my behalf ! 'Instead of seeking mercy in your behalf, we need to seek mercy for ourselves. As it is said: 'And the moon and the sun will be shamed' (ibid. 24).

'He went to the stars and the constellations and said to them: Seek mercy on my behalf !

'Instead of seeking mercy for you, we need to seek mercy for ourselves. As it is said: 'And the hosts of the heavens will be erased' (ibid. 34).

'He went to the mountains and the valleys and said to them: Seek mercy for me !

'Instead of seeking mercy for you, we need to seek mercy for ourselves. As it is said: 'For the mountains will be uprooted and the valleys will be unsettled' (ibid. 54).

'He went to the sea and said: Seek mercy for me!

'Son of Amram ! Why is today different from other days ? Are you not the son of Amram who came upon me with your staff; who smote me and divided me into twelve pathways without my being able to withstand you, because of the Divine Presence which walked by your right hand. And now what has come upon you ?' When the sea reminded him what he had done in his youth Moshe cried out and said: 'Who will make me like (I was in) the months of old?' (Job 29). When I stood against you, I was a king in the world, and now I prostrate myself, and none regards me.

'He went directly to the 'angel-of-the-inner-chamber,' and said to him: Seek mercy for me, that I might not die!

'My teacher Moshe! What will it avail? I have heard behind the curtain that your prayer will not be heard in this matter.' Moshe placed his hands on his head, cried out and wept: To whom shall I go for mercy?

'That hour God was filled with anger against him, till Moshe said: 'Lord, Lord, God who is merciful and gracious...' (Shmot 34).

'The Holy Spirit was placated. God said to Moshe: Moshe! I have sworn two oaths: One, when they worshipped the golden calf, that I would destroy Israel; the other, that you would die and would not enter the land. The oath which I swore against Israel I annulled because of you, for you said: 'Forgive, I beseech!'· Now you again want to nullify My desire and to confirm yours. You now say, 'Let me cross over, I beseech!' You are holding the rope at both ends. If you wish to confirm My request to cross over into the Land of Israel, then nullify your plea for forgiveness for Israel. And if you wish to confirm My forgiveness unto Israel for the sin of the golden calf, then nullify your desire to cross over into the land.' When Moshe Rabenu heard this, he said: 'Lord of the Universe, let Moshe and a thousand like him perish, but let not the nail of a single Israelite be injured.'

'Moshe said before God: 'Lord of the Universe, the feet which ascended to the heavens; the face which greeted the Divine Presence; the hands which received the Torah from Your hand, shall they lick the dust?'

'Such is the thought which rose before me, and such is the way of the world: Each generation has its teachers, each generation has those who sustain it, and each generation has its leaders. The time has arrived for your disciple Yehoshua to serve.'

'Said he: 'Lord of the Universe, if I am to die because of Yehoshua, I will go and become his disciple.'

'If you wish to do so, go and do it !'

'Moshe rose and entered Yehoshua's doorway. Yehoshua sat, expounding Torah. Moshe stood, bent his height, and placed his hand on his heart. The eyes of Yehoshua failed to see him, so that Moshe might grieve, and accept death.

'All Israel went to Moshe's doorway and asked: 'Where is Moshe Rabenu ?' They were told: 'He went to Yehoshua's dwelling.' They went and found him at the entrance. Yehoshua was seated and Moshe stood. They said to Yehoshua: 'What has come upon you ? Moshe Rabenu stands and you sit ?' When Yehoshua raised his eyes and saw him, he immediately tore his clothes, cried out and wept, saying: 'My Master, my Master ! my Father, my Father !'

'The Israelites said to Moshe: 'Moshe Rabenu, teach us Torah.'

'I have no permission.'

'They said to him: 'We will not leave you.'

A *bat kol* (echo of Divine-voice) emerged: "Learn from Yehoshua.'

'They accepted it upon themselves to sit and learn from the mouth of Yehoshua.

'Yehoshua seated himself at the head, with Moshe on his right hand, and the sons of Aharon to his left. And Yehoshua sat and expounded in the presence of Moshe. At that hour, the 'tradition-of-wisdom' was taken from Moshe and given to Yehoshua.

'They went out to walk, and Moshe walked to the left of Yehoshua. They entered the Tent-of-Meeting, and the Pillar-of-Cloud descended and separated between them. When the Pillar-of-Cloud departed, Moshe approached Yehoshua and said: 'What did the Divine Word say to you ?'

'Said Yehoshua: 'When the Word was revealed to you, did I know what it said ?'

'At that hour Moshe cried out and said: 'One hundred deaths and not one jealousy ! Lord of the Universe, till now I sought life, and now my life is given to you.'

'Rabi Yashiah said: That hour Moshe accorded great honor to Yehoshua in Israel's presence, and a proclamation went forth from him to the entire camp of Israel: Come and hear the words of the new Prophet who is to rise up for us this day ! All Israel went up in honor of Yehoshua. After-wards Moshe ordered a gold throne to be brought; a crown of gems; royal headwear, and a purple garment. Moshe stood and arranged the chairs of the *Sanhedrin*; of the heads of regiments; and the *cohanim*. Moshe then went to Yeho-shua, clothed him, placed the crown upon him, seated him on the golden throne, and appointed a translator to explain his words before all Israel and his teacher Moshe.

'Moshe then said to him (to Yehoshua): 'Come and I will kiss you.' He came and (Moshe) kissed him, wept on his neck and blessed him again: 'May you be in peace and may Israel my people be in peace ! They (Israel) never found satisfaction from me during all my days, because of all the forewarnings and admonitions which I addressed to them.' Moshe began to bless each tribe separately. When he saw that his hour was drawing near, he encompassed them all in one blessing and said: 'I troubled you greatly with Torah and mitzvot ! Forgive me !'

'Said they to him: 'Our Teacher, our Master, forgive us ! We too have angered you greatly, and have caused you great trouble. Forgive us !'

'Said he to them: 'It is forgiven.'

'A *bat kol* emerged and said: 'Moshe, why should you grieve ? You have only an hour left of life in the world.'

'When he saw the measure of the world, the great salva-tions and redemptions which God would in the future bring upon Israel, he said to them: 'Happy are you, Israel: Who is like you, a people whose salvation is in the Lord ?'

'He rose, bade them farewell, wept aloud and said to Israel: 'May I see you in peace at the resurrection of the dead !'

'He went forth from them weeping greatly, and all Israel wept and cried out bitterly. Moshe arose, tore his shirt, removed his coat, and covered his head like a mourner. He entered his tent weeping and said: 'Woe to my feet that did not tread upon the Land of Israel ! Woe to my hands which did not pluck its fruit ! Woe to my throat which did not eat of the fruit of the Land flowing with milk and honey !'

'When Moshe readied himself for death, God said: Who will rise for Me, against those who do evil ? Who will stand for Israel, at the time of My anger ? Who will stand for them, when My sons are engaged in war ? And who will seek mercy for them, when they sin before Me ?

'That hour the angel Metatron came and prostrated himself before God, saying: 'Lord of the Universe, when Moshe was alive he was Yours; in his death, he is Yours.'

'Said God to him: 'I will tell you a parable. To what may the thing be likened ? To a king who had a son. Every day he angered his father, and his father wished to slay him. But his mother saved him. His mother died, and the king wept. His servants said to him: Our Lord the King ! Why do you weep ? Said he to them: I weep not only for my wife, but for her and for my son. Many times have I been angry with him, and wished to slay him, but his mother saved him from my hand. Likewise, did God say to Metatron: Not for Moshe alone do I weep but for him and for Israel. For they have angered Me and I have been angered with them many times, but he stood in the breach before me, to turn back my anger.'

'That hour God said to Gabriel: 'Go and bring the soul of Moshe.'

'Said he: 'Lord of the Universe, how can I see the death of one who weighs against six hundred thousand ?'

'Said God to Michael: 'Go and bring the soul of Moshe.'

'I was his teacher, and he was my disciple. How can I see his death ?'

'God then said to Samael: 'Go and bring the soul of Moshe.' The angel Samael, the chief Accuser, had always waited for the soul of Moshe: 'When will the moment come for Moshe to die, so that I might descend and take his soul from him. When will Michael weep, and my mouth be filled with laughter ?'

'He immediately clothed himself in anger, girded a sword, wrapped himself in brutality, and went towards Moshe. He found him seated and writing the ineffable Divine Name in a scroll. His appearance shone with the glow of the sun, and he was like an angel of God. Immediately he (Samael) was filled with fear; trembling seized him, and he could not open his mouth to speak. Till Moshe said to Samael: 'Wicked one ! What are you doing here ?' Said he: 'I have come to take your soul.'

'Who sent you ?'

'He Who created every creature.'

'Go from here, for I wish to praise God 'I shall not die, but I shall live, and I shall recount the deeds of God' (Tehilim 118).

'Moshe, why are you haughty ? He has those who can praise Him — 'The heavens declare the glory of God' (Tehilim 19).

'Said Moshe to him: 'I will silence them, and praise Him — 'Hear you heavens, and I shall speak, and let the earth hear the words of my mouth' (Dvarim 32).

'The souls of all the world's inhabitants are handed over to me.'

'Said Moshe to him: 'I have more power than all the world's inhabitants.'

'And what is your strength ?'

'I am the son of Amram who prophesized at the age of three, that I was destined to receive the Torah through flames of fire. I entered the palace of the King and removed the crown from his head (Pharaoh). When I was eighty I performed signs and wonders in Egypt and brought forth six hundred thousand before the eyes of all Egypt. I split the sea into twelve segments and rose to trod a path in the Heavens. I engaged in war with the angels, vanquished the Heavenly Hosts and revealed their secrets to Man. I spoke face to face with God, received a fiery Torah from His right hand and taught it to Israel. I waged war with Sichon and Og, two of the mightiest among the nations of the world and smote them unto death with a staff in my hand. I caused the sun and the moon to stop in their heights. Is there anyone among the world's inhabitants who can do the same ? Go and flee from me. I will not give you my soul !'

'Samael returned and brought back word to God. God (again) said to him : 'Go and bring the soul of Moshe.' Samael drew his sword from its sheath, went and stood over Moshe. Immediately Moshe was filled with anger against him. He took the staff of God in his hand, on which the ineffable Name was engraved and struck Samael with all his strength, till he fled. Moshe pursued him with the Divine Name, and blinded his eyes.

'A *bat kol* emerged and said : 'The moment has come for you to depart from the world.' He answered : 'Blessed is His Name : He lives and endures for eternity !'

'He said to Israel : 'I ask of you, when you enter the land, remember me and my bones and say : Woe for the son of Amram who ran before us like a horse, and whose bones fell in the wilderness.'

'A *bat kol* emerged and said : 'Within half a minute you are to depart from the world.' He lifted his two arms, and said to Israel : 'See the end of one of flesh and blood !'

'At that hour Moshe rose, sanctified himself like an angel,

and God descended from the highest heavens to take Moshe's soul. Three angels were with him: Michael, Gabriel and Zagzael. Michael spread Moshe's bed, Gabriel spread a precious white linen cloth under his head, and Zagzael placed one under his feet. Michael stood on one side and Gabriel on the other.

'God said to Moshe: 'Moshe, close your eyes.' He closed his eyes. 'Place your hands on your breast.' He placed his hands on his breast. 'Bring your feet together.' He brought his feet together.

'At that hour God called to the soul of Moshe, saying to her: 'My daughter, I have assigned one hundred and twenty years for you in the body of Moshe.' Your time has now come to depart. Emerge, do not delay!'

'She said to Him: 'Lord of the Universe, I know that you are the God of all spirits, and the Lord of all souls. You created me and you put me in the body of Moshe for one hundred and twenty years. Is there at present a purer body in the world than the body of Moshe? I love him, and do not wish to depart from him.'

'God said to her: 'Emerge, and I will raise you to the highest heavens, and seat you beneath the Throne of My Glory, near the angels.'

'At that hour God kissed Moshe and took his soul with a kiss.

'The Holy Spirit wept and said: 'And there never again rose a Prophet in Israel like Moshe' (Dvarim 34).

'The Heavens wept, saying: 'The pious man has perished from the earth' (Michah 7).

'The earth wept and said: 'And there is none (any longer) among men, who is upright' (ibid.).

'The ministering angels wept and said: 'The righteousness of the Lord, did he do' (Dvarim 33).

'Israel wept and said: 'And his judgments were with Israel' (ibid.).

'These and those said: 'Let him go in peace, let him rest in his abode !' (Yeshayahu 57. Dvarim Raba 7, 11; Yalkut Shimony Vayelech; Midrash Tanchuma; Chronicles of Moshe Rabenu).

'And He buried him in the valley' (Dvarim 34): How did Moshe merit that God should be engaged with him (in his burial)? When Israel was engaged in gathering plunder (in Egypt), he went about the city for three days and three nights, to find the coffin of Yosef, but did not find it. After he had exerted himself greatly, Sarach, the daughter of Asher, met him, and said to him: 'Our teacher Moshe, why do you exert yourself so ?'

'He answered: To seek the coffin of Yosef — but I cannot find it.'

'She said to him: 'Come with me.'

'She led him to the river Nile, and told him: 'In this place they made an ark of lead weighing five hundred *kikar*. They placed him (Yosef) in it and sealed it, and then threw it into the river — the magicians saying to Pharaoh: If it is your will that this people should never depart from your hands, see to it that Yosef's bones may not be found. They will never depart from here, for he made them swear thus.'

'Immediately, Moshe stood by the river and said: 'Yosef ! Yosef ! You know the oath which you placed upon Israel: 'He-shall-surely-remember.' Accord honor to the God of Israel and do not restrain Israel's redemption. You have good deeds to your merit. Seek mercy before your Creator and come up from the depths !'

'Immediately, his coffin rose upwards, and it came up from the depths whole. He took it on his shoulder and carried it, while all Israel followed him, laden with their silver and gold.

'God said to him: Though your lovingkindness may be a small matter in your eyes — in My eyes it is great — that you showed no regard for silver and gold. I, myself, will therefore also ascend to show lovingkindness towards you, at the time of your departure from the world' (Yalkut, end of Vezot Habrachah).

THE CUSTOMS OF THE SEVENTH OF ADAR

It is customary in many Jewish communities for the *Chevrah Kadisha* (burial society) to observe the seventh of Adar as a day of gathering for all members of the *Chevra*. On the seventh of Adar they hold a festive banquet, in which the entire community participates. *Gaba'im* (officials) are appointed, and regulations are adopted for the coming year.

The reason for this custom reflects praise upon Israel, and upon those who are engaged in the practice of mitzvot. Men of all occupations rejoice when their work increases, and are saddened when their work diminishes. In the case of the *Chevrah Kadisha*, though its members faithfully practice lovingkindness with the dead and the living, they never rejoice in their work. When do they rejoice ? When their work ceases.

On the seventh of Adar their work ceased. For upon the death of Moshe Rabenu no creature was engaged in his burial, except God in His Glory alone.

Another reason : It also happens that the seventh of Adar never falls on Shabat.

THE EXTENT OF DIVINE JUDGMENT

'Come and see how exacting and precise God is towards the righteous, and how grave a curse spoken by a Sage is. When Israel sinned with the golden calf, Divine wrath would have befallen them had it not been for the plea for Mercy which Moshe, God's elect, spoke before the Lord. With total disregard for himself, he said : 'And now if you forebear their sin — and if not — erase me, I beseech, from your book which you have written' (Shmot 33).

'In the Midrash it was stated, that we may learn from Moshe Rabenu that even a conditional curse has an effect. For Moshe Rabenu said : 'Erase me' — and though Israel was forgiven for the sin of the golden calf, his name was nevertheless erased from the *sidra Tetzaveh.*' (Moshe's name is unmentioned in *Tetzaveh.*) — (Rabenu Bechayey).

Why was Moshe Rabenu's name 'erased' particularly from the sidra of *Tetzaveh* ? Most years, *Tetzaveh* is read during the week in which the seventh of Adar, the day of Moshe Rabenu's death, falls (The Gaon of Vilna).

Adar REMEMBER WHAT AMALEK DID TO YOU

PARSHAT ZACHOR ❖ AMALEK ❖ AMALEK'S HATRED FOR

ISRAEL ❖ THE FIRST ONES ❖ AND AMALEK CAME ❖ THE FIRST

OF NATIONS ❖ THE POWER OF AMALEK ❖ REFIDIM ❖ TESTING

AND QUARRELLING ❖ IDOLATRY IN THE CAMP ❖ REMEMBER

WHAT AMALEK DID TO YOU ❖ AND IT SHALL BE WHEN THE

LORD WILL GIVE REST ❖ A COMMAND-HATE ❖ FROM THE

TEACHINGS OF THE SAGES ❖ THE DAY OF TURYANUS.

CHAPTER TWO

The Shabat which precedes Purim, two Torah scrolls are taken from the ark; in one the regular *sidra* of the week is read, and seven are called to the Torah; and in the other *maftir* is read — 'Remember what Amalek did to you' (Dvarim 25). Because of this reading, it is called, *Shabat zachor* (remember). The Prophetic portion also deals with Amalek.

It is a positive *mitzvah* in the Torah — upon all Israel — to hate Amalek and his descendants; and to orally recall his iniquity. We are to tell our children in each generation what he did to us, upon our departure from Egypt. This mitzvah will be fulfilled completely, only when we shall have caused his memory to perish, and his name to be erased from the world, together with the slightest remnant of anything that bears his name. It is written in the Torah: 'Remember what Amalek did to you on the way, upon your departure from Egypt'... 'You shall erase the memory of Amalek from beneath the heavens, you shall not forget.' Upon which the Sages have expounded: 'Remember,' orally — 'You shall not forget,' at heart.

For the purpose of fulfillment of this commandment, the Sages have prescribed the public reading of this passage from a Torah scroll, once every year, on the Shabat which precedes Purim — so that the 'wiping-out' of Amalek might 'be adjacent' to the 'wiping-out-of-Haman;' the latter being a descendant of Amalek.

Although this passage is read yearly, in the order of the weekly Torah readings, in the *sidra* of *Ki Tetzeh* (which we read towards the end of the summer), it is nevertheless obligatory for us to read this passage separately in its prescribed time before Purim; in fulfillment of the Torah's

31

commandment to remember the hatred of Amalek and to erase his memory.

Since the reading of *parshat zachor* in its designated time is a *mitzvat aseh* (a positive Torah commandment), the reader must intend to enable the congregation to fulfill the *mitzvah* through hearing his reading, and the congregation is required to have the intention of fulfilling the mitzvah through hearing the Reader. (As if they were reading it themselves.)

Some authorities say that if one fails to hear *parshat zachor*, he fulfills his obligation through hearing the prescribed Torah reading on Purim: ('And Amalek came').

A minor who has not yet reached the age of Bar-Mitzvah should not be called to the Torah for maftir on parshat zachor. Nor should he read the parshah for others. For since he is free of the obligation of mitzvot, he cannot enable others to fulfill their obligation through him. Some abide by the stringent ruling of not calling a minor to *maftir* during all the four special parshiyot.

The coming of the women to the synagogue to hear the reading of *zachor*, is only a custom and, is not a formal requirement of the *din*. The mitzvah of *zachor* was addressed to the males, for the obligation of waging war to wipe out the seed of Amalek rests upon them alone. And since women are not subject to the commandment to wage war, they are also not subject to the commandment of 'remembrance.' Some of the authorities hold however, that it is obligatory upon the women to hear this Reading, as a formal requirement of the *din*, since the above distinction between men and women only applies to 'voluntary war,' but not to a commanded war.'

If a person is ill and unable to leave his home, or if he is imprisoned, it is prohibited to remove a Torah scroll from the synagogue for him to hear the Torah read. In the case of Shabat zachor, however, since the reading of *zachor* is a Torah-commandment it is permissible to move the Torah scroll for his sake. Some even hold that this *din* applies on *Shabat parah* as well.

AMALEK

The first Amalek was a grandson of Esav. His father was Esav's eldest son, Elifaz. His mother was Timna, a daughter of one of the dukes of Seir, who was a concubine to Elifaz. Tradition states that Timna was an illegitimate daughter. When Timna grew up she wanted to cleave to the seed of Avraham, because of their renown among the neighboring peoples. She came to Ya'akov and he would not accept her because of her illegitimacy. Whereupon she came to Elifaz — her own father — and became a concubine to him. Her son Amalek was therefore an illegitimate son of an illegitimate mother. Elifaz grew up in the care of Itzchak and was circumcised at the age of eight days. For while Itzchak still lived, Esav circumcised his children, and all the children born in his household. Elifaz himself still retained a residue of decency. Amalek, his son, however, was born after the death of Itzchak, and grew up in the care of Esav, from whom he inherited an abiding hatred to Ya'akov and his descendants.

'Esav said to Amalek : 'How I have exerted myself to kill Ya'akov, but I have not succeeded ! Resolve to exact vengeance for me !'

'Said Amalek : 'How can I hope to prevail against him ?'

'Let this tradition be in your hand. When you see them (Ya'akov's descendants) commit some misdeed, leap upon them !' (Yalkut Chukat 764).

The first Amalek lived long. He saw Ya'akov and his sons go down to Egypt, and he saw the departure of the children of Israel from Egypt two hundred and ten years later. When he saw them in bondage in Egypt, he said in his heart : The vengeance of my grandfather is already attained. They will never emerge from their bondage. And if they will, I

will meet them on the way like a predatory bear and annihilate
them.

His descendants were fruitful and increased like thorns in
the field and became a people, and Amalek planted in their
hearts a relentless hatred towards Israel, unto death. When
Amalek saw the Israelites marching from Egypt, his hatred
erupted like a flame. He took his people and set an ambush
for Israel on the way. Israel was tired and weary and Amalek
leaped upon them from ambush: 'And Amalek came.'

AMALEK'S HATRED FOR ISRAEL

The hatred which Amalek has for Israel is not comparable
to the hatred felt by all other anti-Semites. The hatred of
other anti-Semites subsides at times. Amalek's hatred never
subsides, and as long as he exists he constantly plans only our
destruction. Our other enemies, accept bribes and are placated. No bribe in the world is sufficient to placate him. When
other nations rose against Israel, and saw the hand of God
inflicting penalty upon them, they at times experienced awe
and fear, and submitted. In the case of Amalek, even the
sight of God's mighty wonders in behalf of Israel, and the
vengeance He exacted from His people's enemies; even the
knowledge that his attack against Israel would bring him
to grief and destruction, could not deter him. For the very
essence of Amalek is hatred of Israel; without prospect of
self gain; hatred without cause or motive; hatred for the
sake of hatred alone; a hatred which never ceases.

When our father Avraham's sun began to shine, and all
the world's peoples saw that God's name was upon him, they
viewed him as the source of their blessing, and regarded
him as a 'prince of God' in their midst. Avraham's greatness
consisted of his denial of idolatry, and of his becoming a
servant to God alone. He instructed his sons and household
to observe the way of the Lord, to do righteousness and
justice. Ishmael was born from him, and refused to go in
the ways of his father, but he laid no claim to Avraham's

greatness, and left Avraham's spiritual inheritance to Itzchak his brother. Esav was born from Itzchak, and committed all manner of abominations, including robbery, murder and adultery, but nevertheless wanted to inherit both worlds. When God ordained the blessing for Ya'akov alone — who was wholehearted, and all whose days reflected holiness and human love — Esav saw that his designs upon the birthright and the blessings were of no avail, and departed to the land of Seir. He did not however despair of regaining his father's inheritance. And he hated Ya'akov with the zeal of eternal hatred.

When Esav saw that Ya'akov was beyond the reach of his hand, he bade his sons to exact vengeance for him. Some of his sons despaired of being able to do so, for they said: We shall never prevail against this one, over whom Divine protection constantly hovers. Our own possessions are sufficient for us, and we do not want the inheritance of the house of Avraham or Itzchak. We want neither the obligations of that inheritance, nor its merit. And they drew far away from the path of Avraham and Itzchak, and walked on a path of ever growing evil. One abominable branch of Esav rose — one who came himself from a poisoned source of illegitimacy and evil — and he said to his grandfather Esav: I do not fear the Lord. I feel no shame over your deeds, or over my deeds. I will accord no honor to the deeds of the righteous. I will deride them and I will deride their conduct. Greatness and strength are mine. I will go out to wage war against your brother's sons, who have inherited your greatness. I will wage war against them openly and in ambush. I will kill among them those who will fall behind, and I will cut down their great — till I annihilate them.

As long as there remained within Esav and his sons, a residue of the decency that had adhered to them in the house of Avraham and Itzchak, they did not dare to seek to destroy all that was good in the world. When Amalek was

35

born — the very incarnation of evil — immediately, 'Amalek came and waged war with Israel.'

Therefore, in the future all the nations of the world are destined to forsake their wrongdoing and to seek protection under the wings of the Divine Presence. Amalek however, will never repent. He will pursue his path of evil to the very end — till he perishes totally. 'For there is a hand on the throne of God, a war unto the Lord with Amalek from generation to generation' (Shmot 17).

THE FIRST OF NATIONS

Bilaam was a prophet unto the nations, and it is written of him that, 'he saw Amalek ... and he said : The first of nations is Amalek and in the end he will perish.' Was then Amalek the 'first of the nations ?' Was he not preceded by the seventy nations who were descended from Shem, Cham, and Yefet. The verse is however understood thus : 'The first of those to wage war against Israel was Amalek.' At the time of Israel's departure from Egypt, Amalek was the first nation to wage war against Israel. None of the other nations dared to do so before his example. 'The peoples heard, they trembled, fear seized the inhabitants of Philistia, the dukes of Edom were confused, the mighty ones of Moab seized with shuddering. All the inhabitants of Canaan melted. Awe and fear fell upon them; when Your arm grew great, they became stilled like a rock' (Shmot 15).

When the Lord made manifest His signs and wonders in the land of Egypt;

When He split the sea, and all the world knew that it was God who had performed wonders for Israel, His children;

When His name became great in the world, and all the corruption and the wrong which had been committed by the world's inhabitants, were about to be rectified;

When God was to reveal himself at Mt. Sinai and to give the Torah to Israel, thereby making them a kingdom of *cohanim* for all the other kingdoms of the earth;

When they were about to enter the chosen land, in order to make of it a dwelling place for the Divine Presence — a place to which all the nations would stream in quest of Divine guidance;

When the pride of the mighty kings of the nations, with Pharaoh at their head, was broken, and the inhabitants of Philistia and Canaan were reconciled to return the land of Avraham to the rightful owners, his descendants;

When all the world was ready to join in Israel's song, 'The Lord shall reign unto eternity;'

What did Amalek do at that hour?

'And Amalek came and waged war with Israel in Refidim.'

Are you then stronger than Pharaoh, than Sichon and Og, than the 31 kings of Canaan, than your brothers the Dukes of Edom, than your relatives the mighty ones of Moab?

Why did you alone embark on war at a time when those others submitted? Did Israel ever enter your domain in the past, or are they planning to do so on the morrow? Are they perhaps now passing through your land? Are there not 400 *Parsah* separating you from them, in addition to five other nations, who dwell between your land and this great awesome wilderness, bereft of water or bread?

Your serpent-like character has brought you to this. You are prepared even to be uprooted from the world, if only you might succeed in extinguishing the flame of the awareness of God's wonders which has encompassed Israel; if only you might succeed in casting confusion and doubt in the hearts of the nations and of Israel.

You too Israel — reply to him measure for measure! He came to destroy and hate. You have no other recourse but to respond with like hate. 'You shall surely erase the memory of Amalek from underneath the heavens — you shall not forget!'

THE FIRST ONES

Both Israel and Amalek are called 'first': Israel is called 'first', as it is said, 'Israel is holy unto the Lord, the first of His produce' (Irmeyahu 2). By contrast Amalek is also 'the first of nations.'

The Sages have said: 'First' refers to *trumah* (literally: heave-offering). The essence of any object is 'first' to it; and hence may be called its *trumah*. And just as there is trumah on the 'side of holiness,' likewise, is there trumah on the 'side of defilement.'

The essence of all that is pure and holy in God's creation is to be found in Israel. The essence of the defilement cast into the world by the *nachash hakadmoni* (the primordial serpent), is personified by Amalek. Amalek too is therefore called 'first.' On one side Israel stands; the 'root of holiness.' On the other side Amalek stands, as the 'root of defilement.' All the remaining nations of the world stand between the two extremes. When the hand of Israel falls low, Amalek inclines the world towards his extremes, and causes it to submerge in defilement and evil; nevertheless, he remains unable to erase the name of Israel. In the future, when the hand of Israel will be mighty, the entire world will be inclined to the side of good: Amalek alone — whose very root is evil, will lose its capacity to exist, and his name will be erased from beneath the heavens.

'AND AMALEK CAME'

The Sages have said: 'Amalek' in this verse refers literally to the first Amalek — to Amalek, the son of Elifaz, who grew up in the care of his grandfather Esav. He was still alive then, and came at the head of his people to wage war against Israel.

'And Amalek came:' He came with a stratagem. He gathered the nations of the world and said to them: Come and help me against Israel! They said: We are incapable of

standing against them. For Pharaoh opposed them and he
and his army were drowned in the sea. How then shall we
stand against them ? Said he: I will advise you as to what
you may do: If they should vanquish me — flee. If not,
come and help me against Israel' (Yalkut Beshalach 262).

'It is said of Esav: 'And he went to a land, because of
Ya'akov his brother' (Breishit 36). He went there because
of the bill of debt which Itzchak's descendants were required
to pay: ('For your children shall be strangers in a land not
theirs for 400 years.')

'He said: I will depart from here. I have no part either
in the gift of this land to Itzchak's children, or in the payment of this debt. His departure from the land was further
motivated by the shame he felt for having sold his birthright to Ya'akov. His grandson Amalek, seeking vengeance
in his behalf — waited till Israel emerged from Egypt and
their 'bill of debt' had been paid, and then: 'Amalek came'
(Chizkuni Beshalach).

What did Amalek do to them ? He came to the chamber
of the Egyptian archives. He took the records on which the
names of the tribes were inscribed; he came and stayed outside the cloud (which providentially accompanied Israel in
its wanderings) and called out: Reuven ! Shimon ! We are
your brothers; come out ! We wish to do business with you.
And whenever one of them would emerge, he would be slain'
(Yalkut Tetze 938).

'From eternity Amalek was a scourge to Israel:

'When Israel came to Refidim prior to the giving of the
Torah and they said: 'Is the Lord in our midst or not ? —
immediately, 'Amalek came.'

'At the time of the sending of the spies — 'and Amalek
descended...and smote them till Chormah !' — When Amalek heard that Aharon had died, and the protective 'clouds
of glory' had departed, he immediately sought to inflict harm
upon Israel.

'In later generations, the Babylonians came to destroy Israel, Amalek thought at heart: If Israel prevails, I will say: 'I have come to help you.' If Babylonia will emerge victorious, I will turn upon Israel and slay them' (Yalkut Chukat 864).

THE POWER OF AMALEK

What was the source of Amalek's power against the people of Israel, while the latter were under the protection of the Divine Presence?

The Sages say: 'And he waged war with Israel in Refidim.' — 'Can the rush shoot up without mire? Can the reed-grass grow without water?' (Job 8). Likewise, can Israel endure if it is not engaged in the study of Torah? When they forsook the words of the Torah, the enemy came upon them. For the enemy comes only because of sin and transgression' (Yalkut Beshalach 262).

REFIDIM

Amalek was ever loyal to the testament of his grandfather Esav: 'Whenever you see them stumble, leap upon them.'

When the people of Israel came up from the sea and went out to the wilderness of Shur, they knew that they were drawing near to the mountain of God in order to receive the Torah. They were about to become 'kingdom of *cohanim*' and a holy people, destined to live not on bread alone but by God's word. After they crossed the Red Sea, they came to the wilderness of Shur, and they journeyed in the wilderness for three days without water. They did not complain nor murmur, and retained their faithfulness and trust in God. They knew that the Torah they were about to receive could only be acquired through travail; that through the casting away of sensual pleasure in order to experience the joy of God, they would merit, in the end, even the pleasures of this world. The entire people ... almost 3 million men, women, and children stood in ready anticipation of receiving the Torah, and of bearing its yoke.

When they came to Marah and found water there, they faced a new test. 'And they were unable to drink the water from Marah because the waters were bitter.' Their patience snapped 'and the people complained to Moshe.' 'The people' — not its sages or leaders. And then the people expressed only a moderate complaint: 'What shall we drink ?'

They passed the first crisis. 'And they came to Elim, and there, there were twelve springs of water and seventy palm trees, and they encamped there upon the waters.' As long as some of the bread they took along on the way out of Egypt was still left, they were unconcerned over bread. Since however they had already suffered thirst for three days, they rejoiced greatly over finding the twelve springs in Elim. 'And they encamped upon the waters.'

After satiating themselves completely with the waters of Elim, they journeyed to the Wilderness-of-Sinai. By now they no longer had any remaining bread. There were no waters either in Sinai, but they still had some remaining water from Elim. Now they complained, not over water, but over bread for their children. How could an entire people live without bread even a single day ? 'In the end,' they thought, 'He will surely give us bread. Why should He impose hunger upon us first almost unto death ? If the Torah will demand of us this kind of life constantly, it is extremely doubtful whether the entire people will be capable of enduring it.' 'And the entire community of Israel murmured against Moshe and Aharon in the wilderness.'

In the first test in the Wilderness-of-Shur, all Israel passed the test. When the second test occurred in Marah, the common people complained, but their Sages and leaders remained steadfast. When the third test occurred, the faith of the entire people was 'broken.' Indeed, their situation was beyond endurance. If tests such as these were destined for them repeatedly, it was clear that such a path was too difficult for an entire people to walk in.

And yet their request and their complaints were still proper ones, for they asked only bread and water.

The *Manna* descended and their daily bread was given to them — the people felt reassured, and were pacified. They were ready to receive the Torah provided daily sustenance would be given them. But once again they were left without water.

The water they had brought from Elim was also gone. 'And they camped in Refidim, and there was no water for the people to drink.' Immediately, 'and the people quarrelled with Moshe.' Previously they had all — great and small — come to only complain against Moshe. Now they began to quarrel.

Their tests seemed beyond endurance. The bread of affliction without water — bitter water — water by measure without bread, bread without water. Whenever one was given, the other was taken away. And when the other was given, the first was taken away. Is this to be the way of the Torah ?

'And they encamped in Refidim:' Their hands became weak (Refidim — *rafu yadayim*, the hands became weak). Their hands became too weak for holding the Torah. There were now many among the people who despaired of ever being able to bear the yoke of Torah under such harsh conditions.

TESTING AND QUARELLING

'And he called the name of the place 'testing and quarrelling,' over the quarrelling of the children of Israel and their testing of the Lord, saying: Is the Lord in our midst, or not ?'

How are we to understand this question on the part of the people for whom God had performed so many mighty miracles ?

'What quarrelling occurred there ?

'Rabi Yehudah said, the people of Israel said: If He is the Master over all existence, just as He is our Master we shall serve Him. But if not, we shall rebel against Him.

'Rabi Nechemiah said: If He provides sustenance for us like a king who dwells in a country... we shall serve Him. But if not, we shall rebel against Him. The Rabis said: If He shows that He knows our inner thoughts, we shall serve Him. If not, we shall rebel against Him.

'God said to them: You wished to examine Me — let the evil one come and examine you! Immediately, 'and Amalek came' (Shmot Raba 26).

According to Rabi Yehudah Israel was prepared to accept the entire yoke of Torah, however heavy it might be, provided that God's conduct towards them should not be arbitrarily imposed upon them alone, but should be His manner towards all other peoples.

Rabi Nechemiah added to his words. Israel was prepared to live differently than any other people in the sense that they were willing to give up all personal possession for the sake of receiving their sustenance from their King — provided that they would not be required to plead for their food every morning and every hour.

The Rabis go still further. They hold that Israel said as follows: However difficult our lives may be; however differently we might be called upon to live than all other nations, we are prepared to do and to obey. Even if we shall be required to plead for our food every single hour — we are still prepared to do and to obey. We ask only one thing, — that our lack might not be so grave as to bring us near to loss of life. For then no person can be expected to retain control over himself, and he must come to quarrelling and complaining, as is the case with us today. If He will know our needs immediately as we feel them in our hearts, and will fulfill them for us, we will do and obey and serve Him constantly. If however, we will be brought to the point of crying out unto death for the fulfillment of our needs, we will be unable to endure such a condition, and in the end we will rebel against Him.

They did not rebel out of disloyalty. They rather felt too weak to be able to abide by the conditions of life which the acceptance of the Torah seemed to impose upon them. And they posed as a condition for accepting the Torah that they might be assured of being able to abide by it.

God then said: You make conditions with Me, and seek to investigate Me lest I ask something of you that is beyond your capacity. Let Amalek come and examine whether you have followed Me in whatever was within your power.

IDOLATRY IN THE CAMP

Your going after Me in the wilderness in an unknown land is a temporary labor, till your new Torah is lastingly implanted within you. Afterwards you shall enter the land which is My palace, and you shall plow, sow and reap; each in their proper time. I shall then bestow greater blessing upon you, than upon any other people. However, the labor of removing from your midst all traces of paganism and of serving God alone, is a labor both for the time and for generations. Have you already removed the alien gods from your midst? Have you all entered under My wings? Have you broken down all your idols? Let Amalek come and examine you. If you are wholehearted with Me, you need not fear him. If there is among you any man or woman whose soul still cleaves to the Egyptian gods and their execrations, let them come and save you from the hands of Amalek. Immediately, 'and Amalek came... and he ambushed among you all those who fell behind you, in weakness.' 'And he ambushed among you' — said Rav Nachman: Whomever the 'protective cloud' cast out, was caught by Amalek. The Rabis said: The tribe of Dan was cast out by the cloud because they all worshipped idols. The idol of Michah was in their midst, and there were many among them who had not resolved wholeheartedly to serve God alone.

It was therefore as if God said to them: Over what you are capable of doing, but do not do, I am patient. Over what

I am capable of doing, you are impatient. Let Amalek come and examine you ! Amalek was hence like a fly, who locates any place on which a wound has been inflicted, and seeks to draw blood from it.

Sin and transgression — these are the strength of Amalek. He is a source of sin, and from him the resultant calamity comes. For this is the way of Satan (the Accuser). First he poses a stumbling block, then he ascends before God to condemn, then he descends to destroy.

REMEMBER WHAT AMALEK DID TO YOU

'The Rabis said : '... *asher karsha*' — 'how he met you' and also : 'how he chilled you.' Amalek chilled the people of Israel before the nations of the world. The matter may be likened to a boiling basin which no one could enter. Finally an evil person came and jumped into it; though he was scalded, he nevertheless chilled the basin for others. Likewise, when Israel emerged from Egypt, dread befell all the nations. As it is said : 'The Dukes of Edom were confounded... dread and fear befell them...' When Amalek came and engaged them — though he took his (punishment) at their hands — he chilled them before the nations' (Yalkut Tetze 938).

Before the sun of our father Avraham began to shine, the entire world was desolate. It was as if the lamp of the world had been extinguished, and its destiny was sealed for submergence in the abyss of evil and paganism.

Avraham came and fired a coal. His children came after him and fanned the coal till a bright, warm fire began to rise from the coal. Israel emerged from Egypt attended by a miraculous revelation of the Divine Presence. All Israel, all Egypt, all the world's peoples then knew that the Lord alone rules and there is none beside Him. All existence waited expectantly for the exalted stand of God's revelation at Sinai, and His speaking to man. Man's pride was about to be humbled, and God alone would remain exalted. The idols were about to vanish. God had revealed himself to His people and was about to designate them as His emissaries to Mankind. Would there still be found a people who would say: 'Who is the Lord that I should hear His voice ?' Amalek, the *rasha*, (wicked) then came and undid everything. He leaped into the fire — a fire feared by everyone — and was burned, but he also chilled it a bit. What would all the nations now say ? The war will continue. We have submitted only for the hour. The world's *tikun* (rectification) is again postponed for many days, till the Messianic End of Days. As for Israel —though Amalek was scalded as a result of his attack upon them, he nevertheless chilled their fire, and the strength of their faith. The war still continues. Fear of men of flesh and blood have not yet been replaced by reverence for God's majesty. Those who fell behind, he ambushed; in the hearts of the weak he aroused fear; within the strong he caused anxiety. When their feet later stood beneath Mt. Sinai, something was already missing of their wholeheartedness. This slight failing later left its mark on many, grave actions. Israel's *tikun* and the restoration of the world to its originally intended character, were postponed. It is now more than 3000 years since then, and the final redemption has not yet come. The world still hovers over the abyss — such was the effect of that winding serpent, Amalek the *rasha*, may his name and memory be blotted out.

'AND IT SHALL BE WHEN THE LORD WILL GIVE YOU REST'

Is anything impossible for Him who performs great acts beyond count or measure ? Was He not capable of subjugating Amalek too, and of paralyzing him like a stone ?

There is however a matter of deep import here. The subjugation of the nations of the world before God, is a source of merit to them. Egypt, Philistia, the mighty ones of Moab — all bent their height before the majesty of God, and were instruments, whether they wanted it or not, for the revelation of God's Sovereignty over the world. The merit that is thereby theirs, will enable them to have a portion in the Messianic fulfillment at the End of Days. Amalek, however, is totally bereft of good. It is not for him to have a share in acknowledging God's sovereignty. He remains totally bereft of fear of God, in order to be eternally distant from Him.

'And it shall be when the Lord your God will give you rest from all your enemies about you,' when there shall no longer be any fear of war; when the fear of Amalek will also vanish, and nothing will be lacking in the world, to prevent its reverent submission before God — then, 'you shall wipe out the memory of Amalek from underneath the heavens;' as if he had never existed in the world. The world is to be perfected and rectified like a new creation — a world without Amalek.

A COMMAND-HATE

Till that day when God will grant us rest from all our enemies and will transform all our enemies into friends, we have no relation of hate towards any people, other than with Amalek alone. This Torah which consists wholly of lovingkindness, and compassion, has commanded us to hate Amalek and to wage war against him, collectively and individually. We are to wage against the filth and poison which he has injected within all the nations; against the defilement which he injected even among us — and whose results are, that we too are vulnerable to the attraction of evil.

Ours is a war of annihilation against Amalek; not a war of conquest or subjugation. We want no benefit or pleasure from him or anything that is his. We are to destroy him and his money, and we are not to stretch forth our hand to touch his plunder.

As long as we are incapable of destroying him utterly we are to hate him with an implacable hatred. This very hatred — is his destruction. For we are bidden to put the greatest possible distance between his evil and ourselves, and there is no greater distance than that engendered by enmity. We are to make him utterly distant from our heart, and from the hearts of all the world; and the greater our enmity towards Amalek, the greater the love that will rise within us towards God, and the deeper our adherence to worship of Him.

FROM THE TEACHING OF THE SAGES

The Evil One, seen or unseen, who stands at the crossroads of all who serve God, and offers an obstacle to their worship — he is the root of Amalek. Whenever there is some minute negligence in the service of God — immediately, the strength of that *rasha* increases. Therefore, every person is bidden to guard all the more against committing sin, in order to cut down Amalek's strength.

'There is a war unto the Lord against Amalek from generation to generation.' For God has reserved, for each generation, revelations of His light. And only Amalek's evil stands in the way of the revelations that are intended for each generation. Therefore God abhors him, for he withholds Divine good from creation. And every servant of God who yearns for the revelation of Divine light, and fails to merit that light because of the effect of Amalek, likewise utterly hates him.

The strength of Amalek consists in making the yoke of worldly activities as oppressive as possible in a person's life. Where there is serenity of soul, he has no dominion. Therefore it is written: 'And it shall be when the Lord your God will give you rest... you shall wipe out the memory of Amalek !' For when a person achieves serenity of soul, he sees the utter nothingness of evil. For this reason *parshat zachor* is read on Shabat, which is the day of rest, and is hence suited for uprooting Amalek from the soul. Therefore, at the time of the miracle of Purim, when Israel vanquished Haman — who was of the seed of Amalek — the Yom Tov was fixed not on the day of victory, but rather on the day when 'they rested from their enemies.' For the rest which comes after victory serves to conclude the wiping out of Amalek.

The final 'wiping-out-of-Amalek' at the time of final redemption, will occur immediately preceding the month of Nisan. A trace of that 'wiping-out' is felt each year during the days of Mordechai and Esther, which fall in the month preceding Nisan. The reading of *parashat zachor* was therefore also prescribed for this time of year.

Rosh Chodesh Nisan is the Rosh Hashanah for the kings of Israel. And the establishment of the kingdom of Israel, depends on the establishment of the kingdom of Heaven. For this reason the two mitzvot of designating a king and of destroying Amalek are adjacent in the Torah.

THE DAY OF TURYANUS

In Megilat Ta'anit the twelfth of Adar is mentioned as a day on which God exacted vengeance from a bitter enemy of Israel named Turyanus, through two righteous brothers, Luliyanus and Papus — who had offered their lives for the sanctification of God's Name, thereby saving the lives of their brethren. The day was designated as a day of rejoicing, on which there was to be no fasting, and as a day on which eulogies were not to be delivered. In later times the joyous character of the day was anulled, because two other pious brothers, Shmayas and Achiyah, were slain the same day.

Turyanus was a Roman ruler who harshly oppressed the Jews. One day his daughter was found slain in the city of Lod, but the identity of her murderer was unknown. Turyanus said: The only enemies I have here are Jews. They must have killed her. And he decreed death against all the Jews of Lod.

There were two righteous brothers in Lod named Luliyanus and Papus, who came forth and said to Turyanus: We have slain your daughter and her blood is on our heads!

Turyanus knew that they had not killed her, and that they were seeking only to save their brethren. He nevertheless accepted their confession, and was thereby restrained from pouring forth his wrath against all the Jews.

When Luliyanus and Papus were brought forth for execution, it is related that Turyanus said to them: If you are of the people of Chananyah, Mishael and Azariah, let your God come and deliver you from my hand, as He saved Chananiah, Mishael and Azariah, from the hand of Nebuchadnetzar. They answered ! Chananiah, Mishael and Azariah were *tzadikim*, and they were worthy of a miracle. Nebuchadnetzar was an eminent king, and was worthy that a miracle be performed through him. But that Wicked One (Turyanus) is a commoner, and is not worthy of a miracle. As for ourselves, we have been condemned to death before God. And if you will not slay us, He has many executors and many bears and lions, who will strike us down and slay us. Nevertheless, God has handed us over to you, only because it is destined that He should exact payment for our blood from your hand !

Turyanus killed them nevertheless.

It is told that later, two men who appeared to be high government officials came to the palace and killed Turyanus with a brutal death. They beat him on the head with wood clubs till he died. The words of Luliyanus and Papus came true.

That day, the twelfth of Adar, was fixed as a festive day and was known as 'the day of Turyanus.'

The two brothers, Luliyanus and Papus, are frequently referred to anonymously as 'the slain of Lod.' And of them it was said: 'No one can stand in the place of the 'slain of Lod in the Garden of Eden.'

As for the details of what occurred to the brothers Shmayah and Achiyah, who were also slain that day, there is no description of the event, nor is there mention as to why they were killed.

Adar PURIM

A DAY OF MOBILIZATION FOR WAR — A DAY OF FASTING ❖ THE
FAST OF ESTHER ❖ THE HALF-SHEKEL ❖ THE DAY OF NIKANOR
❖ THE DAYS OF PURIM ❖ THE OBSERVANCE OF THIS DAY ❖
A TRIPLE PURIM ❖ THE READING OF THE MEGILAH ❖ THE
BRACHOT OF THE MEGILAH ❖ ONE WHO JOURNEYED TO ANOTHER
CITY ❖ FROM THE COMMENTARIES OF THE SAGES ON MEGILAT
ESTHER ❖ HOW HAMAN ENGAGED ACHASHVEROSH AGAINST
THE JEWS ❖ TEN THOUSAND SILVER KIKAR ❖ FASTING ON
PESACH ❖ WHY DID ESTHER SUMMON HAMAN TO THE FEAST ❖
HAMAN'S LETTER TO ALL THE PEOPLES AND PROVINCES, IN
THE NAME OF KING ACHASHVEROSH ❖ HAMAN AND THE
SCHOOL CHILDREN ❖ THREE VERSES ❖ WHICH CORRESPOND TO
THESE WARS ❖ THE VOICE OF THE SHEEP ❖ MORDECHAI'S
PRAYER ❖ ESTHER'S PRAYER ❖ ESTHER IN THE INNER COURT-
YARD ❖ THE ADVICE OF ZERESH ❖ HAMAN'S TREE ❖ THE
KING COULD NOT SLEEP ❖ THE DREAM OF ACHASHVEROSH
AND ITS INTERPRETATION ❖ MATTERS PERTAINING TO THE
MEGILAH ❖ FEASTING AND REJOICING ❖ TOWARDS EVENING ❖
THE SIGNIFICANCE OF THE PURIM FEAST ❖ 'AD DE'LO YADA' ❖
BETWEEN 'CURSED-IS-HAMAN' AND 'BLESSED-IS-MORDECHAI' ❖
❖ OTHER COMMENTS ON 'AD DE'LO YADA' ❖
❖ WHY DO WE WEAR DISGUISES ON PURIM ❖ 'AL HANISIM' ❖
❖ GIFTS FOR THE POOR ❖ 'MISHLOACH MANOT' ❖ LOVE AND
UNITY — A SHIELD AGAINST AMALEK ❖ HUMILITY AND
GRATITUDE ❖ PURIM ALLUSIONS ❖ THE DAYS OF PURIM AND
THE MEGILAH OF PURIM WILL NEVER CEASE.

CHAPTER THREE

On the 13th of Adar, the Fast of Esther is observed in memory of the Fast observed by Mordechai and Esther and all Israel. On that very day, the enemies of the Jews had planned to subjugate and destroy them. 'The opposite, however, occurred, whereby the Jews ruled over their enemies.' The practice of fasting was observed by the people of Israel whenever they were faced by war. Thus Moshe Rabenu also fasted when he came to wage war against Amalek. The aim of the fast was to affirm that a man does not prevail by physical or military strength, but only by lifting his eyes heavenward in prayer so that Divine Mercy might give him the strength to prevail in battle. This then was the purpose of the fast observed by Israel at the time of Haman, when they gathered to defend themselves against those who sought to destroy them. And in memory of that Fast, a yearly Fast was fixed for generations on the same day. We are to recall thereby that God accepts each person's prayer and penitence in the hour of his trouble.

The acceptance of this Fast of the 13th of Adar on the part of Israel for later generations, is alluded to in the Scroll of Esther: 'And as they accepted upon themselves and upon their children, the matters of their fastings and their cry' (Esther 9).

The Fast is called by the name of Esther because it was she who first requested the observance of a fast, of Mordechai: 'Go and gather all the Jews who are found in Shushan and fast over me, and do not eat and do not drink three days, night and day; and I and my maidens will also fast thus' (ibid. 4). The fast which we observe is nevertheless not observed for a three-day period, as was the case with the original Fast, nor is it observed on the same date. Originally the Fast was observed by Esther and the entire people of Israel on the 14th, 15th and 16th of Nisan, immediately after Mordechai was informed of Haman's decree and of the letter of annihilation which Haman wrote on the 13th of Nisan. Our Fast however, is observed on the 13th of Adar, in memory of the Fast observed by Israel on the day of their mobilization for war against the enemies. The Fast is nevertheless called by the name of Esther since it was she who first proposed its observance.

Others hold the view, that even our Fast is also primarily a memorial to the original three-day Fast observed by the Jews when the decree was announced. But since the Fast could not be permanently fixed for later years in its proper time (because fasting is not permitted during Nisan), the Sages therefore fixed it for the 13th of Adar — which was also a Fast day for the Jews, who then gathered to wage war against their enemies. And although the Fast of Esther is therefore a memorial to the original three days of fasting, the Rabis were nevertheless lenient in fixing it for only one day.

In deference to this view, there are some who fast an additional three days; on Monday, Thursday and Monday after Purim. Others voluntarily fast the night as well as the day on the 13th of Adar, since the original three-day Fast was observed night and day.

THE FAST OF ESTHER

Since the Fast of Esther is not one of the four Fast days which are specifically mentioned in the Prophetic Writings, it is observed with greater leniency than the other Fast days. Pregnant women, nursing mothers, as well as others of generally weak health, (who would suffer by fasting) do not fast therein. The additional penitential prayers, and the Torah

Reading, which are prescribed for the other Fast days are also required for the Fast of Esther.

If the 13th of Adar falls on Shabat, the Fast is observed the preceding Thursday which is the eleventh of Adar. Because of Purim, the Fast is not postponed to the following day, nor is it observed Erev Shabat: Since it is no longer observed in any event in its proper time, it was not fixed for Erev Shabat, in deference to the honor of Shabat. (A Fast whose prescribed date can fall on Erev Shabat such as the 10th of Tevet, is neither postponed nor observed earlier, but it is observed on its fixed day).*Tachanun* is not said during *minchah* of the Fast of Esther. And because of the Reading of the Megilah, which follows shortly after *minchah* some dress in Shabat clothes for *minchah* on the Fast of Esther.

THE HALF-SHEKEL

On the 13th of Adar during *minchah*, it is customary to give three halves of the coin which is the basis of the local currency. The money is turned over to the poor to do with it as they wish. This contribution is made in memory of the half-*shekel* given by Israel when the *Beit Hamikdash* still stood; and whose forthcoming collection was announced on Rosh Chodesh Adar.

This memorial act is performed before the Reading of the Megilah, because all Israel gathers for the Megilah Reading in the Synagogues. It is proper to give the half-*shekel* before *minchah*, since 'the diligent perform *mitzvot* earlier.' Those who live in 'open-cities' give the half-shekel before the Megilah Reading on the night of the 14th, whereas the inhabitants of Yerushalayim give the half-shekel before their Reading of the Megilah — the night of the 15th.

In a place which has no coin that is designated a 'half' coin, it is customary for the *gabaim* to bring three halves of silver coins which are issued elsewhere, and to give these coins in exchange, to anyone who makes his contribution in the coins available to him. After the latter has performed his *mitzvah*, he returns the three 'halves' to the *gabaim*, so that others might also be able to observe the custom properly.

Those who seek to observe mitzvot with *hidur* (literally — enhancement) give the half-shekel for each of the members of the household including minors, and in the case of an expectant mother, for the unborn child as well. Once a father has begun to give a half-shekel for a minor child, he is required to continue to do so each year.

The reason for the giving of three 'halves' is that the term *trumah* (contribution) is mentioned three times in the portion of Ki-Tisa, in the account of the mitzvah of the half-shekel.

The established practice is to consider the giving of the half-shekel as not freeing one from the mitzvah of giving charity to the poor, which is specifically prescribed for Purim.

THE DAY OF NIKANOR

The 13th of Adar is also mentioned in the Talmud as the day on which vengeance was executed (during the time of the Hasmoneans) against a tyrant who oppressed the land of Yehudah cruelly and arrogantly blasphemed the city of God. The name of the tyrant was Nikanor and he fell by the hand of Yehudah, the son of Matityahu, on the 13th of Adar, which was hence celebrated as a festive day.

THE DAYS OF PURIM

In some places, Purim is observed exclusively on the 14th of Adar and in others, exclusively on the 15th.

The observance of Purim was thus originally ordained by the Sages who established the festival for generations. 'To observe these days of Purim, in their times.' 'In their times:' In the specific time of each. The reason for the different dates designated for the observance of Purim is that, the Jews of Shushan originally observed the festival on a different day than the Jews who lived elsewhere. In all other provinces the Jews waged war on the 13th and observed the 14th as a day of festivity and rejoicing. Whereas Jews in Shushan waged war both 13th and the 14th of the month, and observed the 15th as a day of festivity and rejoicing.

It was therefore proper to distinguish only between Shushan and all other places in accordance with the original event. The Sages of that generation wished, however, to accord honor to the Land of Israel which then was desolate. They therefore determined as follows : The capital city of Shushan, in which the miracle occurred enjoys special preeminence and the festival is to be observed there on the 15th; despite the fact that in the days of Yehoshua, Shushan was not yet surrounded by a wall, and hence enjoyed only minor status as a city. All other cities which were already settled and were surrounded by walls in the days of Yehoshua, are to be accorded the preeminence of Shushan — although they might presently lack surrounding walls and might be in a state of ruin — and they are to observe Purim the 15th. Cities which were not surrounded by walls in the days of Yehoshua though they may have surrounding walls presently — are not to be accorded the status of Shushan, and they are to observe the festival on the 14th.

What then is the criterion for judging the status of a city? The condition of the given city during the days of Yehoshua. That is to say, cities either found by Yehoshua in the Land of Israel, or built in his time, are considered as assured of eternal existence. Their present destruction is viewed as passing. Cities outside the Land of Israel — though they later acquired the status of walled cities — are not regarded as assured of permanent existence.

Therefore the Purim which is observed on the 14th is called 'Purim-of-the-open-cities;' and the Purim observed on the 15th is named the 'Purim-of-the-walled-cities.' In our times, the only city besides Shushan in which Purim is observed the 15th of Adar is Yerushalayim. In a number of other places, the Megilah is also read the 15th — but only

because of doubt. In these communities, the essential observance of Purim is fixed for the 14th, and though the Reading
of the Megilah is repeated in them the 15th as well, the
required *brachah* which precedes the Megilah-Reading, is not
recited.

THE OBSERVANCE OF THE DAY

There are four *mitzvot* which are prescribed for Purim,
and which were promulgated by the *Sanhedrin* and by Prophets. The Reading of the Megilah, festivity and rejoicing,
the mutual sending of gifts and gifts to the poor.

The Sages have further prescribed the reading of the passage 'and Amalek came' for Purim morning, as well as the
recalling of the miracle of Purim in Prayer and in *birkat
hamazon (al-hanisim)*.

Halel is not, however, said on Purim; the Megilah-Reading
being regarded as the *Halel* of the day.

A second reason: Halel is not recited over a miracle which
occurred outside the Land of Israel. To which the objection
is raised: Is not Halel said over the miracle of the exodus
from Egypt? The answer given however is that, till they
entered the Land of Israel, every land was suitable for the
saying of *shirah* (song of praise — *Halel*). Once they entered
the land, only the Land of Israel was regarded as appropriate
for the saying of *shirah*.

In the Talmud a third reason is given: In Halel we say,
'Praise Him, you servants of the Lord' — you are now
servants of the Lord and no longer servants of Pharaoh.
After the miracle of Purim, however, we still remained the
servants of Achashverosh and in exile.

All the mitzvot of the day apply to the 'open cities' and
to the 'walled cities' in their respective times exclusively.

Eulogies and fasting are prohibited on Purim, and in a leap
year, they are prohibited in the first Adar as well. A mourner
likewise does not practice mourning publicly on Purim. He

does not sit on the ground nor remove his shoes, and observes the private aspects of mourning, as is the case on Shabat.

It is legally permissible to work on Purim, but is nevertheless not considered proper. The Sages have said: 'Whoever works on the day of Purim does not see any sign of blessing (through his work).' In a place in which it is the established custom not to work on Purim, the *Beit Din* penalizes one who does work.

The type of work that is referred to is work which results in profit. Work involving a mitzvah, however, or work for the sake of Purim, is permitted even initially. Likewise, is there no restriction against work in the 'open cities' on the 15th and in the 'walled cities' on the 14th.

A TRIPLE PURIM

When the 15th of Adar falls on Shabat, the 'open cities' — whose Purim is observed on the 14th — observe Purim on the prescribed day — which is Friday. The 'walled cities,' however (the inhabitants of Yerushalayim and Shushan,) 'divide' their observance of Purim into three days: On Erev Shabat (the 14th) the inhabitants of the 'walled-cities' read the Megilah, and give gifts to the poor.

On Shabat (the 15th) they read the passage 'And Amalek came,' in the Torah, and they recite *al hanisim* in their prayers and in *birkat hamazon.* On Sunday, (the 16th) they hold the Purim Feast and they send gifts to friends.

The reason for this manner of observing Purim on their part, is as follows:

The Sages have prohibited the reading of the Megilah on Shabat, lest one carry the Megilah through a public domain, in order to bring it to one who is competent to read it for him.

The Sages have also deduced from specific verses in the Megilah, that whenever the Reading of the Megilah in its proper time is impossible, it is read earlier, rather than later.

For it is said: 'And it shall not pass' — you are not permitted to 'pass' its proper time.

As for giving gifts to the poor, the earlier the better, so that the poor might enjoy their gifts on Purim.

On the other hand, the Purim festive meal is not held on Shabat since we do not commingle 'one joy with another.'

The sending of mutual gifts is impossible on Shabat because of the prohibition against carrying either from one domain to another, or through a public domain. But since there is no prohibition against delaying the sending of gifts (as is the case concerning the Reading of the Megilah), the sending of gifts is postponed for the day following Shabat; which also serves the distinction between 'open cities' and 'walled cities' every year. The inhabitants of 'walled cities' who read the Megilah — in this instance — on the 14th, do so in a *Minyan* of ten. Since their Reading of the Megilah is not done at the prescribed time, they are required to read it publicly, and not privately.

Although the inhabitants of 'walled cities' send gifts to one another on the 16th of Adar, they nevertheless also send some gifts on the 14th as well — as the inhabitants of the 'open cities' do. They also make their Shabat meals more elaborate in honor of Purim.

'And Amalek came' is read as maftir on Shabat, from a second Torah scroll, after seven persons are called to the reading of the regular *sidra* in the first scroll.

On Sunday (the 16th of Adar), they dress in festive clothing; and after *minchah*, they hold the Purim feast. They do not, however, say *al hanisim* during prayer or *birkat hamazon* on the 16th. They partake of sumptuous foods and extend Yom Tov greetings to each other.

THE READING OF THE MEGILAH

One is required to read the Megilah at night, and to repeat it by day. The Megilah may be read all night till the coming of dawn. By day, the Megilah may likewise be read from sunrise till sunset. Post factum, however, if one has read the Megilah even before sunrise, but at least after dawn, he has fulfilled his obligation to read the Megilah.

Both men and women are obligated to read the Megilah (or hear it read).

The most preferred manner of fulfilling the *mitzvah* is to read the Megilah publicly, and in the Synagogue. Even if there are many persons in one's company, he should not read the Megilah at home, but should rather go to the Synagogue, since, 'In a multitude there is Majesty;' and the miracle is made known more widely.

Positive Torah commandments are all deferred for the sake of hearing the Megilah. Even the study of the Torah is suspended for the Megilah Reading. The only mitzvah which is not deferred by the Reading of the Megilah, is the mitzvah of providing burial for a person found dead, who has no one else to do so.

If one hears the Megilah read, he fulfills the obligation as if he were to read it himself; provided that the Reader is himself obligated to perform mitzvot. It is, however, necessary to hear every single word, for if one has not heard the entire Megilah, he has not fulfilled his obligation.

It is proper for every person to hold a Megilah on parchment before him and to read alone in a whisper, as he hears the Reader. If he misses hearing a word, he may read it himself from his own Megilah. And if he holds a printed Megilah before him and he misses hearing a word from the Reader, but reads it himself from the printed book he still fulfills his obligation — *bedi'avad* (post factum). It is the established custom to spread the Megilah wide on the table, and to double one sheet of parchment under another, so that the individual sheets may not hang below the table. The Megilah should not be read rolled on either side, as a Torah Scroll is read. The reason for this custom is that the Megilah is called a letter: 'To fulfill this Purim letter.'

And it is the way of one who reads from a letter, to hold the letter completely open before him. Further, the miracle is more widely publicized through this variation in the manner of holding the scroll. And although this custom applies essentially to the Reader rather than to the hearer, it is nevertheless customary for all to spread their scrolls like a letter, though they hear the reading from another.

It is customary for the Reader to pause when he reaches each of the four 'verses-of-redemption' which are found in the Megilah. As he pauses, the congregation reads each verse aloud, and the Reader then repeats it from his Megilah — since those who fulfill the obligation of reading the Megilah by hearing it read, are required to hear the entire Megilah read. The following are the four 'verses-of-redemption:' 'There was a Jew in Shushan...' 'And Mordechai went forth from before the King in royal garments...' 'Unto the Jews there was light...' 'For Mordechai, the Jew, was second to the King...' The purpose of this custom is to keep the children from slumber so that the great miracle performed for Israel in the days of Mordechai and Esther, might enter their hearts.

The passage, 'That night the sleep of the King was disturbed,' is customarily read aloud, and with a variation in the melody, because therein the salvation of the Jews begins to be revealed.

The names of the ten sons of Haman together with the four preceding words ('500 men and'), and the word 'ten' which follows, are all read in one breath: Thereby indicating that they were all lain and hung together. The 500 men mentioned with them, consisted of ten groups — each under the command of one of Haman's sons — who were charged with executing their wishes.

If the reader fails to hold his breath for the duration of the entire passage, he nevertheless fulfills the obligation of the Megilah Reading.

THE BRACHOT OF THE MEGILAH

The reader of the Megilah recites three brachot prior to the reading, and one afterwards, and he should intend to discharge the obligation of the congregation thereby. The hearers answer 'Amen,' and they should likewise intend to fulfill the mitzvah. They do not say 'Baruch Hu u'varuch Shemo' — in order not to interrupt in the middle of the brachah. Before the Megilah-Reading three brachot are said:

'Who sanctified us with His commandments, and commanded us concerning the Reading of the Megilah . . .'

'Who made miracles for our fathers in those days at this time . . .'

'Who kept us alive and sustained us . . .'

Afterwards, one brachah is said:

'Who waged our quarrels . . .' Two concluding passages follow, as indicated in the 'sidur.' The second of these contains the word: 'Cursed be Haman and blessed be Mordechai . . . and also Charvonah shall be remembered for good.' The prayer is an allusion to the Sages' injunction to utter words of curse against Haman, and of blessing upon Mordechai and Charvonah. The first of the two concluding passages ('asher heni') is not said after the Megilah-Reading by day.

The brachot preceding the Megilah-Reading are said before the reading of the Megilah by day as well; except that in saying 'shehecheyanu,' ('who kept us alive'), the Reader should intend to apply his 'brachah' to the other mitzvot of the day — the Purim Feast, the sending of gifts, the giving of gifts to the poor.

There are some who do not say 'shehecheyanu' by

*day, and they have the above intentions when saying
'shehecheyanu' at night.*

*If one reads the Megilah alone, he recites the 'bra-
chot' which precede it, but not the one which follows.
If one has already fulfilled the obligation of reading
the Megilah, and he wishes to read it a second time
publicly for the sake of others, he recites all the
'brachot' beginning and end — and the hearers
answer 'Amen.' If one reads the Megilah for another
individual hearer, he recites only the first brachot.
And if the hearer knows the brachot well, he says
them himself.*

*Before the brachah which follows the Megilah-
Reading, the Megilah is rolled together, since it is
not respectful to keep the Megilah open after the
reading. When the Megilah is read before women,
the first brachah is changed. Since women are obligated only to hear the Megilah read, but not to read it
themselves, the word 'lishmoa' (to hear) is used, instead of 'al mikra Megilah' ('over the Reading of the
Megilah'). In Sephardic communities, the Megilah is
read for women without a brachah.*

FROM THE COMMENTARIES OF THE SAGES ON MEGILAT ESTHER

Not all Israel participated in the feast
of Achashverosh — 'Unto all the people who are
found in Shushan' — Rabi Chama Bar Chanina said: We
learn from this that only the common people participated
in the feast, while the great of Israel fled from the occasion.
Rabi Shimon Bar Yochai said: We learn from this that they
were forced to eat foods cooked by non-Jews. The Persians
said to the Jews: Is your God capable of offering you a
feast such as this in the future world? They said: 'No eye
has seen, except for you, God! He shall do it for those who
wait for Him' (Yeshayahu 64). And if He will make feasts

for us such as this, we shall say: We have already eaten one like this before Achashverosh' (Yalkut Esther 1048).

'And the drinking was according to the law' — according to which law ? The Sages have said: According to the law of the Torah namely that there should be more eating than drinking. For thus do we find in the case of flour-offerings and wine-libations, that the measure of flour was larger than of the wine. Similarly, it was strictly prescribed at the feast of Achashverosh, that the guests were to eat more than they were to drink, in order that they might not become intoxicated.

But it might be asked: What difference did it make to Achashverosh whether or not they would become drunk ? The answer is that Achashverosh wanted to cause Israel to be judged as sober people are judged, and not as drunkards.

Haman's anger drove him to distraction — 'And Haman wished to annihilate all the Jews :' The matter may be likened to a bird who built his nest at the seashore, but the sea rose and flooded it. What did he do ? He began to fill his mouth with water and spit out the water upon the sand, and then he repeatedly did the same. His friend came, stood by him and said: 'What is it that you are doing unto exhaustion ?'

'Said he: 'I will not budge from this place till I make of the ocean sand, and of the sand, ocean.'

'Likewise, 'And Haman wished to annihilate all the Jews.' God said: Wicked one ! I wanted to, but was unable — 'And He (God) wanted to annihilate them, were it not for Moshe his chosen one who stood in the breach' (Tehilim 106) — And you seek to do so ?' (Yalkut Esther 1056).

How Haman Enraged Achashverosh against the Jews — Rava said: No one knows how to slander like Haman :

'*Yeshno am echad*' — ('There is a people.') 'yeshno' —

'there is,' but the letters of 'Yeshno' may also be formed to read yashnu, which means, 'they slept.'

'Haman said to Achashverosh : Come and let us destroy Israel. Said he : I fear lest their God do to me as He did to my predecessor. Said Haman : 'Yashnu min hamitzvot' — (they slumbered from the practic of mitzvot). And they no longer have any merit by which their God might save them.

'One people' — Achashverosh said to him : 'There are among them Rabanim and Tzadikim who do not commit sin.' Said Haman : 'They are one people. And the Tzadikim among them incurred guilt together with the wicked among them.'

'Scattered' — Do not say : I am emptying part of your kingdom, since they fill an entire province. Not so : For they are scattered among all the peoples, and their lack will not be noticeable.

'In all the provinces of your kingdom' — perhaps you will say that they inhabit some small city by themselves and you are unwilling to destroy it ? 'They dwell commingled with all others, but not by themselves.

'And their religious practices differ from those of all other peoples.' They do not eat what we cook, and they do not marry our daughters, nor do they marry their daughters to our sons.

'And the laws of the King they do not perform.' All year they avoid the King's work with the excuses : 'Today is Shabat, today is Pesach, and we are forbidden to work.'

'And it is of no value to the king to let them remain.' For they eat and drink and deride the king. If a fly falls into one of their cups, they throw the fly out and drink the wine. But if my Lord, the King were to touch one of their cups, he would dash it on the ground and refuse to drink it.' (Tr. Megilah 13).

Ten Thousand Silver Kikar — 'What cause did Haman have to pay ten thousand silver Kikar in order to destroy the Jews ? Thus did Haman say : The merit of the

Jews consists in their each having donated a half-shekel for the service of the *Mishkan*. I alone will give the equivalent of what all 600,000 of them gave for the *Mishkan* throughout their lives. For a Jew becomes obligated to give a half-shekel upon reaching the age of twenty, and their life span consists of seventy years. All that they give together from the age of twenty till the age of seventy adds up exactly to ten thousand silver *kikar*. Let my shekalim annul theirs' (Chizkuni Ki-Tisa).

On the other hand, 'Resh Lakish said: It was known before Him who created the world that Haman would weigh out shekalim to destroy Israel. He therefore caused their shekalim to precede his. And for this reason we learn in the Mishnah: 'On the first day of Adar announcement is made concerning shekalim' (Tr. Megilah 13).

Fasting on Pesach — 'Esther said to reply to Mordechai... and fast over me, and do not eat or drink for three days.' The three days are: The 13th, the 14th and the 15th of Nisan. Mordechai said to her: Is not the first day of Pesach — on which fasting is prohibited — one of the three days ? Said she to him: Elder in Israel ! Of what use would then Pesach be ? (Without Israel, Pesach has no meaning) Mordechai immediately admitted that she was right' (Esther Raba).

Why did Esther summon Haman to the feast ? — 'The Rabis have expounded: What caused Esther to invite Haman ?

Rabi Eliezer said: She prepared a net for him. As it is said: 'Let their table be a net before them' (Tehilim 69). 'Rabi Yehoshua said: She learned from her father. As it is said: 'If your enemy is hungry feed him bread, if he is thirsty give him water to drink; for thereby you heap burning coal on his head' (Mishley 25).

'Rabi Meir said: So that he might not undertake a conspiracy against the king.

'Rabi Yehudah said: So that it might not be discovered that she was a Jewess.

'Rabi Nechemyah said: So that Israel might not say, 'We have a sister in the king's palace,' and therefore turn away from seeking Divine Mercy.

'Rabi Yosi said: So that he might be available to her at all times — she might thereby somehow find a way to trap him into some misdeed before the king.

'Rabi Shimon Ben Menasia said: Perhaps God will see (she said) that I too am forced to flatter this *rasha*...He might therefore perform a miracle for us.

'Rabi Yehoshua Ben Karchah said: (Esther said:) I will show him friendliness, so that the king might suspect us both, and that he might slay both of us.

'Raban Gamliel said: He was an unstable king and constantly withdrew his word. She said: Perhaps I will be able to ensnare him and kill him. And if the opportunity should be lacking, the hour might pass, and he might change his mind.

'Raban Gamliel... quoted Rabi Eliezer Hamodai: She caused the king to be jealous of him, and she incited the nobles to envy him (by inviting him alone).

'Raba said: 'Before the downfall — there is pride' (Mishley 16).

'Abayey and Rava both said: 'In their heat I will set their drinks, and I will intoxicate them so that they might exult, and that they might sleep an external sleep and not reawaken' (Irmeyahu 51). (This occurred to Belshatzar, king of Babylon, and Esther likewise thought: When the wicked drink calamity befalls them.)

'Raba Bar Avuha found Eliyahu, the Prophet, and said to him: In accordance with which of the Sages did Esther see fit to do? Said he: In accordance with all the *Tanaim* and *Amoraim*.'

HAMAN'S LETTER TO ALL THE PEOPLES AND PROVINCES,
IN THE NAME OF KING ACHASHVEROSH

'Endless peace be unto you!

*'Let it be known to you that there is one man in
our midst who is not of our place, but is of royal
ancestry — of the seed of Amalek. He is among the
greatest of the generation and his name is Haman.
And he has made a minor request of us. There is
a people among us which is the lowliest of all peoples,
but they are arrogant; they seek our harm, and their
mouths are filled with curses against the king. What
is the curse with which they curse us? 'The Lord
reigns unto eternity, the nations shall perish from his
land.' And they also say: 'To inflict vengeance upon
the peoples, reproof against the nations.' And they
refuse to acknowledge gratitude towards those who
bestowed good upon them.*

*'Come and see what they did to poor Pharaoh.
When they went down to Egypt, he welcomed them
cordially and settled them in the best part of the
land. He fed them in the years of famine, and gave
them the best food in his land. He had a palace to
build, and they did the building. Nevertheless, he
could not prevail against them. More than this, they
came with a pretext and said to him: 'We shall go to
sacrifice unto the Lord our God, a distance of three
days. Afterwards we shall return. If you wish to, lend
us silver and gold, utensils and clothing.' Whereupon
the Egyptians loaned them their silver and gold, and
all of their fine clothes. The Jews loaded mules without number with their belongings, till they emptied
all Egypt and fled. When Pharaoh heard that they
had fled, he went after them to return his money.
What did they do to him? There was a man in their
midst by the name of Moshe, the son of Amram.*

69

With the use of magic, he smote the sea with a rod till the sea became dry. Whereupon they all entered the bed of the dry sea and crossed the sea. And I do not know how they crossed the sea and how the waters became dry. When Pharaoh saw it, he entered after them to return his money. And I do not know how they pushed him into the sea, but he and his entire army were drowned in the sea. They did not remember the good he bestowed upon them. Do you hear what ingrates they were?

'Further, see what they did to Amalek, my grandfather, when he came to wage war against them. 'And Amalek came and waged war with Israel in Refidim.' From where did Amalek come? Rabi Kruspedai said in the name of Rabi Yochanan, that he came from Bilaam, to whom he had gone for advice. He had said to Bilaam, 'I know that you know how to give counsel; that you are a master of (evil) thoughts; that whoever takes advice from you does not fail... See what this people have done to the Egyptians who bestowed so many favors upon them. And if they did thus to the Egyptians who were so kind to them, how much more will they do to the other nations. What advice do you give me?'

'Bilaam said, 'Go and wage war against them. And if you do so you will prevail. For they rely on the merit of their Father Avraham, and since you too are a descendant of Avraham, you can also rely upon his merit.' Immediately, he came to wage war against them.

'What did Moshe their leader do? He had a disciple by the name of Yehoshua Bin Nun, who was exceedingly brutal, and utterly merciless. Said Moshe to him, 'Choose for us men and go out to wage war against Amalek.' I do not know whether the men he chose were magicians or heroes. What did Moshe do?

He took a staff in his hand, and I do not know what he did with it. When they came upon Amalek, I do not know what incantation he whispered over them; and their hands were weakened and they fell before them.

'They (Israel) came upon Sichon and Og, the mightiest of our land, before whom none could stand, and I do not know how they killed them.

'The Kings of Midian came upon them, and I do not know how they killed them.

'What else did the disciple of the man Moshe do? He brought Israel into the land of Canaan, and not alone did he take the land but he slew thirty one Canaanite Kings. He divided their land among Israel and had no mercy over them. Those whom he did not choose to slay, became servants of his.

'Sisera and his multitude came upon them, and I do not know what they did to Sisera and his army. The river Kishon swept them away and cast them into the great ocean.

'Their first king, Shaul by name, waged war against my grandfather Amalek. He killed one hundred thousand riders among them in one day. He had no mercy on man, woman or child, and I do not know how he killed them.

'What else did they do to Agag, Haman's grandfather? First they were merciful towards him. Then a certain man by the name of Shmuel came, severed his body, and gave his flesh for food to the birds of the sky. I do not know how he killed him...

'Afterwards, they had a king named David Ben Ishai. David destroyed all the kingdoms without mercy. After him, there rose his son Shlomo, who built a house for Israel which he called the Beit Hamikdash. And I do not know what they had inside.

When they embark on war, they enter it and practice sorcery there; and when they emerge they kill, and they destroy the world.

'Out of abundance of good they rebelled against their God. Further, that God of theirs became aged, and Nebuchadnetzar came and burned the house of theirs. He exiled them from their soil and brought them among us. But they have not yet changed their repulsive practices. And although they are in exile in our midst, they scoff at us and at the faith of our gods.

'And now we have come to a common resolve. We have cast lots to destroy them from the world, and to determine the most suitable time for us to destroy them. The lot fell on the month of Adar, on the 13th of the month, and now, when these letters reach you, you are all to be prepared on that day to annihilate all the Jews in your midst, young and old, infants and women, in one day. And you are not to allow any remnant to remain of them' (Esther Raba 7).

HAMAN AND THE SCHOOL CHILDREN

'When those letters were sealed and given to the hand of Haman, he and his companions rejoiced. On the way, they met Mordechai walking before them. Mordechai saw three children walking from school, and he ran after them. When Haman and his company saw Mordechai running after the children, they followed Mordechai in order to find out what Mordechai would ask them. When Mordechai reached the children, he asked one of them: Recite the verse you learned today. Said he: 'Do not fear a sudden dread, or the storm of the wicked when it comes' (Mishley 3). The second said: Today I read and dwelt upon the following verse at school: 'Take counsel and it shall be nullified, speak a word and it shall not stand, because God is with us' (Yeshayahu 8).

'The other began and said: 'And unto age I am, and unto

hoary age I shall bear, I have done, and I shall bear; I shall endure, and I shall save' (ibid. 46).

'When Mordechai heard this, he laughed and rejoiced greatly. Said Haman to him: What is this great joy of yours over the words of these children: Mordechai answered: Over the glad tidings which they have brought me — that I need not fear the evil counsel which you have contrived against us. Immediately Haman-the-wicked was enraged and said: I shall stretch forth my hand first only against these children' (Esther Raba 7).

THREE VERSES — AS AGAINST THREE WARS

'Why did Mordechai see fit to rejoice over these three verses which he heard from the children? These verses allude to the three wars which Amalek waged against Israel. And Scripture thereby informed Israel that the conspiracy of Haman would be nullified just as the plans of Amalek were nullified in earlier generations.

'The first time that Amalek came to wage war against Israel, he attacked suddenly, as it is said: 'Who met you unexpectedly on the way.' The first verse cited by the children corresponds to Amalek's first war: 'Have no fear of sudden dread.'

'During the second attack of Amalek against Israel, Amalek came disguised as Canaanites in order to confuse Israel, so that they might not know who their enemies were, and how to pray. As it is said: 'And the Canaanite heard.' (The Amalekites were disguised as Canaanites) ... and he waged war against Israel...' It was to this war, that the second of the children's verses alluded: 'Devise a plan and it shall be nullified.'

'Concerning the third war on which Haman embarked, in the thought that God had become 'aged' (see above, 'A letter by Haman'), the third verse states: 'And unto old age I am' (The Gaon of Vilna).

THE VOICE OF THE SHEEP

'After the building of the scaffold, Haman went to Mordechai and found him in the *Beit Midrash*, with the children seated before him, wearing sackcloth, studying Torah and weeping. He counted them and found twenty two thousand children. He had them all chained and appointed guards over them, saying: Tomorrow, I will first slay these children; afterwards, I will slay Mordechai. Their mothers brought them bread and water and said to them: Our children, eat and drink before you die, so that you might not die of hunger. They placed their hands on their *sefarim* and swore: By the life of our teacher Mordechai, we shall not eat or drink, but shall die fasting !'

'They all burst into weeping, till their cry ascended above. And God heard the sound of their weeping... At that hour, God's mercy was awakened, and He rose from the 'seat-of-judgment' and sat on the 'seat-of-mercy.' Said He: What is this loud sound I hear, that is similar to kids and sheep ? And Moshe Rabenu stood before God saying: Lord of the Universe, these are not kids or sheep. They are the little ones of Your people who have been fasting for three days and three nights. Tomorrow, the enemy wishes to slaughter them like kids and sheep.

'At that hour, God took the decrees He had issued against them which had been sealed with clay, and tore them. That night He cast confusion upon the king. 'That night the sleep of the king wandered' (Esther Raba 9).

MORDECHAI'S PRAYERS

'And Mordechai prayed to God, saying: It is revealed and known before the Throne of Your Glory, Lord of the Universe, that what I did in not bowing down to Haman, was not done because of arrogance and pride, but rather for fear of You. For I fear You and would not give the honor due You to honor flesh and blood, and I therefore would not bow down to anyone besides You.

'For who am I that I should not bow down to Haman, in behalf of the deliverance of Your people Israel . . .

'And You are our God — save us from his hand ! Let him fall into the pit he dug; let him be trapped in the net he set for your pious ones. Let that agitator know that You have not forgotten the promise You gave us : 'And yet for all that, when they are in the land of their enemies, I will not reject them, neither will I abhor them, to destroy them utterly, and to break My covenant with them; for I am the Lord their God' (Vayikra 26).

'What did Mordechai do ? He gathered the children and withheld bread and water from them. He clothed them in sackcloth, seated them in ashes; they wept and studied the Torah' (Esther Raba 8).

ESTHER'S PRAYER

'At that time Esther was exceedingly fearful of the evil which had befallen Israel. She removed her royal garments and dressed in sackcloth. She uncovered the hair on her head and filled it with dust and ashes. She afflicted herself with fasting, and fell upon her face before God, in prayer.

'Lord God of Israel, Who has dominion from eternity, and Who created the world ! Help your maidservant, for I am an orphan, without father or mother. I am compared to one impoverished, one who goes begging from house to house. Likewise do I seek your mercy, in the house of Achashverosh, from window to window. Now O Lord, grant wellbeing, I beseech You, to Your lowly maidservant. Save Your flock from these enemies who have risen up against us. For there is nothing to restrain You from saving — the many, or the few. Father of orphans ! I beseech You to stand by the right hand of this orphan, who has placed her trust in Your lovingkindness. Grant me mercy before this man, because I fear him. Cast him down before me, for You cast down the haughty' (Esther Raba 8).

ESTHER IN THE INNER COURTYARD

'On the third day Esther dressed in her finest clothes and most precious jewelry. She took with her her two maid-servants, and placed her right hand on one maiden, and leaned upon her — in the manner of a queen. The second maiden walked behind her mistress, and held her jewelry, so that the gold she wore might not touch the ground. Her face was radiant, and she concealed her anxiety. She came into the inner courtyard facing the king, and stood before him. The king was seated on his throne dressed in gold and precious gems. He lifted up his eyes and saw Esther facing him. And his wrath burned exceedingly over her coming before him uncalled — in violation of his rules.

'Esther lifted her eyes and saw the King's face; his eyes were like glowing fire, for all the wrath within him. On perceiving his anger, she became frightened and faint, and leaned her head upon the maiden supporting her on the right.

'God saw, and had mercy over His people. He turned towards the anguish of the orphan who had placed her trust in Him. He granted her favor before king, and added beauty to her beauty and majesty to her majesty.

'The king arose in agitation from his throne. He ran towards Esther, and embraced her and kissed her. He cast his arm about her neck and said to her: Queen Esther, why are you fearful? This rule which we have established does not apply to you, since you are my beloved companion. And he said to her: Why did you not speak to me when I saw you? And Esther said: My Lord King! When I saw you I was frightened because of your majesty. And the king said to her: What is your wish, Queen Esther, and what is your request...? And Esther said: If it is good unto the King, let the King and Haman come to the feast...' (Esther Raba 9).

THE ADVICE OF ZERESH

'When Haman saw Mordechai seated in the King's gate and Mordechai would not rise or turn aside before him, he was filled with anger but restrained himself ... And he brought together all who loved him and Zeresh his wife ... Among them all, there were none who could advise him like Zeresh his wife. For he had 365 advisors, after the number of the days of the sun. His wife said to him: This man about whom you ask, if he is of the seed of the Jews you will not prevail. Approach him with some tactic, which none of his people have experienced. For if you cast him into a fiery furnace, Chananyah and his companions have already been saved from one. If unto a lions' den — Daniel has already risen from one. If you imprison him, Yosef has already emerged from one. If you put him into an iron box and kindle a fire beneath it, Menashe has already emerged from one after praying to God. And if you will exile him into the wilderness, his forefathers have already been fruitful and have multiplied in the wilderness. They were indeed tested by many tests, all of which they withstood and were saved from. If you should blind his eyes, there is Shimshon who slew many Philistines while he was blind. Rather, hang him on a tree scaffold — for we do not find that any of this people have ever escaped from such a death. 'And the matter was good before Haman and he made the tree-scaffold' (Esther Raba 9).

HAMAN'S TREE

'What sort of tree was it ? The Sages have said: When Haman came to prepare it, God summoned all the trees of creation: Who will volunteer for this rasha to be hung on him ? The fig tree said: I will offer myself, for the people of Israel bring Bikurim from me, and they themselves are compared to a fig tree. The vine said: I offer myself. For Israel is compared to me. The pomegranate said: I offer

myself, for Israel is compared to me. The nut tree said:
I offer myself, for Israel is compared to me. The *etrog* said.
I offer myself, for the Israelites take me for the performance
of a *mitzvah*. The myrtle said: I offer myself because Israel
is compared to me. The olive, the apple tree and dekel tree
each said: I offer myself for Israel is compared to me. The
palm and cedar said: We offer ourselves because we are
compared to one who is righteous. The willow said: I offer
myself, for Israel is compared to me, and they use me for
the mitzvah of the four species.

'At that hour the thorn said before God: Lord of the
Universe, I, who have no merit on which to base my claim
— I offer myself, and let this defiled one be hung on me.
For my name is 'a thorn,' and he is a thorn which causes
pain. It is fitting that a thorn should be hung on a thorn !
And the tree which they found was a thorn, and from it
they made a scaffold.

'When they brought the tree before him (Haman) he sat
at the entrance to his home and measured himself upon it
to show his servants how Mordechai would hang on it. A *bat
kol* (Echo-of-a-Divine-voice) replied to him: This tree is
fitting for you; it is prepared for you ever since the six days
of Creation ! (Esther Raba 9).

THE KING COULD NOT SLEEP

'That night the King could not sleep.' Rabi Tanchum said:
The King of the Universe did not sleep. Does God sleep
then ? Has it not been said: 'Behold the guardian of Israel
neither slumbers nor sleeps?!' But, when Israel suffers and
the nations of the world are at peace, it is said: 'Awaken,
why do you sleep, Lord ?'

'The Rabis have said: Those above were awake, those
below were awake. Those above were awake to seek mercy.
Those below were awake — Rav Chama Bar Guria said:
None capable of sleep were able to sleep that night. Esther
was busy preparing the feast for Haman. Mordechai was busy

with his sackcloth and fasting. Haman was busy with his scaffold. At that hour, God said to the angel appointed over sleep : My children are in travail shall this *rasha* sleep on his bed ? Come and trouble his sleep. The angel descended, stood over Achashverosh and beat on his heart saying : Ingrate ! Go and gratify the one to whom it is due !

'Rava said : The sleep referred to in this chapter, is the real sleep of King Achashverosh who began to think at heart : Why has Esther invited Haman ? Are they perhaps conspiring to kill me ? He further thought : If they were conspiring against me, do I not have a single loyal friend who would have informed me ? Then he thought : Perhaps there is a person who has done me a favor and I have not repaid him : Perhaps it is for this reason that people refrain from revealing things to me anymore ? 'And he said to bring the book of remembrance.'

'Rabi Levi said : Haman's son was the king's scribe. When he read in the script before him : 'And it was found written what Mordechai had told about Bigtana and Teresh,' he rolled the scroll further. The king said to him : 'How long will you keep rolling the scroll ? Read what is before you !' He answered : 'I cannot read.' But the verses were read of themselves : 'What Mordechai told...' When Mordechai's name was pronounced, sleep befell the king' (Various Midrashim).

THE DREAM OF ACHASHVEROSH AND ITS INTERPRETATION

'Towards morning, the king dreamt : Haman was standing over him with a drawn sword; Haman was removing his royal robe and crown, and was seeking to kill him. At that very hour, Haman himself came and knocked on the door. The king awoke from his sleep and said : 'Who is in the courtyard ?' They said to him, 'Behold Haman is standing in the courtyard.' Said he : 'This is not a dream but the truth.' And the king said : 'Let him come.' When he entered, the king said to him : 'What shall be done with the man whom the king wishes to honor ?' Haman was filled with conceit and thought: 'Who is greater than I? Who is more honorable than I? Whatever I ask — I shall be asking for myself.' He said: 'My Lord the King ! The man whom the king wishes to honor, let them bring the royal garments and the horse on which the king rode... and the crown.' When he asked for the crown, the king's face was altered, and he thought: This is the one of whom I saw in my dream, that he wishes to slay me. The king said to him: 'Hurry, take the garments and the horse, and deliver them to Mordechai.' Said he: 'My Lord, the King ! There are many Mordechais in the world.'

'To Mordechai the Jew.'

'Many are called Mordechai among the Jews.'

'The one who sits in the gateway of the king.'

'If so, one village or one stream are sufficient for him.'

'The king roared like a lion at him and said: 'Do not omit anything from all that you have spoken !'

'The king called Hatach and Charvonah and instructed them to go with Haman. He said to them: 'Be careful that he should not omit anything from all that he spoke.' They went with Haman.

'At that hour, Haman entered the king's storage chamber bent in height, mourning, with head hanging... darkened eyes, contorted mouth, dulled heart and knees shaking. He took the king's cloak and the royal vestments. He came out agitated; entered the king's horse stable, and took a horse standing at the head of the stable — on which a gold chain hung. He took hold of the reins, loaded all the royal vestments on his shoulders and went to Mordechai.

'When Mordechai saw Haman leading the horse, he said. 'It seems to me that this *rasha* comes only to trample me with his horse.' His disciples were sitting before him studying. He said to them: 'Rise and flee that you might not be burned by my coal !' They said to him: 'We shall not part from you; whether for life or death, we are with you !' He wrapped himself in a *talit* and rose to pray. In the meantime,

Haman came and sat among the pupils. He said to them:
'What subject are you engaged in ?' They said to him: 'In
the subject of the mitzvah of *omer*, which Israel offered when
the *Beit Hamikdash* still existed.' (The occurrence took place
on the 16th of Nisan, on which Israel offered a measure of
barley in the *Beit Hamikdash*, and Mordechai had been
teaching his pupils the subject of the day.) He said to them:
'And what is this measure ?' Is it of silver or of gold ?' They
said to him: 'Of barley.'

'And what was its worth ?'

'Much, ten *maot* (farthings).'

He said to them: 'Your ten *maot* prevailed against my
ten thousand silver *kikar*.'

'When Mordechai finished his prayer, Haman said to him.
Rise, Mordechai the Just, the son of Avraham, Itzchak and
Ya'akov! Your sackcloth and ashes have prevailed against
my ten thousand silver *kikar*. Arise from your sackcloth and
ashes, dress in the king's garment and ride on the king's
horse !' Mordechai answered: '*Rasha*, the son of Amalek's
seed ! Wait one hour, and I shall eat bitter bread and drink
bitter water. Afterwards, take me out and hang me on the
tree.' Haman said to him: 'Come rise, Mordechai the Just !
From your earliest days, great miracles have been performed
for you. The scaffold was prepared for my harm. And now,
rise and dress in this royal cloak; place this crown on your
head and ride on this horse, for the King wishes to honor
you.' Mordechai immediately understood that God had performed a miracle for him. He answered and said to him:
'World's fool ! I sit on ashes, and my body is dirty. Shall
I dress in royal garments ? It is not proper to do so. I shall
not dress till I wash and cut my hair.' He went to seek a
bath-attendant and a barber, but failed to find any. Haman
brought him into the bath-house and became his bath-attendant. He brought all spices and fine oils. He bathed him
and rubbed him with oil. He also brought him a pair of
shears from his home and became his barber. While shearing

81

him, Haman began sighing. Mordechai said to him: 'Why are you sighing?' Said he: Woe to that man — a man who was the greatest of the Nobles, and whose seat was above theirs — he has become a bath attendant and a barber.' Said Mordechai: 'Rasha! Did I not know your father who was a bath attendant and a barber in the village of Krinus for twenty-two years? These are his tools!'

'Having dressed him, Haman said: 'Go up and ride this horse.'

'I'm old and weak because of the fast.'

'Haman bowed low for him, and offered his neck. Mordechai stepped on him, and mounted the horse. In mounting, Mordechai kicked him. Said Haman: Mordechai! 'When your enemy falls, do not rejoice.' Mordechai answered: Rasha! It is said: 'And you shall tread on their height!'

'Mordechai rode, with Haman walking before him and announcing: 'Such is done to the man whom the king wishes to honor!' 27,000 slaves from the palace, with gold cups in their right hands and silver on their left hands, also walked, proclaiming: 'Such is done to the man whom the king wishes to honor.' All praised him, and torches were lit facing him.

'Haman's daughter looked through the window; seeing her father so shamed, she fell and died.

'When the Jews saw Mordechai's glory, they walked to his right and left, saying: 'Thus shall be done to the man whom the King in Heaven wishes to honor!'

'And Mordechai praised God, saying: 'I will exalt you, Lord, for You have saved me, and You have not rejoiced my enemies over me.'

'His disciples said: 'Sing to the Lord, His pious ones, and give thanks to His holy name. For His anger is but for a moment, His favor is for a life-time.'

'Esther said: 'To You, Lord, I called, and to the Lord I pleaded. What profit is there in my blood?'

'Israel said: 'You have turned my mourning into dancing.'

'Haman staggered back to his house — with four trades

in hand — now a bath attendant, a barber, an orderly and an announcer.' (Tr. Megilah 16; Esther 10; Vayikra Raba 28).

MATTERS PERTAINING TO THE MEGILAH

Noise making upon mention of Haman's name in the Megilah — Haman was a descendant of Amalek, of whom it is written: 'I shall surely wipe out the memory of Amalek.' And it is also written: 'You shall erase the memory of Amalek.' (The Hebrew terms for 'erasing' and 'beating' are phonetically alike.)

And Mordechai would not kneel or bow down — Why did Mordechai endanger his people by arousing Haman's anger? The Sages have said that an idol hung on Haman's heart, in order to trap Israel into sin, while bowing down to him. And idolatry is one of the three transgressions which one may not commit even on pain of death. Why is it said, 'He *would not* kneel or bow down,' in the future tense, rather than, 'He *did not* kneel or bow down'? We learn from this that Mordechai sought to let Haman know that he would never bow down to him. For he could have avoided his presence. Instead he intentionally appeared before Haman to demonstrate his refusal to bow down. It has been suggested that, since Mordechai was descended from Binyamin, who had not yet been born when Ya'akov bowed down to Amalek's grandfather, Esav — therefore Binyamin's descendants refused to bow down to Esav's descendants.

Others explain the use of the future tense as indicating that the king's orders specifically exempted Mordechai from having to bow down before Haman. As it is written: 'And all the king's servants who were in the king's gate, kneeled and bowed down to Haman, for thus did the king command concerning him; and Mordechai was not to kneel or bow down.' Haman, however, hid the matter from Mordechai. He, therefore, did not slander Mordechai before the king for

83

having failed to abide by the king's decree, but rather looked for some other cause for complaint against the Jews.

'In the plunder they did not send forth their hand.' — Why? And why is this mentioned three times in the Megilah? The reason is that those who were slain were all descendants of Amalek, from whom any manner of benefit is prohibited; so that the Jews might possess nothing to remind them of Amalek.

'The Jews affirmed and accepted.' — If they affirmed, they certainly accepted. Why then is it related that, 'they accepted?' Thus did the Sages say: 'They affirmed now what they had accepted earlier.' That is to say: They now voluntarily reconfirmed their acceptance of the Torah — which they had originally accepted involuntarily at Sinai.

We see thereby that the miracle of Purim brought Israel to a second 'acceptance-of-the-Torah.' For the merit of wiping out Amalek always leads to the acceptance of the Torah. After the war of Yehoshua againt Amalek in Refidim, the giving of the Torah took place; after the war of Mordechai against Haman, the Torah was accepted a second time.

FEASTING AND REJOICING

It is a mitzvah to have a sumptuous meal on Purim, including meat dishes and wine.

This 'command-feast' should be held during day time. And if one holds it at night, he fails to fulfill his obligation. Nevertheless, after the reading of the Megilah on the night of the 14th (in 'unwalled cities'), or on the night of the 15th after the Megilah-Reading (in 'walled cities'), one's meal should be somewhat more festive than usual. Lamps should be lit; one should wear festival clothing and rejoice.

The main Purim meal is held Purim afternoon and is preceded by Minchah. The meal is extended into the night. Most of the meal should, however, be had during the day.

When Purim falls on Erev Shabat, the meal is held early, and is concluded sufficiently before Shabat for one to be able to partake of the Shabat meal with a good appetite. Some follow the practice of extending their meal till Shabat arrives. They then place a Shabat tablecloth on the table, recite *kidush,* and continue their meal.

The miracle of Purim occurred through wine. Vashti was removed from her throne because of a wine-feast and Esther replaced her. The downfall of Haman was brought about through the wine feasting which Esther held. And through the repentance of the Jews, they expiated their sin in having drunk wine at the feast of Achashverosh. Our Sages of blessed memory, therefore, prescribed the drinking of wine on Purim till intoxication, and they said: 'A person is obligated to drink on Purim till he no longer knows the difference between 'cursed-is-Haman,' and 'blessed-is-Mordechai.' In the case, however, of one whose health may be harmed by excessive drinking of wine; or who fears that he might come to levity thereby; or that he might forget the required brachot or prayer — drinking till intoxication is not required. It is sufficient for such a person to drink a little more than is his usual habit, and to take a nap. He thereby fulfills the precept of the Sages: For one who sleeps does not know the difference between a curse and blessing.

It is customary to eat vegetables on Purim, in memory of the fact that Esther ate vegetables in the king's palace in her unwillingness to eat non-kosher food. As it is written 'And he gave her and her maidens preferred treatment...' That is, he gave her the food she preferred; as Daniel, Chananyah, Mishael and Azariah had done in the palace of the king of Babylonia.

'Although it is a Rabinic precept to eat more fully on Purim, it is preferable for one to extend charity to the poor. For there is no greater joy than to rejoice the hearts of the poor, the orphaned, the widowed, and strangers. And one who rejoices the hearts of these unfortunates is likened to the Divine Presence. As it is said (of God) : (He) 'enlivens the spirit of the lowly, and restores the heart of the down trodden' (Rambam, Hilchot Megilah Chapter 2).

TOWARDS EVENING

The reason for holding the Purim feast towards evening rather than in the morning, as is the case with other 'command-meals' on Shabat or Yom Tov is that people are busy sending gifts to their friends during the morning hours.

The Gaon of Vilna gave an explanation which is alluded to in the Megilah : The Purim feast is held in memory of the feast held by Esther for Achashverosh and Haman. She held her feast the third day of the fast, two hours before the advent of night. All Israel fasted the full three days and three nights. Esther alone did not fast the entire third day because of the feast. And this matter is alluded to in Esther's words to Mordechai : 'And I and my maidens will also fast thus.' The Hebrew equivalent for 'thus' is *'ken,'* and the numerical value of the two letters which comprise the word *'ken,'* is seventy. That is to say — 'I will fast only seventy hours, whereas all Israel are to fast seventy-two hours.'

THE SIGNIFICANCE OF THE PURIM FEAST

The Purim feast is especially significant in that it elevates the soul as it provides pleasure to the body. It is thus stated in the Zohar that on Purim one may accomplish through bodily pleasure, what he can accomplish Yom Kipur through bodily affliction.

The people of Israel are invested with bodily holiness as well as with spiritual holiness. And it is proper for their physical actions to be sanctified always, and to be done for the sake of God alone. As long, however, as Amalek exists, he corrupts the purity of Israel's actions. When Amalek's power is weakened and he is subjugated, the physical actions of Israel are again purified.

And the joy of the people of Israel over this feast is

especially great. For it bears witness that the penalty they paid in the days of Haman has completely expiated the sins they had committed. Otherwise, bodily affliction would have been prescribed for them rather than bodily pleasure.

It is proper to engage in some study of Torah prior to the meal. As it is said: 'Unto the Jews there was light and joy.' Upon which the Sages have commented: 'Light' refers to Torah.

'AD DELO YADA' ('Till one Does Not Know')

The precept of our ancient Sages to the effect that, 'A person is required to drink on Purim till he no longer knows the difference between 'cursed-is-Haman' and 'blessed is Mordechai,' appears strange, and we find no parallel to it anywhere else. Why did the Sages require us to drink till the loss of mental clarity ? The later Sages have explained the matter as follows :

Israel's salvation in the days of Mordechai and Esther was not merely a temporary one. We thus say in the praise after the Megilah-Reading: 'You were their salvation unto eternity, and their hope in every generation.' Till that salvation, the destiny of Israel hung on the balance of sin and repentance. And they might have incurred, Heaven forbid, the penalty of destruction, had they sinned greatly and failed to repent.

In that generation, the people of Israel did indeed incur the penalty of total destruction for many desecrations : They bowed d wn to Nebuchadnetzar's idol; they derived pleasure from Achashverosh's feast — in which he desecrated the sacred vessels of the Beit Hamikdash; they committed other evil actions after having imbibed Achashverosh's wine, till they were subject to the penalty of total destruction. When, however, they wholeheartedly repented, Divine mercy was forthcoming to them, and a path of salvation was opened.

At that hour, the 'attribute-of-Divine-mercy' came and said before God: 'Lord of the Heavens ! Your sons have sinned and a harsh decree was issued against them. The righteous Mordechai and Esther came, and awakened your sons to perfect repentance, whereupon the decree was nullified. But perhaps your sons will sin again, and there may not be among them *tzadikim* like Mordechai and Esther — and Israel may not know how to expiate their sin. Would you say that your sons, Israel, will perish, Heaven forbid, at that hour, and will not be granted mercy? Immediately, the path of salvation was widened for them, and their salvation became an eternal one for all generations. From then on — even if their sin should be exceedingly great, their enemies will be unable to destroy them. And the gates of Divine mercy which then opened for them, will never again be closed.

Just as Israel's redemption in those days was brought about not through our own merit, but through Divine mercy, likewise do we demonstrate through our manner of rejoicing, that we do not rely on our own merits but only on God's compassion. For this reason, we eat and drink on this day till 'loss-of-mind.' It is as if we were saying: 'Our salvation does not rest with us. For we do not know the distinction between our right hand and our left one.' We trust only that God will shield us against every enemy.

BETWEEN 'CURSED-IS-HAMAN' AND 'BLESSED-IS MORDECHAI'

In seeking to attain sufficient loss of awareness for us to be unable to distinguish between cursing Haman and blessing Mordechai, it is as if we were saying to God:

Even if — Heaven forbid, we no longer know anything of Your ways; even if we no longer know how to distinguish between such great extremes as these; nevertheless we do not despair of salvation, for we seek protection in You alone. Whether we are sober or intoxicated, we do not fear evil, for You are with us forever.

OTHER COMMENTS ON 'AD DELO YADA'

Everyone knows how to distinguish between 'cursed-is-

Haman' and blessed-is-Mordechai.' A person is to know, however, the various intermediate stages between these two extremes, so that he might always know whether a matter inclines towards good or bad. If one has drunk enough on Purim that he no longer knows the various stages that are 'between' Haman's cursedness and Mordechai's blessedness, then he is considered sufficiently intoxicated to have fulfilled his obligation.

Still another explanation : There are two ways in which holiness is revealed in the world : Either through the victory of the just or through the downfall of the wicked. As our Sages have said : 'Just as God's praise rises from the mouth of the just in the Garden of Eden, likewise does it rise from the mouth of the wicked in *Gehinom.*' God however, desires the praise of the just. When Israel acts justly, the righteous are exalted, and God's praise rises from them. When Israel lacks merit, salvation comes to them through the downfall of those who are more wicked than they. But then there is lack of joy in the world. The joy which emerges from 'blessed-is-Mordechai' is greater than the one which results from 'cursed-is-Haman.'

The Sages have, however, required us to rejoice on Purim till we no longer know the difference between the two types of salvation. For the downfall of Haman is not like the downfall of other *resha'im.* The joy which results from this downfall is as perfect as that which results from the victory of the just. For Haman is a descendant of Amalek, of whom it is said : 'When the wicked perish — there is song.' And whenever Amalek is wiped out, it is as if the Divine Presence were revealed in the world, — which is certainly a reason for perfect joy. And in order that a person might not feel downcast over having failed to merit salvation through his righteousness, but only through the greater evil of the wicked, we say to him : 'Drink and forget the difference between these two ways of salvation.'

WHY WE WEAR DISGUISES ON PURIM

The custom to wear disguises on Purim and to appear as
non-Jews is related to our father Ya'akov's wearing of Esav's
clothes when he received the blessings that were due him.
It is as if we announce that just as Ya'akov only had the
outer appearance of Esav, but was inwardly holy and pure,
so are all appearances of evil in Israel only external, and
inwardly we remain a holy people. At the time of Purim,
Israel was likewise loyal to God at heart, and only pretended
to worship Nebuchadnetzar's idol.

'The disciples asked Rabi Shimon Ben Yochai: 'Why were
the people of Israel liable to destruction in that generation ?'

'Said he: 'You tell me !'

'Because they derived enjoyment from Achashverosh's
feast.'

'If so, those in Shushan, the capital, should have incurred
death; but not those who lived elsewhere.'

'Said the disciples: 'You tell us!'

'Because they bowed down to the idol.'

'Is there arbitrary judgment in the matter ?' (and how
could they be forgiven ?)

'They only did so for appearance sake. And God also
acted towards them only for appearance sake' (Tr. Megilah
12).

This custom has also been related to a verse in the Torah:
'And I shall surely hide My face on that day,' on which
the Rabis comment: 'Where does the Torah allude to
Esther ?' It is said (Dvarim 31): *V'anochi haster astir
panai...*' ('And I will surely hide My face...' *'haster'* = 'to
hide' — and *'haster'* and 'Esther' are phonetically alike).
From this we learn that hiding one's face is proper on the
day of Esther.

Another reason: Amalek's hatred to Israel came to him
from his grandfather Esav. Esav's clothes upon entering to
receive Itzchak's blessing — which Esav had regarded due

him. Now we again disguise ourselves, to indicate that that disguise was not an unrighteous act, but that Ya'akov and his descendants justly receive the inheritance which Esav wanted.

Israel and Amalek are two extremes in the history of the nations. They are furthest apart from each other, but as is sometimes the case with extremes, at times they seem similar to each other. It is the way of Esav, and of Amalek his descendant, to disguise himself in garments which are not his; to talk smoothly, to pretend to be pious and just, while inwardly harboring only evil, deception and cunning. You thus find it said of Esav: 'For there is hunt in his mouth.' His mouth and his heart are not equal. The same trait but totally inverted, is found among the righteous of Israel. You thus find of David, King of Israel, that he appears like a sinner, whereas in truth he excelled in piety. The same trait characterized our father Ya'akov, whose righteousness was so much concealed from all eyes, that even his father Itzchak failed to recognize his true self; till Rivkah revealed his hidden traits and caused the blessings to be given to Ya'akov — who alone was worthy of them.

'AL HANISIM' ('For the Miracles')

Since the Purim festival is a Rabinic precept, it is obligatory to recall the miracle by reciting 'al hanisim' during 'birkat hamazon' — more so than during Chanukah. For if one forgets to say 'all hanisim' on Chanukah during 'birkat hamazon,' he is not required to repeat it since the Chanukah meal is not obligatory. On Purim, however, at least one meal is obligatory and therefore if one forgets to say al hanisim even once during birkat hamazon, he is required to repeat birkat hamazon. He is not however required to do so, if he says al hanisim at least after one meal during Purim. But some are of the opinion that one is not required to repeat al hanisim in any case; since the drinking of wine, rather than the feast itself, is the essential part of the mitzvah and al hanisim is not recited over wine. In any event when one reached 'harachaman' ('the Merciful One'), he should say: 'May the Merciful-One perform miracles and wonders for us... In the days of Mordechai and Esther...' Since the Purim meal is obligatory, al hanisim is added to its birkat hamazon, despite the fact that the meal extends into the night. The Sephardim, however say al hanisim only while it is yet day. (For the other rules concerning al hanisim in prayer, see the chapter on Chanukah).

GIFTS FOR THE POOR

There is a prophetic precept to give at least two gifts to two poor people on Purim; that is, one gift to each. And even a poor person who himself has to ask for charity, is required to do so. This obligation is fulfilled through any type of gift; whether of money, of food or drink, or even of clothing. One should however try to give a substantial gift. For if one gives a gift of money it should be sufficient for the recipient to buy bread weighing at least three eggs. At the very least, however, one must give a penny or its eqivalent value to each of two poor persons.

These gifts should be given by day.

It is proper to give the gifts to the poor after the Reading-of-the-Megilah. If one sets aside a tithe from his income for charity, he should not give these gifts from those monies. If however, he gives some slight sum from his own funds and wants to add his tithe, he may do so.

If one has set aside money for gifts to the poor on Purim, he may not change their intended purpose and give them to another charity.

A person cannot free himself, through his gifts to

the poor on Purim, from the general obligation of 'tzedakah' (charity) which the Torah places upon him. And even a poor person is obligated to fulfill the mitzvah at least once a year, aside from what he gives to the poor on Purim.

The gifts should be given in sufficient time for the poor to utilize them during Purim — and for their Purim meals. The poor person may however do as he wishes with the gifts he receives.

The special gifts for the poor which one is required to give for Purim, should not be given earlier, lest the poor partake of them before Purim; in which case the giver will not have fulfilled his obligation (In any event the general mitzvah of tzedakah would apply before Purim.)

One is not strict with the poor on Purim in determining whether they are needy or not. Whoever stretches forth his hand, is to be given a gift.

If one fails to find poor persons in his place, he sets the intended gifts aside till he encounters poor people.

Women are also obligated to give gifts to the poor on Purim.

'MISHLOACH MANOT'   ('The Sending of Gifts to One Another')

It is obligatory to send a gift which consists of at least two 'portions' to another person. Both men and women are included in this mitzvah.

Only what is edible or drinkable without further cooking or preparation, is considered a 'portion.' One may therefore send cooked meats or fish, pastry goods, fruit, sweets, wine and other beverages. And it is the more praiseworthy to send portions to as many friends as possible. It is, however, preferable to give more gifts to the poor than to friends.

Even a poor person is required to fulfill the mitz-

*vah of 'mishloach manot.' If one is unable to do so
directly, he may exchange his own food for that of
his friend; both of whom would thus fulfill their
obligations.*

*The mitzvah of mishloach manot may not be ful-
filled with money, clothing and the like, but only
with foods or beverages.*

*It is proper to send portions sufficient to convey
regard for the recipient. One should not send an item
so minute as to be worthless in the eyes of the poor.*

*If at all possible these 'portions' should be sent
by messengers, rather than to be delivered personally.
And though it is said of all other mitzvot: 'It is more
of a mitzvah if done personally, than if done through
a messenger, this mitzvah is different. Since the term,
'mishloach manot' (the sending of portions), is the
term used in the 'Megilah' the proper procedure for
fulfilling the mitzvah, is to do so by messenger. Nevertheless, if one delivers his mishloach manot personally,
he yet fulfills his obligation.*

*The mitzvah of mishloach manot should be per-
formed by day.*

*A mourner is free of the obligation, but some hold
that it rests even upon him, except that one in mourning should not send gifts which would be a source of
rejoicing.*

LOVE AND UNITY — A SHIELD AGAINST AMALEK

The mitzvah of mishloach manot and the giving of gifts
to the poor, during the days of Purim, are prescribed in
order to recall the brotherly love which Mordechai and
Esther awoke among all Jews. And when there is inner unity
among Jews, even the wrongdoers among them become righteous.

For Amalek's entire strength rests on those among the
Jews who become 'weakened' for lack of Torah and mitzvot.

Haman — the essence of Amalek — thought that he could destroy Israel after having misled them into sin; thereby making even the others liable for their children's wrongdoing, since they failed to protest. When a cleavage came about between both groups, Esther requested of Mordechai: 'Go and gather all the Jews.' If Jewish unity would be restored, Haman would be unable to subjugate even those who had committed wrong; since all Israel would feel the slightest pain of each individual among them.

Thus did the Sages say of our father Ya'akov: 'His ingathering and the gathering of his sons saved him from the hand of Esav.' Likewise, whenever Israel comes to grief because of Esav and Amalek, their salvation requires their own 'ingathering,' and the strengthening of brotherly love in their midst.

And just as the Jews who gathered in defense of their lives in the days of Haman, 'were thereby saved from calamity; likewise, are we bidden in every generation to strengthen our inner unity so that our enemies might not achieve dominion over us. And the days of Purim are especially suited for inculcating the striving for Jewish unity; as are the mitzvot of mishloach manot and giving gifts to the poor.

HUMILITY AND GRATITUDE

A person sends a gift to his friend only because he feels some sense of gratitude towards him. Thus, at the time of Purim, when the Jews wanted to express their joy and gratitude on being saved from their enemies — they each thought to themselves: By whose merit were we saved? And each said: Not by my merit, but only by that of my friend. Out of the great gratitude which filled their hearts towards one another, they sent gifts to each other, as if to say: I acknowledge the gratitude I owe you — by your merit was I saved! And it is likewise proper for every Jew to fault himself, and credit his friend whenever we are in need of salvation.

PURIM ALLUSIONS

Our later sages have discovered various allusions in the Festival of Purim. Purim is like Pesach — on both we emerged from bondage to freedom.

Purim is like Shavuot — we accepted the Torah again on Purim.

Purim is like Rosh Hashanah — the book of the living and the dead were opened then.

Purim is like Yom Kipur — the generation of Purim then expiated their sins.

Purim is like Sukot — just as Sukot commemorates the protection accorded us by the Divine 'cloud-of-glory' in the wilderness, likewise did many non-Jews enter under the protecting wings of the *Shechinah* during Purim. (The reference is to many of the gentiles who converted to Judaism.)

YOM KIPURIM — KI-PURIM ('Like Purim')

On Yom Kipurim the people of Israel rise above the nature through 'nullifying' the bodily aspects of their existence; and thereby attaining atonement for the transgressions of the body. Purim achieves the same through feasting and rejoicing. That is to say, even their physical pleasures became sanctified from above on Purim.

If one attains holiness through affliction, and another attains holiness through pleasure — who is the greater of the two ? It may be said that the one who attains holiness through pleasure is the greater, for the attainment of holiness through pleasure requires an infinitely greater degree of striving and effort.

Just as Yom Kipur has a scapegoat, similarly does Purim have one — the feast of Haman.

Just as Yom Kipur contains a mitzvah of eating and drinking which is followed by a mitzvah of fasting, similarly does Purim also contain these two mitzvot; except that their order is inverted. First there is the mitzvah of fasting, and then that of eating and drinking.

THE DAYS OF PURIM AND THE MEGILAH OF PURIM WILL
NEVER CEASE

The Rabis have said : 'All Festivals will one day cease, but
the days of Purim will never cease' (Yalkut Mishley 944).

The Rabis have also said : 'All the Prophetic Writings will
'cease' in the days of the Messiah, excepting for the Scroll
of Esther; which will endure eternally like the five books
of the Torah, and like the oral Torah. And although the
memory of the troubles Israel has known will 'cease'...,
the days of Purim will not. As it is said : 'And these days
of Purim will not pass from among the Jews, and their
memory will not cease from their seed.'

In what respect is Purim greater than all the other festivals ? All the festivals are sanctified by Israel, and in the
future when the world will be completely redeemed —
and all its days will be like Shabat — what value will
there be in adding the 'light of Yom Tov' to the pervasive
'light of Shabat ?' What value is there in the light of a lamp
at midday ? The 'light of Purim,' however, comes from a
revelation of holiness above, rather than from the actions
of Israel below. This holiness will therefore continue to shed
light even in the Messianic age.

In what respect is the Megilah of Esther greater than all
the other Prophetic Writings ? All the words of the Prophets
were intended to support the teachings of the Torah and
to sustain its mitzvot. In the future, Messiah will come and
he will establish the religion of truth on its proper founda-
tions. All the words of the Prophets will then be fulfilled.
And Israel will be engaged in the study and practice of Torah
in utter purity, as before their sins and the ensuing reproof
of the Prophets. The Scroll of Purim, however, is not 'the
end-of-a-chapter,' but rather the beginning of the chapter
of wiping out Amalek; a chapter which will come to an
end in the future redemption. At that time, when the memory of Amalek will have been completely erased, and God's

sovereignty will have become fully revealed, all will recount the mighty actions of God — from Mordechai and Esther till the 'end-of-days' — which brought about the blotting out of Amalek's memory.

Adar THE END OF THE MONTH

CHAPTER FOUR

'God is considerate of His creatures.' He therefore did not require that Israel go up to Yerushalayim in pilgrimage during the rainy season. The three Pilgrim-Festivals occur between spring and the conclusion of summer, during which time the days are beautiful and the nights are pleasant for travellers. For the duration of winter all are engaged in their various pursuits; one with his field, another with his vineyard, the third with his garden. As Nisan draws near all Israel rejoices and they say: Let us go to the house of the Lord. From the beginning of Nisan the people set out upon the roads from all corners of the land. They are on the way to Yerushalayim to offer the Pesach sacrifice; to be seen before the Divine Presence, and to discharge their various other obligations in Yerushalayim.

On the 15th of Adar messengers went forth from the *Beit Din* to repair the roads from the effects of the rainy season, in order to make them fit for the pilgrims, as well as for those who had committed accidental murder and were on the way to their 'cities-of-refuge.' The water cisterns were likewise uncovered, in readiness for the pilgrims and livestock.

The major assembly which took place in Yerushalayim after half a year's interruption, made possible various other public activities. Whoever was engaged in litigation could bring his case before the Great Beit-Din. — Cases involving capital punishment or the administration of penalties for violations of the law could likewise be brought before the Great Beit-Din. Objects consecrated to *hekdesh* (Temple-treasury) could be redeemed. The *sotah* (woman suspected of infidelity) was given the bitter waters. The *parah adumah* (red heifer) was burned. The *eglah arufah* was brought for a person found murdered on the road, whose assailant was unknown. The Hebrew slave who refused to go out free during the seventh year was subject to having his ear bored. The leper who had recovered was purified, and he brought his offerings in the Sanctuary. All these activities were intended to purify Israel from all defilement or transgression as 'they went up to be seen before the Presence of God' during the Pesach Festival.

Not only messengers of Beit-Din were engaged in these activities but anyone desirous of furthering the public good had ample opportunity for service. There were pious individuals who devoted themselves to furthering the public interest. In praise of these men the Rabis said: Whoever benefits the community is assured of Divine protection against becoming a cause of sin.

'The Rabis have related: It happened once that the daughter of Nechunya, the digger of cisterns (thus called because he used to prepare wells for the festival pilgrims), fell into a pit. Rabi Chanina Ben Dosa was informed the first hour (when it was presumed that she could still live in the water). He said to them: *Shalom* (that is, do not worry). The second hour he again said: *Shalom*. The third (when the presumption was that if she had been in water she could no longer live), he said to them: She has come up (from the waters)! She was asked: Who brought you up? Her answer was: The ram (the ram of Itzchak) appeared to me, led by an Elder (our father Avraham). They said to him (to Rabi Chanina Ben Dosa): Are you a Prophet? To which he answered: I am not a Prophet, nor the son of a Prophet. Thus however did I think: A matter for which the *Tzadik* suffered anguish (to benefit the community); can his descendants be hurt thereby?' (Tr. Baba Kama 50).

In Tractate Shekalim it is related: 'It once happened that

the daughter of a pious person — who used to dig wells and cisterns for travelers — was drowned in a river on the way to her wedding. All came to console him but he would not accept any consolation. Rabi Pinchas Ben Ya'ir entered and wished to console him, but he would not accept consolation. Rabi Pinchas said to the people: Do you consider this one pious ? They answered: Rabi, thus and thus happened to him. Rabi Pinchas said: Can it be that one who honored his Creator through water, should suffer harm from the Creator through water ? Immediately, the report spread through the city: The daughter of so and so has come back! Some say that she caught hold of the branch of a tree which miraculously was in her way, and she was saved. Others say that an angel descended in the image of Rabi Pinchas Ben Ya'ir and saved her' (Tr. Shekalim Chapter 5).

THE TWENTIETH OF ADAR

In the days of Shimon Ben Shatach and Choni Ha-me'agel, the 20th of Adar was made a festive day :

'On the 20th (of Adar) the people were thirsty for rain and it fell for them. There had been a famine and drought in the Land of Israel for three consecutive years. They had prayed for rain, but were unanswered. When they saw that most of Adar had passed without rainfall, they went to Choni Ha-me'agel and asked him to pray for rainfall.

'He said to them : 'Bring in the Pesach ovens so that they might not be damaged by the rains.'

'He prayed, but there was no rainfall. He then drew a circle, stayed within it as Havakuk the Prophet had done, and said: Lord of the Universe, Your children look to me for I am like one of Your household. I swear by your Great Name that I will not budge from here till You have mercy upon Your children ! Rain began to fall drop by drop. His disciples said to him : Rabi, this is not what we asked of you; we came to ask for sufficient rain that we might not die of famine. It seems to us that these rains have come only in

order to repeal your oath. Said he: My sons, you shall not
die !

'Lord of the Universe, (said he) Not for this did I ask,
but for enough rains to fill the pits and the cisterns. It then
began to rain in buckets. And the Sages surmised that each
drop was the measure of a log. They said to him: We have
come to you not for this, but to be saved from death. We
think that these rains will destroy the world. Again he
answered: My sons, you shall not die!

'Lord of the Universe ! Not for this did I ask, but for
rains of blessing.

'The rains became then normal. They kept falling however
till Yerushalayim became flooded and the people had to go
up to the Temple Mount, because of the excess rain. They
said to him: Just as you have prayed that they might fall,
pray likewise that they might cease. He said to them one
does not pray against too much good: Rather, go and bring
me an ox for thanksgiving. They went and brought him one,
and he rested his two hands on the ox, praying: Lord of
the Universe: See that Your people — Israel, Your inheritance — whom You brought forth with Your might and outstretched arm — are unable to withstand either Your great
anger or Your great benevolence. May it be Your will that
there might be relief ! Immediately the wind came, the
clouds scattered, the sun shone, the earth became dry, and
all went down to the field: Whereupon they saw that the
wilderness had become filled with truffle and mushrooms.
Shimon Ben Shatach, then sent word to him: If you were
not Choni Ha-me'agel, I would decree excommunication
against you. If these years were like the year of Eliyahu,
the Prophet, (when there was a decree from above that there
would be no rain) would not God's name have been desecrated
through you ?

'But what shall I do ? You plead before God like a son
does before his father, and who always gets his way. If he
says, 'bring me warm food' — the father provides it for him;

'bring me cold food' — he provides it; 'give me nuts' — he gives it to him; 'give me pomegranates,' he gives them to him: ... Of you Scripture says: 'Let your father and mother be happy, and let her who bore you rejoice.'

'That day was declared a festive day, since rainfall is dependant upon Israel's merit. As it is said: 'The Lord shall open for you his good treasure.' 'For you' — the matter depends upon you. It is also said; 'And all the families of the Earth shall be blessed through you and through your seed.' (Tr. Ta'anit 19).

PARAH (The Red Heifer)

The third of the 'Four Parshiot' is that of *Parah*, and is read on the Shabat which immediately precedes *Parshat Hachodesh*, without interruption between the two. If Rosh Chodesh Nisan falls on Shabat, *Parah* is read the last Shabat of Adar. And if Rosh Chodesh Nisan falls during the week, *Parshat Hachodesh* is read the last Shabat of Adar, and *Parah* on the preceding Shabat.

On Shabat Parah two Torah Scrolls are taken out of the ark. To one, seven persons are called for the weekly portion, and from the other the *maftir* of Parah is read (from *Chukat*).

According to some authorities this Torah reading is prescribed by the Torah; hence a minor (one younger than thirteen) is not eligible for this maftir. (A minor is not obligated to perform mitzvot; he cannot therefore enable others to fulfill their obligations.)

The purpose of reading this passage before Nisan, is to remind all who had been defiled by contact with the dead, to purify themselves in order to be able to offer the Pesach-sacrifice in its proper time. The Reading was set sufficiently before Pesach, so that even those who lived distantly from Yerushalayim (and departed from their homes by Rosh Chodesh Nisan), might have been instructed to that effect.

Although, because of our sins, the Sanctuary was destroyed,

and we have neither 'sacrificial-offerings' nor 'purification,' we nevertheless hold fast to the teachings of 'purification,' and we study its precepts in the proper time. It is thus regarded as if we had purified ourselves from our defilement, and rendered ourselves fit for bringing our offerings in their set time.

It is stated in the Jerusalem Talmud: By right, Parshat Hachodesh should precede Parshat Parah since the *Mishkan* was erected the first of Nisan, while the heifer was burned the second of the month. Why then was Parshat Parah prescribed first ? Since it involves purification of the people of Israel, in order to enable them to bring their Pesach sacrifices in the proper time.

'EVERYTHING GOES AFTER ITS ROOT'

The Torah requires purification through the ashes of the red heifer only for those defiled by contact with the dead. Anyone defiled in any other manner could attain purification in the particular manner prescribed by the Torah. For one defiled by contact with the dead, the only valid procedure for purification was that of the red heifer.

This mitzvah was given to Israel on Rosh Chodesh Nisan of the second year after they had departed from Egypt — on the day of the erection of the Mishkan. That particular year all Israel was required to undergo the purification of 'the red heifer,' regardless of their defilement through contact with the dead or not, since they had all been involved in the sin of the golden calf; and idolatry defiles like the dead. After God was reconciled with Israel, and commanded them to build the Mishkan for him, so that He might dwell in their midst, He gave them this mitzvah as a means of purification from all defilement; whether that of contact with the dead, or that of idolatry (which is the root of all death in the world).

Since the practice of the laws of 'the red heifer' is a 'root' of purification for Israel, greater stringency applies to it than to other forms of purification. If a place is presumed to be devoid of all graves, whoever walks thereupon, is not required to suspect that some dead person might be buried deep underneath. (His defilement would then be regarded as ascending to the surface.)

Likewise, any person upon whom the ashes of 'the red heifer' were sprinkled, is regarded as purified, and capable of purifying others as well.

The above is however dependent on one condition: that 'the first root of purification' had been perfect: That in 'the first root of purification,' in the preparation of 'the red heifer,' and its subsequent usage, the required regulations had been completely fulfilled.

From the time when this mitzvah was first given to the people of Israel, till the destruction of the Second Temple, there were nine red heifers altogether. The first one was brought by Moshe Rabenu, and its ashes were used during the entire existence of the first Beit Hamikdash with a little remaining, after its destruction. The second was brought by Ezra the Scribe; and the remaining seven were brought from Ezra till the destruction of the second Sanctuary. The tenth will be brought by the Messiah, who will speedily redeem us. And whenever a new heifer was brought, some of the remaining ashes of each of the preceding heifers were sprinkled on the *cohen* engaged in its burning.

Just as the *Cohen Gadol* was removed from his home seven days before Yom Kipur for the Service of Yom Kipur, likewise was the cohen engaged in burning the 'heifer' separated for the preceding seven days from his house. During this period he stayed in a special chamber which was called 'the house of stone.' All the materials in the structure of this house, and all its vessels were made of stone and earth (which never received defilement). Each of the seven days some of the remaining ashes of all the previous 'heifers' was sprinkled on the designated cohen, in order to purify him from any unknown defilement.

107

Only such a person who had never been defiled by contact with the dead could sprinkle the ashes on the designated cohen. Likewise, the vessels used for the sprinkling were required to be of stone (which could never be defiled).

THE STATUTE OF THE HEIFER

There are many mitzvot in the Torah which are called 'statutes,' for which no reason is stated. Nevertheless their reasons and secret meanings were revealed to the Sages of succeeding generations, beginning with Moshe Rabenu. Of the mitzvah of 'the red heifer' however, it is stated: 'This is the statute of the Torah' — that is to say, 'This,' and there is none like it.

'We have learned: Whoever is engaged in the preparation of 'the heifer' from beginning to end, his clothes are defiled, whereas 'the heifer' itself purifies others. Thus however did God say: I have established a statute, I have made a decree, you may not violate my decree !' (Yalkut Chukat 759).

'All this have I thought I would attain wisdom but it is distant from me' (Kohelet 7). King Shlomo said: I have attained an understanding of the whole Torah. But upon reaching this passage of 'the red heifer,' I expounded it, I asked and inquired concerning it — 'I thought I would attain wisdom, but it is distant from me' (ibid.).

'And they shall take unto you a red heifer.' God said to Moshe: To you I will reveal its reasons, but to others it is a statute' (ibid.).

Come and see that the way of Israel is different than that of the nations of the world. The way of the nations, is, that when they know the reason for a precept, they praise it. When they do not know the reason, they hold it in disregard. In either case, they do not accept the obligation of the mitzvot upon themselves, and they do not observe them. They are particularly critical of Israel over the mitzvah of 'the red heifer;' of this mitzvah the 'Accuser' and the nations of the world say, more so than of any other mitzvah : What is this mitzvah, and what reason is there for it.

The way of Israel is different however. Whether they know the reason for a mitzvah or not they accept the yoke of all the mitzvot and a mitzvah whose reason is unstated, and which is entirely 'a royal decree,' is particularly precious to them.

Since Israel adheres to the mitzvot as Divine decrees, and they accept those decrees in humility — whether or not human reason finds them attractive — they hereby attain the merit of purification from above — which makes them as newborn and lifts them above the limitations of nature — measure for measure. Just as they nullify their own nature and reason in the presence of God's will, likewise does He nullify the laws of nature in their behalf.

SOME ALLUSIONS

Although the meaning of the mitzvah of 'the red heifer' was revealed only to Moshe Rabenu, nevertheless the Sages have pointed out some possible allusions.

'Why are only male animals valid for all the other offerings, while here the female is required ? Rabi Ivo said : The matter may be likened to the son of a maidservant who dirtied the king's palace. Said the king : Let his mother come and clean up the excrement. Likewise did God say : Let the heifer come and atone for the act of the golden calf' (Yalkut Chukat 759).

Another possible allusion from the writings of the later Sages :

By means of this mitzvah the Torah intended to teach us the way of perfect repentance; so that no trace of one's earlier sin might remain.

If a person has committed a misdeed, that misdeed has left its mark on his soul — even if he subsequently regrets having committed it. And one misdeed leads to another; his own misdeeds lead others to wrongdoing; and those others

109

have the same on going effect upon still others without end. His one misdeed is therefore found to have 'cast blemish' upon all of creation. How then is it possible to remove one's wrongdoing from the world, and to completely wipe out its traces and effects.

The way of repentance is as follows : First a person is bidden to forsake his sin and not to repeat it. Afterwards, he should return to the cause which led him to wrongdoing and rectify that cause. To the extent possible, he is to trace the whole chain of such causes to their earliest beginnings. And if one goes back far enough, he will reach a point of utter purity. Having reached that point he will have attained perfect repentance for himself, and the total removal of the 'blemish' which his misdeeds cast upon the world.

This matter is alluded to in the procedure for 'the red heifer :' Israel committed the sin of the golden calf. Having repented, they burned it in fire and 'negated' it completely. Subsequently they returned to the 'source' of the golden calf, the red heifer (red being a symbol of sin). They then burned the red heifer till it became ashes. But even these ashes were not completely free of the taint of sin. Therefore, they put the ashes into spring water — both of which together were poured into a consecrated vessel. They thus reached 'the first root' of all creation — spring ('living') waters — 'the waters of creation' of which it is said : 'And the Spirit of God hovers upon the face of the waters.' Having reached this 'root,' all becomes rectified.

That is to say, one who has committed a sin is required to remove all of its effects and the effects of its causes from himself, till he becomes like a newborn person; like the Earth itself before its dry land appeared, when it was everywhere covered with the living waters of Divine creation; when it had neither earth nor ashes nor any of their derivatives, but only pure waters placed in the vessel fashioned for them by the Creator alone.

110

THE DAYS OF DEDICATION

The seven final days of the month of Adar, from the 23rd of the month till Rosh Chodesh Nisan, are called 'the days of dedication;' for on them Moshe Rabenu dedicated the *Mishkan* after its completion. On the first of Nisan the Mishkan was erected and Aharon and his sons began to serve as *cohanim*. The previous seven days Moshe Rabenu alone served as a cohen. He erected the Mishkan, took it apart; brought the dedication-offerings and ate of their meat.

These days of dedication of the first Divine Mishkan, built by Moshe Rabenu upon God's command, are destined to be renewed when our Messiah comes. His coming, and the rebuilding of the Beit Hamikdash — speedily in our days — will also occur in the month of Nisan. Just as the days of dedication are a memorial to the Mishkan made by Moshe Rabenu, they are also days of prayer for the final redemption, and the building of the Sanctuary, in which the Divine Presence will dwell eternally.

THE SECOND ADAR

All the laws which apply to the month of Adar during a regular year, apply to the second month of Adar during a leap year. Purim and the four special *Parshiot* are then observed in the second Adar. And those who fast on the seventh of Adar in memory of Moshe Rabenu's death, do so the second Adar. It is however stated in Yalkut Yehoshua that the year of Moshe Rabenu's death was a leap year, and that he died during the first Adar — in which case the fast of the seventh of Adar should be observed during the first Adar. In this matter customs vary from place to place.

It is also customary to observe the fourteenth and the fifteenth days of the first Adar with some festive spirit; *Tachanun* being omitted, as are likewise, fasting or eulogies.

If anyone is born during Adar of a regular year, and the year of his Bar Mitzvah occurs during a leap year, he does

111

not become Bar Mitzvah till the second Adar. If however the year of his birth was also a leap year, he becomes Bar Mitzvah in the month of his birth. It is therefore possible, in the case of children born in the same year at a distance of one or two days from each other, for the child born first, to become Bar Mitzvah almost an entire month after the other child. It is likewise possible, in the case of two children born the same year at a distance of almost a month apart, for the child born almost a month before the other, to become Bar Mitzvah after the second child. How ?

If two children were born in a leap year, one on the last day of Adar I, and the other — after him — on the first day of Adar II; and if the year of their Bar Mitzvah is a regular year containing only one Adar — then the child born last, on the first of Adar II becomes Bar Mitzvah on Rosh Chodesh Adar, whereas the one born a day earlier, the last day of Adar I, becomes Bar Mitzvah a month later than the other child — on the last day of Adar.

Likewise, if two children were born in a leap year — one on the 28th of Adar I and the other a month later, on the 27th of Adar II; and if their Bar Mitzvah occurs during a regular year — then the one born a month later, becomes Bar Mitzvah one day before the other, since he becomes Bar Mitzvah on the 27th of the month, whereas the second one becomes Bar Mitzvah the next day, on the 28th.

Why is Purim observed during a leap year, the second Adar? Since the year of Haman's decree was a leap year, and it occurred during the second Adar. Also by observing Purim during the second Adar we place 'one redemption adjacent to another' — the redemption of Esther to the redemption from Egypt.

Why is the month of Adar alone used for a leap year ? It has been stated earlier (see the chapter on Rosh Chodesh) that the purpose of leap years is to make certain that the month of Nisan should always coincide with the advent of spring. For in speaking of Pesach the Torah stated: 'Observe the

month of spring.' The month which immediately precedes
Nisan was therefore intercalated to form a leap year. For
if Shevat or Tevet were intercalated, and spring were to
arrive during the month of Adar, the Beit-Din might have
cause to regret having made the leap year. But by the time
of Adar, it is already apparent whether or not the winter
season is longer than usual; so that a leap year would be
necessary. And although our calendar is based entirely on
calculation and not on observation, we nevertheless do not
depart from the principles by which the Sanhedrin abided,
when they still regulated the calendar by observation.

Nisan

CHAPTER FIVE

The Sages of Israel decreed that on the Shabat before the
first of Nisan, or on Rosh Chodesh itself if it occurs on
Shabat, we should read the chapter beginning with the words
'This month shall be for you the head of the months; it is
the first for you of the months of the year' (Shmot 12).
This reading is in addition to the usual weekly *sidra*.

If Rosh Chodesh occurs on a weekday, seven people are
called up for the reading of the Torah on the previous Shabat. Then an additional person — the *maftir* is called to
read 'This month shall be for you...' from a second scroll.
If Rosh Chodesh falls on Shabat, three scrolls are taken
from the Ark. The weekly *sidra* is read from the first scroll
for which six people are called up, but *kadish* is not said
at the end of the *sidra*. A seventh person is then called for
the reading from the second scroll a passage from *Pinchas*
(in the book of Bamidbar) which deals with Rosh Chodesh.
After this reading *kadish* is recited. Then another person
— *maftir* — is called to the reading from the third scroll
The theme of the last reading, i.e. 'This month shall be for
you...' forms the subject of the *haftarah* which is read afterwards.

Whenever we read from more than one scroll, the *haftarah*
has some connection with the reading from the last scroll.
This *haftarah* is taken from the Book of Yechezkel (Chap.
45). It speaks of this day — Rosh Chodesh Nisan — and
its sacrifices, and mentions also the other offerings brought
by the *Nasi* or King. It tells of the honor which must be

shown to the King when he enters and departs from the Sanctuary.

According to the custom of the Sephardim, whenever a second scroll is read from, *kadish* is said after this reading. If three scrolls are taken out of the Ark, then kadish is said after reading from the second scroll and again after reading from the third scroll. It is not said after reading from the first scroll, but only after seven people have been called to read from the Torah, that is to say, after reading from the second scroll.

In many communities it is the custom, on this Shabat, to recite *yotzrot* during *shacharit* and *piyutim* during *musaf*, but in other places *piyutim* alone are read during *musaf*.

THE PUBLIC ANNOUNCEMENT

It is because of the importance of the month of Nisan that our Sages decreed that we should add a special section of topical interest to the usual reading from the Torah. For Nisan is the first — the king — of all the months. 'This month shall be for you...' The letters of the word 'for you' (*lachem*) are the same as those of the word 'king' (*melech*) and we must honor Nisan more than any other month. We therefore announce it in public on Shabat when people are gathered in the synagogues and we hallow it by special readings from the Torah and by the *haftarah*.

However, it is not this reading which sanctifies the month, for this could only be done by a Beit Din of experts, duly authorized, and by witnesses who had actually seen the new moon appear. But it is a way of showing greater honor to the month of Nisan than to any other month.

Furthermore, this reading which reminded the people that Nisan was at hand, also reminded them of the approach of Pesach, so that they could make preparations for the pilgrimage. To go up on foot to Jerusalem on Pesach was more important than on the other festivals, for the *mitzvah* of bringing the special Pesach-sacrifice was included in this pilgrimage. The offering of an individual for other festivals could be brought at any time within the week, but the Pesach-sacrifice could only be offered on the 14th of Nisan.

The *Beit Hamikdash* was more honored during Pesach than at any other time of the year when the majority of the people, great and small alike, came into its precincts with song and with praise. For this reason, the people and their leader were taught their duties to themselves and to each other, and towards the *Beit Hamikdash* with its holy objects, its services and its sacrifices.

All these ideas are contained in the chapter from the Book of Yechezkel which is read as the *haftarah* on Shabat *parshat hachodesh*.

SOME OF OUR SAGES' INTERPRETATIONS
ON PARSHAT HACHODESH

We read in this chapter (Shmot 12) 'And God said to Moshe and to Aharon in the land of Egypt saying; 'This month shall be for you the head of the months. It shall be the first for you of the months of the year.'

Our Sages have commented on the phrase 'In the land of Egypt.' Why does it not simply say 'In Egypt?' Rabi Chanina said, 'The Holy One, Blessed be He has said, 'In the Torah it is written (Dvarim 24), 'You shall stand outside and the man who is in debt to you shall bring the pledged article outside to you.' I too will act in this manner.' 'In the land of Egypt,' but outside of the city of Egypt, (the name of the city is the same as that of the country). For we learn that the Israelites were given as a pledge to the Egyptians until such time that the promise made to Avraham would be fulfilled; 'And they (the Israelites) shall serve them (the Egyptians) and the latter shall afflict them for four hundred years,' but they were not sold to the Egyptians to be slaves forever. When the time came for the pledge to be redeemed, God, standing outside the city of Egypt, demanded that the

Israelites be given back. But Pharaoh wanted to retain them illegally and God had to use force against him.

Our Sages have also connected the phrase 'In the land of Egypt' with the love that God bears for His people Israel. God came to a land of idol-worship, to a defiled and unclean land, in order to redeem His people. It can be compared to a *cohen* whose *trumah* (which must be kept in purity) has fallen into a cemetry. 'What shall I do ?' he asks himself. 'I cannot defile myself by entering a graveyard, but I also cannot allow the *trumah* to remain there. It is better that I should defile myself on this one occasion and purify myself afterwards, rather than lose my *trumah*.

Israel, the *trumah* of the Holy One, Blessed be He, was in an unclean place. 'How can I redeem them' said God, 'but also, how can I leave them there ? It is better that I defile Myself by going to Egypt and delivering them.' After He had brought them out, He called for Aharon — as one who had become defiled would call for a *cohen* — of whom it is said : 'And he shall make atonement for the place of holiness of the Sanctuary' (Vayikra 17).

'This month shall be for you.' 'For you,' that is to say, 'your very own,' 'for your redemption,' and also : 'It is given over to you.'

'Rabi Yehosua Ben Levi said : 'It can be compared to a king who had a time piece. He used to look at it to know the correct time. When his son was old enough the king handed the time-piece to him. The Holy One, Blessed be He, said, 'Until now, the reckoning of the months and the years was My province. From now onwards this task is entrusted to you' (Yalkut Bo 190).

This is how the Sages interpreted the verse 'You have done great many things, O God. My Lord, Your wonders and Your thoughts are to us' (Tehilim 40). Said Rabi Simon; 'Your thoughts,' that means, 'Your reckonings.' Throughout the two thousand four hundred and forty eight years that preceded the deliverance from Egypt, the Holy One, Blessed be He, calculated the reckonings of the years and the months. As soon as the Israelites went out from Egypt, He handed this task over to them. That is why it says, 'And God said to Moshe and Aharon in the land of Egypt, to say:' What does the phrase 'to say' tell us ? 'Say that from now onwards this task is entrusted to you, 'This month is for you.'

The Rabis further explained the verse 'It is the voice of my beloved one, behold he comes. He skips over the mountains, he jumps over the hills' (Shir Hashirim 2). Said Rabi Yehoshua : 'The voice of my beloved one,' that refers to Moshe. When Moshe told the Israelites that they would be redeemed during that month, they said to him, 'How can we be redeemed? Did not the Holy One, Blessed be He, say to Avraham our father, that we would be slaves to the Egyptians and that they would afflict us for four hundred years ?' Moshe replied to them, 'Since He wishes to deliver you, He does not look at your reckonings, but 'He skips over the mountains,' He skips over — He overlooks — the fixed time, the calculations and the leap years, so that you may be delivered this month.'

THE MONTH FOR REDEMPTION

The word 'redemption' applies only to one who emerges from darkness into light. One who has never experienced the suffering of bondage and oppression cannot appreciate redemption. The very essence of redemption is the freedom which comes from the oppression itself. Had the Children of Israel never been enslaved, they would never have experienced true freedom. Once they were enslaved, the slavery itself gave rise to the redemption and from the midst of the darkness, and only from that darkness, the light burst forth. Thus said our Sages: 'The Israelites said to the Holy One, Blessed be He, 'O Lord of the Universe, when will You deliver us ?' The Holy One, Blessed be He, answered; 'When you will have reached the lowest depths, at that moment I will redeem you' (Yalkut Hoshea 533).

You will find that when Itzchak was born, everyone re-marked, 'This child has been born to be a slave, for did not the Holy One, Blessed be He, tell Avraham, 'Your children shall be strangers in a land which is not theirs.' But Itzchak became the father of a nation of redeemed and free people.

You will find that when Itzchak was bound on the altar, it seemed as if the offspring of Avraham were about to perish from off the face of the earth, and yet this binding of Itzchak became a source of privilege and eternal life for all future generations.

Similiarly, when Ya'akov put on the garments of Esav and went in to receive his father's blessing, he was afraid. 'I shall be in his eyes as one who deceives and I shall bring on myself a curse rather than a blessing.' But when he came out, he was laden with blessings for himself and for all future generations.

Likewise we note in the long history of Israel that troubles and dark sorrows became a basis for salvation and light; and the darker the troubles were, the greater was the light which came afterwards. The future redemption will also burst forth from the midst of darkness. At the very moment when every heart trembles at the point of despair, the glory of God will shine forth. And when will that moment be ? In the month of Nisan, for God has appointed it as a time of redemption. Every misfortune which befalls Israel during this month, is nothing else but an assurance that the deliverance is about to begin.

Our Sages have explained the words; 'This month shall be for you...' by quoting the verses 'The counsel of God remains forever' (Tehilim 33) and 'Happy is the nation whose God is the Lord' (ibid.). When the Holy One, Blessed be He, chose this world, He established for it the order of the months and the years for all time. 'The counsel of God remains forever.' When He chose Ya'akov and his sons, He established for him a month of redemption, a month in which

Israel would be redeemed from Egypt, a month in which they are destined to be redeemed in the future. In that month Itzchak was born, in that month he was bound on the altar, and in that month Ya'akov received the blessings. In that month God hinted to the children of Israel that Nisan would be the beginning of their salvation; 'It is the first for you of the months of the year' and therefore 'Happy is the nation whose God is the Lord.'

THE HEAD AND THE FIRST

'The head of the months.' Whoever counts the months in years to come shall count them only from Nisan. Why is this ? It is because the day of redemption is greater than the day of birth, and the redemption itself is greater than any incident or event. Before the Children of Israel came out from Egypt they used to count from the creation of the world, or from the new lease of life that was given after the Flood, or from the birth of Avraham, or from the covenant that was made with him. However as soon as the redeemed nation came out from Egypt, they abandoned all these reckonings and counted only from the redemption. 'This month is the head of the months for you.'

'It may be compared to a king who made a feast when a son was born to him. The son was taken prisoner and held captive for some time. When he was eventually ransomed, the king marked that day as an anniversary. Before the Israelites went down to Egypt they used to count the years until the slavery would begin, that is to say, they would reckon how many years had passed since the covenant with Avraham when the future slavery had been decreed. But after they went down to Egypt and were enslaved there, and God performed miracles for them and redeemed them, they began counting from the month of that great event, 'This month shall be for you the head of the months' (Shmot Raba 15).

'It is the first — for you.' Whatsoever is called 'first' is

123

for you, for your benefit. Whether it is good for itself — or bad, for you it is good, for what is 'first' is always for your benefit.

'It is the first for you' (i.e. the first is for you). The Holy One, Blessed be He, is called 'First,' as it says, 'I am First' (Yeshayahu 44), Zion is called 'first,' 'On high from the first, the place of our Sanctuary' (Irmeyahu 17). Esav is called 'first,' 'The first one came out' (Bereishit). The Messiah is called 'first,' 'The first for Zion, behold he comes' (Yeshayahu 41). The Holy One, Blessed be He, who is called 'The first' will come, He will build the *Beit Hamikdash* which is called 'first.' He will exact punishment from Esav who was called 'first,' and the Messiah who is called 'first' will come in the month that is first; 'This month shall be for you the first' (Shmot Raba 15).

SOME EXPLANATIONS OF THE LATER SCHOLARS
ON PARSHAT HACHODESH

On the Difference between Shanah (year) and Chodesh (month) — The word *shanah* — 'a year' is connected with the word *yashan* — 'old' and also with the word *shenah* — 'sleep.' That is to say, everything in the year has been established from the time of the creation. The word itself conveys the idea of the laws of nature which the Creator ordained in the world which He created, laws by which nothing changes and in which there is nothing new.

The word *chodesh* — 'a month' is connected with the word *chadash* — 'new.' That is to say, that which you now see, will not necessarily exist in the future, but you may expect new things. The word hints at miracles and wonders, beyond the boundaries of nature, with which the Holy One, Blessed be He, sometimes guides His creatures in order to show them that He is Master over His World.

On the Difference between Israel and Other Nations — For all the nations of the world, the fixed year is the central point of their lives — beginning from the creation of the world. From that time onwards, they are all bound by the laws of nature from which there is no escape. But for the Children of Israel. the Holy One, Blessed be He, set aside the laws of nature and struck a new path and a new way of life, for them alone, — the path of wonders and miracles by which He redeemed them from Egypt. For He took out a nation from the midst of another nation by means of trials, signs, wonders and wars, by a strong hand and outstretched arm, by imposing His awe and revealing His Divine Presence. Those miracles have remained with Israel for all time.

The other nations have only one 'Head of the year,' in Tishrey, the day that reminds us of the creation of the world. On that day the nations are judged. But for Israel there are other 'heads' in the year — the head of each month — and there is one that is the first of all these 'heads' — that is the month of Nisan. In every month the Children of Israel hope that the strength of their youth will be renewed, both by natural and by supernatural means. In the month of Nisan their expectation that the Divine Presence will be revealed, becomes even greater, and more than in any other month, they hope for something new to happen in their lives. Therefore it is written, 'This month is for you', that is to say, this introduction of something new into the plan of the creation, is intended for you alone, and the month of Nisan is the first of those things which are beyond the laws of nature.

First and Foremost — Even though the fixed laws of the creation were given to Israel as well, and the natural way of life is available to them as much as to any other nation, and even though Israel is well able to exist and even to prosper in that way, nevertheless they were also given miracles and wonders that are outside the scope of nature and that take precedence over the laws of nature. This is the meaning of the words, 'It is the first for you of the months of the year,' that is to say; the *Chodesh* — the month, in its meaning of *chadash* — new, will come first for you and will be more important than the *shanah* — the year, in its meaning of *yashan* — old. Israel's survival and valiance in all generations have not come about through natural means but through miracles and wonders, by God, may His name be blessed, revealing His glory to His people. Therefore, when the Holy One, Blessed be He, appeared to them at Mount Sinai, He said, 'I am the Lord your God, Who brought you out from the land of Egypt,' but He did not say, 'I created you and brought you out.' It is as if He overlooked what was of lesser importance and mentioned only the greater event.

'For You' — on Your Behalf — At the time of the departure from Egypt, the Holy One, Blessed be He, changed all the fixed rules of nature to demonstrate that God, may His name be blessed, is the Creator and that He does everything according to His will, and also to demonstrate that the whole world was created for the sake of Israel. When the Creator wished to show His great strength and to change the laws of nature He did so only for the sake of Israel His people.

The Holy One, Blessed be He, could have redeemed the Israelites from Egypt by natural means. He could equally have guided them from the first by natural means so that they would not have been enslaved by the Egyptians. But the sole purpose of the exile was to make clear to Israel, and to the entire world, that the whole order of the universe and all its laws and all power that there is in the world, is bound by the will of God and exists for the sake of His chosen people. At His will, He maintains the natural laws of the world, and at His will He changes them for the sake of Israel, His people. Therefore it is written; 'This month is for you,' — for your sake; new miracles and wonders have been made in order to exalt you and to raise you up, just as My name is exalted throughout the world.

The Torah — Only Source for Renewal —

In what way is Israel different from the other nations ? For their sake, the Holy One, Blessed be He, made changes in His world that He might redeem them. Furthermore He gave them the power to upset the natural order, and to use this power constantly. Is it not written, however, 'There is nothing new under the sun ?' But God, may His name be Blessed, foresaw that Israel would one day accept the Torah and walk in His ways — for the Torah preceded the creation of the world and is superior to all things that have been created. Under the sun there is nothing new, but above the sun, in the Torah, there are new things.

NISAN

There are three names for this month; the head of the months — 'hachodesh harishon' (the first month), 'chodesh ha'aviv' (the month of Spring) and Nisan.

The Torah refers to it as 'the first month,' for it is always reckoned the first of the months of the year. It is also called the month of Spring, for in it all plants and living things flourish and are renewed, and in this month life and riches are given to the world.

The name Nisan is Babylonian in origin. The Israelites brought the name back with them when they returned from their exile in Babylonia. This name too is connected with spring for the word Nisan is similar to the word *nitzan* meaning a bud, and of Spring it is said: 'The buds have appeared in the land' (Shir Hashirim 2). The later Sages found a hidden meaning in the name *Aviv* (spring). Its Hebrew letters mean 'The head of twelve,' that is to say, it is the head of all the twelve months of the year.

The sign of the Zodiac for this month is Aries, a ram, which reminds us of the 'lambs for each household' which the Torah commanded the Israelites to bring for the Pesach sacrifice.

But even before the Israelites were commanded to take the lamb for the sacrifice in Nisan, the other nations, and especially the Egyptians, used the ram, which is clearly visible in the stars during this month, to symbolize the power that is present in Nisan. For the ram is a sign of riches and in our sacred tongue, the word for 'ewes' — *ashtarot* is from the same root as the word for 'riches' because they make their owners rich. In this month the ram is more prolific than at any other time and the source of blessing and life for the whole year is found therein.

The Egyptians, whose entire purpose in life was directed towards riches and physical strength, made the ram into a god, bowed down to it and worshipped it. But the Israelites whose lives are directed towards the service of God, were commanded to take the god of the Egyptians, their master, to slaughter it in that very month and to bring it as an offering to God. For there are no riches and there is no strength, except that which comes from God. The sign of the Zodiac for the month of Nisan is a ram — both for the Israelites and for the Egyptians, but for Israel it is a symbol of the service of God and for the Egyptians it is a symbol of idolatry.

This is how our Sages explained the verse 'Draw out and take for yourselves sheep for your families and kill the Pesach offering' (Shmot 12), that is to say, 'Withdraw your hands from idolatry, take for yourselves sheep, slaughter the gods of the Egyptians and make a Pesach offering.' 'Withdraw from idolatory and cleave to the Mitzvot' (Yalkut Bo 206).

The month of Nisan always contains thirty days and has only one day of Rosh Chodesh.

THE MITZVAH OF RECKONING NISAN AS THE FIRST MONTH

These are the words of Ramban. 'This month shall be for you the head of the months' means that Israel should reckon Nisan as the first month and count the other months from it, e.g. the second (from Nisan) the third (from Nisan) etc. so that it should be a constant reminder of the great miracle of the departure from Egypt. Thus whenever we mention the months we will remember the miracle. Therefore the months have no names in the Torah but are simply referred to by numbers, for example, 'In the third month,' or 'And it was in the second year, in the second month that the cloud was lifted' or 'In the seventh month on the first of the month,' and many similar instances.

'Just as there is a reminder of Shabat whenever we mention the days of the week — which also have no names but are known as 'the first day towards Shabat,' the second day towards Shabat,' — so there is a reminder of the departure from Egypt whenever we mention the months, because we count them from the month of our deliverance.

We do not reckon the months according to where they come in the year — for in reality the year begins in Tishrey, ('And the feast of the ingathering at the turn of the year,' 'When the year ends') but when we call the month of Nisan, the 'first' and the month of Tishrey, the 'seventh,' we mean that the former is the first month of our deliverance.

There are some who say that it is not right when using the non-Jewish dates on documents or official papers, to refer to them by numbers, 'first month,' 'second month,' etc. For the Torah has commanded us to call Nisan the first month. There can be no month other than Nisan that can be called 'first.' The non-Jewish months should be called by their names, January, February, March etc.

DAYS OF CELEBRATION

One may not fast during the month of Nisan except for the first, the tenth and the twenty sixth of the month when the righteous abstain from food, and of course, the fast of the first born on Erev Pesach. A bride and bridegroom fast on the day of their wedding during this month, even on Rosh Chodesh. One may also fast after a bad dream. No eulogy may be said at the funeral of one who dies during Nisan, nor does one say the prayer justifying God's action (*tziduk hadin* — said usually at a time of a misfortune).

Throughout the month of Nisan, we do not make memorials for the dead, except on the last day of Pesach. We do not say *tachanun*, nor *av harachamim* on Shabat morning, nor *tzidkatcha tzedek* on Shabat afternoon, for there is an extra holiness that pervades the whole of that month, and all its days are days of celebration. The reason for omitting *tachanun* from our prayers is that during the first twelve days of Nisan, the *nesi'im* (head of tribes) brought their offerings for the dedication of the altar, and each day was a festival for the one who brought an offering. These days are followed by Erev Pesach, then Pesach itself, and then Isru Chag (the day after each of the Pilgrim festivals). Thus, since most days of the month are sacred, we treat the whole month as sacred.

In Tractate Sofrim we read; 'It was the custom of our teachers in the west to fast on three separate days, in memory of the three-day fast of Esther and Mordechai. Why did they not fast in the month of Nisan (when the events actually took place)? Because of the first of Nisan when the Mishkan was set up, the twelve *nesi'im*, one from each tribe, brought their offerings on twelve successive days and each *nasi* made a celebration on the day of his offering. In days to come the *Beit Hamikdash* will be rebuilt during the month of Nisan, in fulfillment of the verse; 'There is nothing new under the sun.'

Therefore we say no *tachanun* throughout Nisan, nor do we fast until the month is over — except for the first born who fast on Erev Pesach, and some others who also fast on that day so that they may carry out the mitzvah of eating *matzah* with greater relish.'

NISAN AS THE TIME FOR A BLESSING

'*If one goes out into the fields or gardens during Nisan and sees trees in blossom, and buds appearing, he must say the blessing; 'Blessed are You, O Lord, our God, King of the Universe, in Whose world no-*

thing is lacking, and *Who has created in it good creatures, and good and beautiful trees from which mankind may benefit'* (Rambam, Hilchot Brachot, Chap. 10). Our version of the blessing is slightly different but the Sephardim use almost the same wording as that laid down by Rambam.

This ruling applies particularly to fruit trees, but not to other types of trees. Because it is usual for trees to produce flowers during Nisan, the latter specifically applies to this month, but if one sees trees in blossom during other months, one should pronounce the blessing. However there are some authorities who say that this blessing should be said only during Nisan.

This blessing should not be said on Shabat, or on festivals, but only on a weekday, and especially when one sees at least two fruit trees which are four years old. The blessing is said only once during the year. If one has not seen any trees in blossom by the time fruit grows, some say the blessing should be said then, but others say it is not necessary, since there is a separate blessing for each type of fruit and one must also thank God for having kept him alive to see the fruit, ('shehecheyanu'). Whenever there is a doubt about a blessing, one takes the lenient view.

THE BLESSING FOR THE SUN

The blessing for the sun can only be said in Nisan, but not every year — only once in twenty eight years, as we shall explain.

The Rabis have taught; 'If one sees the sun at its turning point, the moon in its power, the planets in their orbits and the signs of the zodiac in their orderly progress, one should say 'Blessed is the one who made the Creation.' When does such a time occur? Every twenty eight years' (Tr. Brachot 59).

However it is our custom to say this blessing only

131

when we see the sun at its turning point, for this time can be calculated by everyone, whereas the time when the moon is in its power, the planets in their orbit and the signs of the zodiac in their orderly progress is known only to experts and not to the ordinary person. Therefore the law has been established that this blessing should be said only when the sun is at its turning point.

This is how Rambam expresses it in Hilchot Brachot, chapter 10. 'He who sees the sun at its turning point in Nisan at the beginning of the cycle of twenty eight years, when this turning point occurs early on Tuesday evening, should say this blessing when he sees the sun on the Wednesday morning.' The wording of the blessing is 'Blessed are You, O Lord, our God, King of the Universe, Who makes the works of the creation.' We say it when the sun has fully risen and can be properly seen, and not when it has just risen. It may be said until the third hour of the day, but if there was no opportunity of saying it by then, it may be said until noon. There are some who dispute this and say that is must be said by the third hour. After that time one may say the blessing without mentioning God's name.

If the sun is covered by clouds, there is difference of opinion as to whether the blessing may be said.

It is preferable that this blessing should be said together with many other people, but if there is a possibility that the sun will be observed by clouds before a crowd can be gathered together, then one may say the blessing alone.

Women do not have to say this blessing, for we find that during the days of Irmeyahu, the women used to offer incense to the 'queen of the heavens,' i.e. the sun, and some might think that even now they are doing homage to the sun.

It is the custom to announce on the previous night that people should rise at dawn on the following morning for prayers and for the blessing of the sun. When 'shacharit' is ended early in the morning, the entire congregation goes out into the open and recites this blessing with great rejoicing. They also sing songs and praises, both before and after the blessing, and finish with thanksgiving 'We give thanks that You have kept us alive . . .'

THE SUN AT ITS TURNING POINT

According to the way it appears to us on earth, the annual revolution of the sun — apart from its daily circuit — takes three hundred and sixty five days and six hours, in which time the sun makes a complete circuit from west to east, unlike its daily circuit which is from east to west. On each daily revolution the sun moves slightly to the east and when it rises on the morrow, it does not do so from exactly the same spot that it did on the previous day, but slightly to the east of it. It appears to move a little each day until it makes a complete circuit and returns to its original place after three hundred and sixty five days and six hours. This period is known as a solar year.

In ordinary speech we say that a (solar) year has fifty two weeks, although in reality there is one day and six hours more than that. When all these discrepancies of thirty hours accumulate then the turning point of the sun will occur on the same day of the week and at the same hour of the day that it did when it was created. This takes place only once in every twenty eight years.

There is a dispute among the early Sages as to whether the world was created in Tishrey or in Nisan. The law that states that the blessing for the sun should be said in Nisan is based on the opinion of Rabi Yehoshua who maintains that it was created in that month.

All are agreed that it was at the first hour of the eve of

the fourth day of the week that the lights were fixed in the heavens and twelve hours later the sun shone in the sky above the Land of Israel, that is at the first hour of the fourth day of the week. According to Rabi Yehoshua, that was the beginning of the circuit of the sun, and every twenty eight years, as night falls on the eve of the fourth day of the week, it returns to the place in which it was first seen. The following morning it appears to begin a new circuit, and at that moment we pronounce the blessing for the sun.

This turning point of the sun usually occurs in Nisan, but not always on the same day of the month. It is sometimes at the beginning, sometimes in the middle and sometimes at the end of the month. It is only once in five hundred and thirty two years that the turning point of the sun occurs on the same day of the month, for the month is calculated according to the phases of the moon, whereas the solar year is divided according to hours, days and years. But even though the twenty eight year cycles do not always coincide as far as the day of the month is concerned, nevertheless a new circuit has begun at that moment and it is our duty to give praise to the Creator as if it was on that day that the sun was created.

In the year 5741 (1981), the two hundred and fifth circuit of the sun will be complete, and in Nisan of that year — may it be a good year for us — we will have the privilege of saying the blessing for the sun. Even though two hundred and five multiplied by twenty eight is only equal to 5740, our Sages have already explained to us that during the Flood, the natural order of the world was suspended.

THE FIRST OF NISAN

Rosh Chodesh Nisan has a special glory of its own, more than any other day of the year, for it is the first day of the month which was designated as the first of all the months. God chose that day for the dedication of the Tabernacle and as the day on which His Divine Presence began to rest in

the midst of Israel. Eight sections of the Torah were told to
Moshe on that day and in time to come, the sacrifices will
again be brought from the first of Nisan in the third *Beit
Hamikdash* — may it be rebuilt speedily in our days — as
described in the book of Yechezkel (Chap. 45).

If it happens that the first of Nisan falls on the first day
of the week, then it is exactly like the first Rosh Chodesh
Nisan, from which all the goodness and blessing of the whole
year are derived — for the day on which the Mishkan was
dedicated in the days of Moshe was also the first day of
the week.

Our Sages have said; Rosh Chodesh Nisan has ten crowns.
It was on that day (i.e. the first day of the week) that the
creation of the world began. It was the day on which the
first of the Princes, Nachshon Ben Aminadav, brought his
offering. It was the day on which Aharon began his duties
as a priest — for hitherto the *avodah* had been the task of
the firstborn. It was the first day on which the congregation
participated in the *avodah* by means of communal offerings.
It was the first day on which fire came down from heaven,
('And fire came out from before God and consumed on
the altar'). It was the first day on which the *kodashim* (portions of sacrifices) had to be eaten within certain sanctified
limits, for until now sacrifices which had been offered on
the *bamot* (private altars) could be eaten anywhere. It was
the first day on which God's Presence dwelt among the people
— as it says concerning the *Mishkan*, 'I will dwell in their
midst.' It was the first day on which the *cohanim* blessed
the people with their special blessing, 'And Aharon lifted up
his hands and blessed them.' It was the first day on which it
became forbidden to use *bamot* but all sacrifices had to be
offered at the entrance of the Mishkan, and finally, it was
marked out to be the first of the month.

Rabi Levi said; 'On the day on which the Mishkan was
set up, eight sections of the Torah were told to Moshe, and
these are they: The chapter concerning the cohanim, (Va-

yikra 21) in which they are warned about their service in
the Mishkan; the chapter concerning the Levites, ('Take the
Levites from the midst of the children of Israel') so that they
could be taught the laws which they would need on that day,
for they were required to sing at the time when the sacrifices
were brought. The chapter concerning those who were defiled,
('And there were certain men who were unclean...') because
their offering of the Pesach sacrifice would be affected; the
section containing the instructions given after the death of
the two sons of Aharon. (Even though this section is read
on Yom Kipur, it was told to Moshe on Rosh Chodesh Nisan,
for it warns against coming at any time into the Holy Place.
The sons of Aharon died because they entered the Holy of
Holies unnecessarily.); the section concerning those who were
drunk, ('You shall not drink wine or strong drink, neither
you nor your brothers' — a warning to the cohanim when
they come into the Mishkan; the chapter on the Menorah,
('When you light the lamps...,' for it was on Rosh Chodesh
Nisan that the lamps were first lit) and finally, the section
on the red heifer, for on the morrow of that day the heifer
was slaughtered so that people could be purified to bring
their Pesach offerings' (Tr. Gitin 60).

'And he that presented his offering on the first day...'
Rabi Yosi said: When did the dedication of the Mishkan
begin? On the 23rd of Adar, and on Rosh Chodesh Nisan it
was completed. Throughout the seven days of the dedication,
Moshe would erect the Mishkan and dismantle it each day,
but on the eighth day he did not dismantle it. That day was
the first day of the week and also Rosh Chodesh Nisan. On
that very day, Aharon and his sons arose and bathed their
hands and feet in the laver and carried out the avodah
according to the correct procedure. On that day the children
of Israel brought their vowed offerings and their free-will
offerings, their sin offerings and their guilt offerings, their
first fruits and their tithes. It is to this day — the eighth
day of dedication, Rosh Chodesh Nisan, that the verse from

Shir Hashirim applies, (Chap. 4) 'Awake, O north wind; and come, thou south; Blow upon my gardens, that the spices thereof may flow out. Let my beloved come into his garden and eat his precious fruits' (Bamidbar Raba 13).

A NEW YEAR FOR FIVE SEPERATE THINGS

The first of Nisan is the beginning of a new year for kings, for the pilgrim festivals, for reckoning the months, for calculating the leap years and for giving the *shekel*

For kings: The kings of Israel used to count the years of their reign from Nisan. Even if a king began his reign at the end of Adar, as soon as the first of Nisan arrived, this would be considered as the second year of his reign.

For the pilgrim festivals: The pilgrim festival that occurs in this month which begins on Rosh Chodesh Nisan, namely *Pesach*, is the first of the three festivals. A man may not delay the fulfillment of a vow. If he vowed to bring an offering but did not do so, there are some who maintain that he has not transgressed a negative command until three festivals have elapsed, commencing from Pesach because the month in which it occurs is the first month.

For months: We count it as the first and reckon the other months from it.

For calculating the leap years: If the *Beit Din* wishes to declare a leap year and to add an extra month, this month is inserted before Rosh Chodesh Nisan. If this was not done by that date, then that year could not be declared as a leap year.

For giving the *shekel*: All communal sacrifices which are offered up from the first of Nisan onwards, are bought with the shekalim collected in the new year, i.e. from Rosh Chodesh Nisan, and not with the money left over from before that date.

THE FAST OF THE RIGHTEOUS

Even though the first of Nisan is crowned with glory, as we have explained above, and being Rosh Chodesh it is forbidden to fast, especially so on Rosh Chodesh Nisan when no fast may be held during the entire month, nevertheless that day Rosh Chodesh was fixed as a fast for the righteous, that is to say, a day on which we fast because of the death of the righteous, for 'the death of the righteous is as grievous as the burning of the House of our God.'

On the very day when the Mishkan was erected and the Divine Presence rested on Israel, and the love of the Holy One, Blessed be He, was as great for the children of Israel as was the love of the newly betrothed, and the joy of those who dwell above and those who dwell on earth was as great as the joy of those who accompany a bride and bridegroom, on that day an incident occurred which marred the rejoicing. 'And the sons of Aharon, Nadav and Avihu, took, each one, his fire-pan and they put fire upon them, and they placed incense upon it and they offered up before God strange fire which He had not commanded them. And a fire came out from before God and consumed them and they died before God' (Vayikra 10).

Nevertheless the rejoicing did not cease nor was the service interrupted. Aharon saw his sons lying dead, but he put aside his mourning in honour of God and His service. The sacrifices were brought in their correct order, the priests carried out their duties, the Levites sang on their platform, Nachshon Ben Aminadav brought his offering, the Israelites stood in their position and the glory of God appeared to the people. 'I have come into my garden, my sister, my bride, I have gathered my myrrh with my spice, I have eaten my honeycomb with my honey, I have drunk my wine with my milk. Eat, O friends, drink, drink abundantly, O beloved' (Shir Hashirim, 5).

Yet, shall there be no mourning for these two great and righteous men who died on the day of the 'wedding?' Shall they be forgotten from the hearts of men? Their glory will not be diminished nor will their righteousness be forgotten, but now the rejoicing cannot be mingled with mourning.

'Your brethren, all the house of Israel, shall weep for that which God has burnt.' In future generations, whenever the memory of that day comes before you, when the first of Nisan arrives and there is great happiness because of the eternal bond of love which was made on that day between the Children of Israel and their Father in Heaven, then the memory of that mourning will also come before you, the memory of those two great and righteous men who were to have accompanied the bride and bridegroom on their wedding day. They were not privileged to do this but they died at a most exalted moment in world history, and they left all the rejoicing for others. There was no mourning for them because all Israel was rejoicing, and they left no children to weep for them.

Great is the mourning for which there is no outlet at the right time. Just as mourning for them did not disturb the rejoicing, so it is only right that the joy of future generations should not extinguish the memory of these two righteous men. Therefore it says; 'Your brethren, all the house of Israel, (in all generations) shall weep.'

A PARABLE ABOUT NADAV AND AVIHU

The story of Nadav and Avihu may be compared to the tale of a mighty monarch who made himself known to the citizens of his state. He said to them, 'Although I am king over many lands and provinces, and all their inhabitants are subject to me, nevertheless I have chosen you from all my peoples and I desire to dwell in your midst. Make me a small dwelling place among you and I will leave all my palaces and castles and live with you. I will leave all my entourage of many honorable princes and you will be my associates. All the other citizens of my states will be your servants. When you finish building this dwelling for me, I will make a great celebration. I will rejoice myself and I will make all my subjects and all my servants as happy as on the day of my wedding.'

139

The citizens were delighted to hear this command of the king and all of them volunteered in the task of making a tabernacle for him to dwell in. When they had finished it and beautified it, and put into it every precious and desirable object, they were exceedingly happy and looked forward to the day when they would behold the glory of their king in this house.

However, not everyone rejoiced in equal measure. Some rejoiced because they said, 'The king has taken delight in us because we fear him and honor his name more than others do. It is therefore becoming that from now onwards we should fear him even more and serve him more and honor him more so that he may make our name praiseworthy.'

Others said, 'It is because we are of goodly descent that the king has taken delight in us. Therefore we will walk in the ways of our ancestors so that he will never turn aside from us.'

There were yet others in that kingdom whose joy knew no bounds, for they said, 'It is not because we serve him, nor because of our ancestry. The king has taken delight in us only because he loves us. Even if we are righteous, what can we give him, for he loves constantly with a love that is independent of any cause. We will love him in the same way. We will ask from him, neither greatness nor honor, neither goodness nor blessing, neither livelihood nor life. It is sufficient for us if we are near to our king, even if we die because of that nearness.'

On the day when the erection of the royal house was completed, all the people gazed in awe as the king appeared before them and as his glory filled the place. Each one trembled as he stood in his place because of the awe in which he held the king and none stepped out of his position. But those people in whom the love of the king burnt very deeply could not restrain their love for him, even while fearing him. And this love which was as fierce as death itself, burst from their hearts like a flame of fire. They asked advice of no man, nor did they consult each other, nor did they even question the matter themselves, but unprepared and uninvited, they presented themselves to the king just as they were. 'Let us behold the king,' they said 'even if we die.'

At that moment the king turned on them angrily and ordered them to be put into chains as if they had rebelled against his authority and had insulted his honor. So great is the honor due to royalty that even the greatest love is not permitted to offend it.

After they had been put into chains, the king said, 'I do not wish my happiness to be spoilt by the arrest of these men. Rejoice yourselves and make me happy, according to the royal command. As for these men who came into my chamber without permission, you must not disparage them. They were near to me, they loved me and they gave their lives for that love of me. Take them away and mourn for them as befits great men, men who held high positions in the state. Whatever honor you render to them, it is as if you had rendered it to me.'

AS IN THE DAYS OF EZRA AND NECHEMIAH

In the days of Ezra and Nechemiah, the first signs of the second redemption also appeared in Nisan, and moreover, on the first day of that month, the first group of people went up from Babylon to return to Jerusalem.

We also learn from the Book of Nechemiah that it was in the month of Nisan that he (Nechemiah) 'received permission from the king to go up to Jerusalem and to rebuild the city and its walls, and the king sent officers and horsemen with him.'

The second redemption began on the first of Nisan and it was also completed and perfected on that day. For those who returned from Babylon could not be considered as fully redeemed until they had purified themselves from the uncleanliness of the heathens and until they had separated themselves from their foreign wives. It was to this purpose that Ezra and his associates directed their attention, as we read in the Book of Ezra, 'And they brought back word to Darius on the first day of the tenth month, and all the men finished sending back their heathen wives by the first of the first month,' so that by the time Nisan started in that year, their redemption was complete, the redemption of the body and the redemption of the soul.

SOME CUSTOMS ASSOCIATED WITH THE FIRST OF NISAN AND THE DAYS FOLLOWING

It is customary on the first thirteen days of Nisan to read the sections from the Torah which tell us of the offerings that the Princes brought to the Mishkan. The verses about each Prince in turn are read, in order, on successive days — but from a printed book and not from a Torah Scroll. (However some people do read from a Scroll, but without saying the usual blessings). On Rosh Chodesh we read of the offering of Nachshon Ben Aminadav from the tribe of Yehudah; on the second of Nisan we read of the offering of Netanel Ben Tzu'ar, the Prince of the tribe of Issachar. And so on for twelve days. On the thirteenth of Nisan we read the chapter beginning 'When you light the lamps...' This was said in honor of the tribe of Levi for the Levites were not reckoned among the twelve tribes.

Although some people oppose this custom of reading from the Torah in public without saying the blessings, (basing their objection on a statement in the Talmud Yerushalmi), nevertheless many scholars support this practice for reasons of their own.

One of the reasons is as follows:

Since the tribes of God may be compared to the months of the year, so the first twelve days of Nisan may also be compared to the coming twelve months. The Princes of each tribe brought their offerings on successive days and, by so doing, each Prince opened the Gates of Purity and Blessing of one special month. Thus by reading of that particular offering in public from a Torah Scroll we call to mind the first blessing (given when *Rosh Chodesh Nisan* was originally proclaimed as a day of importance) and we receive an abundance of goodness for all the months.

Among the righteous there are some who are gifted with foresight. They are able to see in these twelve days all the events that will take place in the corresponding twelve months ahead. It is told of one great *tzadik* that, under the influence of God's spirit, he would write down on each of these twelve days everything that would happen during the appropriate month of the coming year. One year he wrote only until the fifth of Nisan, and in Av, the fifth month of the year, he was called upon by the Most High to restore his soul to his Maker.

Many people have the practice not to eat *matzah* from Rosh Chodesh Nisan so that they may eat *matzah* of Pesach with greater relish.

In the days when the Beit Hamikdash stood in Jerusalem, the couriers used to go to the outlying districts of the capital with messages from the king and his judges, telling the people that all who possessed flocks of sheep and cattle should hasten to bring them to Jerusalem, so that the pilgrims would have sufficient supply for their sacrifices and for food.

'WHEAT MONEY'

It is a widespread custom in Israel that during the first few days of Nisan, 'wheat money' is collected from everyone in the town, according to his ability to give. This money is used to purchase flour which is distributed to the poor according to their needs for Pesach. Other items are also supplied to them, wine, meat and fish, or they are given money with which to buy these themselves.

This custom has nothing to do with the mitzvah of

giving 'tzedakah, (charity)' for that mitzvah has to be performed throughout the whole year. It is rather because of the idea of freedom which is inseparable from Pesach. Even if a man has already fulfilled the mitzvah of 'tzedakah,' in complete accordance with the law, he cannot appreciate the full implication of freedom if he knows that his neighbor is hungry and in need. If he knew that there were hungry people in his town and he had not bothered to come to their assistance, he would be guilty of telling lies — God forbid — on this 'watch night' when he says at the beginning of the 'Hagadah,' 'Let all who are hungry come and eat.' If, however, he has busied himself to supply the needy with food, and then he says, 'Perhaps there are still some poor people of whom I know not, I am ready to receive them at my table,' then his words are clearly sincere and he is rewarded for saying this just as if he had only now fed the hungry and gladdened the hearts of the poor.

Everyone in the town is compelled to give 'wheat money' to the poor of his own town, and those who refuse can be compelled to comply. This money is collected even from scholars who are exempt from other taxes. No one can excuse himself on the grounds that he has given to the poor of another town.

All the needy of the town have a right to receive 'flour for Pesach' from the money raised in that town. The overseers may not say to a poor man, 'You have come from another town. Collect your share from there.'

We learn from the Talmud Yerushalmi; 'Rabi Yosi, by Rabi Bon, said, 'Where wheat for Pesach is concerned, the time limit is twelve months, both for giving and for receiving.' That is to say, if one has lived in a town for twelve months, he is considered a member of that town. If he is rich he must give and if he is poor he should be given.'

Later the law was formulated as follows. If one lives in a town for thirty days, he is considered a member of the town where 'wheat money' is concerned. How is this law to be applied? It refers to one who has no intention of settling in the city. But if one intends to settle in a place, then he is counted as a member of the town immediately, whether he is rich or poor.

If he lives in one town but has regular business in another, he has to pay 'wheat money' in the second town too. We have a proof for this in the story of Naval the Carmelite, who although he dwelt in Maon, he was known by the name of the town in which he worked. 'There was a man in Maon whose work was in Carmel' (First Shmuel 25).

It was the custom in most Jewish communities to collect the 'wheat money' in a businesslike way. After the termination of the Shabat before Rosh Chodesh Nisan, the Rabbi of the town, together with seven goodly citizens, would sit together and, as a shepherd counts his flock, so they would survey the names of every member of the congregation. Some would be estimated according to how much they should give and others, according to how much they should receive. No name was missed from the survey. On the morrow, the Rabi with the seven worthy citizens, would rise early and go themselves to the houses of the townsmen to collect from them according to their estimation. There was no escape from this tax. If a rich man was mean and pleaded that he had no money, they would say to him, 'If you have nothing, you will receive from us. Either you give or you take.' Then the rich man would be ashamed and would give his share. If a poor man was too embarrassed to accept,

they would find a clever ruse by which to help him,
either as a loan or as a gift, in such a way that he
would not know who sent it. Both the collection and
the distribution would be completed before Shabat
Hagadol.

It was also the custom in many Jewish communities
for the women of the town to participate personally
in this mitzvah. They would gather in groups and go
to the bakeries to bake matzot for the poor people
of the town. They would work happily, asking no
reward for their services and in the evening they
would distribute the matzot to the poor, secretly and
unobtrusively. In addition to the matzot, they would
also share out eggs and other necessities for the fes-
tival — as much as they could afford.

A CUSTOM AND ITS ORIGIN

It was customary in many Jewish communities, and it is
still widely practiced today that before Pesach people pickle
beetroots and other vegetables to eat on Pesach.

Every custom of Israel has its origin in the Torah and this
custom too, shows us how we accept from our Sages their
interpretations of the mitzvot. For any part of Jewish life
which is not based on the teaching of our Sages is valueless.

The Torah has commanded; 'You shall not eat anything
that is leaven (fermented),' and our Sages of blessed memory
have explained that this prohibition applies only to various
kinds of corn, but the *tzedokim* (saducees) who denied the
Oral Law, explained the verse literally and forbade any
food that had fermented, not only corn. Although they interpret the law more strictly, nevertheless their very strictness
is in itself a denial of the Torah. Therefore we make a point
of eating these fermented goods to show that we reject the
interpretation of the *tzedokim* and follow the teachings of
our Sages.

146

Nisan SHABAT HAGADOL

THE HAFTARAH OF SHABAT HAGADOL ❖ WE REMEMBER THE

MIRACLE ON SHABAT HAGADOL AND NOT ON THE TENTH OF

NISAN ❖ FURTHER REASONS FOR THE NAME 'SHABAT HAGADOL'

❖ CUSTOMS OF SHABAT HAGADOL ❖ THE TENTH OF NISAN ❖

TOPICAL EVENTS WHICH ARE REMEMBERED FOREVER ❖ SOME

MIDRASHIM ABOUT THE VIRTUOUS MIRIAM ❖ THE WELL OF

MIRIAM.

CHAPTER SIX

SHABAT HAGADOL — (The Great Shabat)

The Shabat before Pesach is called *Shabat Hagadol* for a variety of reasons which we will record, and there are a large number of special customs associated with this day.

It was in Egypt that the Israelites celebrated the very first Shabat Hagadol, on the tenth of Nisan — five days before their redemption. On that day the Israelites were given their first mitzvah, a mitzvah which applied only to that Shabat, but not to future generations.

'On the tenth day of the month... each man shall take a lamb for a household, a lamb for each house' (Shmot 12). This mitzvah of preparing a lamb for the Pesach offering four days before slaughtering it, applied only to that first Pesach in Egypt, but the Torah did not command us to take this lamb four days before every future Pesach. Nevertheless, the people used to do this in order to make sure that the lamb had no blemish. Many miracles were performed for the Israelites on that Shabat. Each person took a lamb and bound it to a bedpost. The Egyptians, who saw this activity, asked 'What is this lamb for?' and the Israelites answered them, 'In order to slaughter it as a Pesach sacrifice according to God's command' And the Egyptians who deified the lamb would gnash their teeth in anger but would not utter a sound.

Many other miracles were performed in connection with this offering and we therefore call this day 'Shabat Hagadol' because of the great miracles (*gadol* — great).

In the Sefer Hapardes which is ascribed to Rashi, we read:
'People are accustomed to refer to the Shabat before

Pesach as Shabat Hagadol, but they do not know why this Shabat is greater than any other Shabat of the year. The Israelites went out of Egypt on a Thursday, as we find in Seder Olam. They took the lamb on the tenth of the month, i.e. on the previous Shabat, the Israelites declared, 'If we sacrifice that which is sacred to the Egyptians before their very eyes surely they will stone us,' but the Holy One, Blessed be He said to them, 'Now you will see the wonderful thing which I am about to do for you.' Whereupon each man went and took his Pesach offering and kept it for four days. When the Egyptians saw this, they wanted to rise and take revenge but they were stricken with all kinds of bodily suffering and could do no harm to the Israelites. So on account of the miracles which were done on that day, the Sabbath before *Pesach* is known as *Shabat Hagadol.*'

Even before the Israelites took the lamb for each household to guard it until it was time for it to be slaughtered, the Egyptians knew that the death of their first-born was about to take place, but they did not know on which day this would happen. The words 'Yet one more plague will I bring upon Pharaoh and upon Egypt' were spoken on Rosh Chodesh Nisan. When the Egyptians heard that there was a bound lamb in every Israelite household, they became greatly afraid. 'The plague is about to descend on us, for our gods are bound with ropes in the houses of the Israelites and cannot defend us.' Then the first-born of the Egyptians came in panic into the houses of the Israelites on that first Shabat Hagadol to find out what was in store for them.

In Tosfot (Tr. Shabat 87), in accordance with the Midrash we read; And therefore we call it Shabat Hagadol because a great miracle was performed on that day. When the Israelites took their Pesach offerings on that Shabat, the first-born of all the nations of the world crowded round the Israelites and asked them what they were doing. They answered, 'It is a Pesach Sacrifice for our God Who is about to kill the first-born of the Egyptians.' The latter immediately went to their leaders and to Pharaoh to request him to send the Israelites away, but neither Pharaoh nor his princes wished to do this. Then the first-born made war on other Egyptians and slew many of them. That is why it says in Tehilim, 136, 'Who slew the Egyptians with their first-born,' it does not say, 'Who slew the first-born of Egypt,' but 'Who slew the Egyptians with their first-born,' that is to say, the first-born were the ones who slew the other Egyptians.

THE HAFTARAH OF SHABAT HAGADOL

It is the custom in most communities to complete the reading of the Torah with the chapter from the end of the Book of Malachi; 'Then shall the offering of Yehudah and Jerusalem be pleasant unto the Lord as in days of old.' Even if Pesach begins on the following day, this Haftarah is read.

The reason for this is that it announces the future redemption of the world. This reminds us of the announcement of the first redemption which began on the last Sabbath before the Israelites went out from Egypt.

A further reason is that on Pesach the world is judged for its crops. The Sages have said; 'For not observing the laws of tithes, the heavens are closed, scarcity ensues, people run about in vain in search of livelihood and there is famine abroad . . . ,' but if people give their tithes, then they are blessed, as it says; 'Bring all the tithes into the storehouse that there may be meat in my house, and prove Me now with this, says God, if I will not open for you the windows of the heavens and pour out for you a blessing without end' (Malachi 3).

These verses occur in this haftarah and we therefore read it before Pesach to warn the people about the tithes before the final judgment is given concerning the crops, so that they should not be punished for neglecting this mitzvah.

It is fitting for the Rabbi to admonish the people on Shabat Hagadol about the mitzvah of trumah, tithes and gifts to

151

the poor, so that if they then undertake to carry out these mitzvot it will be considered as if they have already done so, and the verse which says, 'I will pour out for them a blessing without end' will be fulfilled on the first day of Pesach when the judgment about the crops is given.

THE SHABAT BEFORE PESACH — RATHER THAN THE TENTH OF NISAN

Why do we associate this miracle especially with the Shabat before Pesach rather than with the tenth of Nisan on whichever day of the week it occurs? The Torah itself speaks only of the 'tenth of the month' and makes no mention of the day of the week.

It is because the miracle is closely connected with the Shabat. The Egyptians knew full well that the Israelites kept the Shabat and would not busy themselves with animals on that day, so when they saw them taking the sheep and binding them to the bedposts on Shabat, they were surprised and came to enquire the reasons for this. The Israelites were in great danger at being thus confronted and were saved only by a miracle. We therefore remember this miracle on Shabat and not on the tenth of the month.

Had it not been Shabat, they would not have required a miracle to save them, for if the Egyptians would have come on a weekday and asked them the purpose of these animals, they could have diverted their attention and given them any kind of answer, so as not to endanger their lives. On Shabat, however, they could not do so, for our Sages have said that even an ignorant man, out of respect for Shabat, does not tell lies on that day. So we see that it was on account of the Shabat that they were involved in danger and needed a miracle to save them.

A further reason for remembering the miracle on Shabat and not on the tenth of Nisan is that, forty years later, Miriam died on that day and the well which had accompanied the Israelites through the wilderness, ceased to exist. When this anniversary occurs on a weekday, it is kept as a fast for the righteous.

FURTHER REASONS FOR THE NAME SHABAT HAGADOL

We find that the scholars, throughout the ages, have given many and varied reasons for this name, reasons that befit those who give them and are pleasant to those who hear them.

Some explain the word *hagadol* (great) as a title descriptive of *Shabat*. Even though the word *Shabat* is feminine and *hagadol* is masculine, this need not disturb us, since we often find the feminine form changes to the masculine when it denotes something great and important.

Here is a selection of the wisdom of the Sages on this subject:

'Just as a child who is of the age to keep the mitzvot is called *gadol* (an adult), so the day on which the whole people of Israel had to keep their first mitzvot, (on the tenth of this month ... each man shall take a lamb ...') is called *Hagadol*, (Chizkuni, Abudraham and later scholars).

'When the Israelites were in Egypt, Moshe asked Pharaoh to give them one day's rest a week, the Shabat. Each week, as soon as Shabat was over, the Israelites immediately returned from their pleasant rest to their wearisome toil. On this Shabat, however, they did not return to their slavery and we therefore give it this title *Hagadol*' (Rabi Yeshayah of Trani, in the name of his father).

'According to the tradition of the Sages, the verse in the Torah which says, 'You shall count for yourselves from the morrow of the Shabat' refers to the morrow of the first day of Pesach, and from then we begin to count the *Omer*. However the *tzedokim* (Saducees) denied this tradition and maintained that the words 'from the morrow of the Shabat' meant literally 'Shabat.' In order to discount this idea completely, the Shabat before the first day of Pesach was called Shabat Hagadol to tell us this day is followed by another

153

Shabat, viz. the first day of Pesach, even though this latter 'Shabat' is not as great as the previous one' (Beney Issachar).

'The *haftarah* from the Book of Malachi ends with a verse about redemption, 'Behold I will send to you Eliyahu the Prophet, before the coming of the great and terrible day.' The word *hagadol* is the last of the utterances of the prophets, (apart from the word terrible which could obviously not be given as a title of that day). We therefore call this Shabat '*Hagadol*,' just as we call Shabat *Chazon* and Shabat *Nachamu* after words that are found in the *haftarot* for those days' (Mateh Moshe).

'On the tenth of Nisan, which was a Shabat, the Israelites crossed the Jordan' (Taz).

On this Shabat large congregations would gather to learn the laws of Pesach and this day was therefore called 'Shabat Hagadol' because on it people learned great (important) laws' (Tzedah Laderech, by Rabi Moshe Ben Zerach).

'The Rabbi, the most important person in the town, would address the congregation on this day. It was therefore called 'Shabat Hagadol,' meaning the Shabat of the great man' (Later scholars).

In Sefer Hapardes ascribed to Rashi we find an additional reason:

'The people used to make the Shabat before Pesach last longer than any other. They would remain in their synagogues for a long time, until they had learned all the details about observing the Pesach properly. As this day therefore seemed to them longer than any other day, it was called 'Shabat Hagadol.'

In the 'Customs of Maharil' we read of another reason for this name: Just as we call Yom Kipur 'the great fast,' because we pray at great length on that day, so we call this the great Shabat, because we have a lengthly address on it.

The Sages of a later age have also given their reasons for the naming of this day.

There are two reasons in the Torah for the mitzvah

of Shabat. The first time that the Ten Commandments are mentioned in the Torah, we are told, 'Remember the Shabat day, for in six days God made the heavens and the earth...' and the second time we are told, 'Keep the Shabat... so that you may remember that you were slaves in the land of Egypt...' Until the Israelites were redeemed they kept Shabat only for the first reason, but on this last Shabat in Egypt — Shabat Hagadol — the second reason was added, and as the reasons for keeping Shabat were increased, so the Shabat itself became greater in their eyes.

When the days of the week were created, each day had its partner. The first day was paired with the second, the third with the fourth and fifth with the sixth. Only the Shabat was alone. The Holy One, Blessed be He, said: 'The people of Israel will become your partner.' From the moment that Israel became a free people, it became the partner of the Shabat. This Shabat, the beginning of the redemption, thus became greater than any other Shabat and was therefore known as Shabat Hagadol.

CUSTOMS OF SHABAT HAGADOL

It is the custom in many communities to say *Piyutim* (liturgical poems) on this day, during *shacharit*. The main theme of these *piyutim* is the laws of Pesach — in verse form — and their purpose is to make it easy for people to become acquainted with the laws of the festival. Psalm 104 (Bless the Lord, O my soul) and Psalms 120—134, (the Songs of Ascents) which are said every Shabat throughout the winter, are said for the last time of the year on Shabat Hagadol. We also read part of the Hagadah on this day, from the section 'We were slaves to Pharaoh in Egypt' until the words '... to atone for all our sins.'

One reason for this is that the redemption began on Shabat Hagadol. Another reason is to make the youngsters familiar with its contents in fulfillment of the mitzvah 'You shall tell your children on that day...'

This custom is not known among the Sephardim, nor was it practiced by the Gaon of Vilna.

A further reason is that it is like a rehearsal for the Seder night, so that the text may be more fluently read. If the eve of Pesach occurs on Shabat, one may read the *Hagadah* by the light of a candle, even if he is alone, for he need not fear that he will tamper with the light.

Some people in Sephardi communities are very particular, when greeting people on this day, to use the title of the day in their greeting.

From as far back as the days of the Tana'im and Amora'im it was the custom, wherever Jews lived, for the outstanding scholar of the town to address all the people on Shabat Hagadol. He would instruct them in the ways of God and teach them how to behave. He would explain to them how to prepare vessels for Pesach, how to remove the *chametz* and the laws concerning the baking of *matzot*. His purpose was to ensure that the people did not err, in the slightest degree, in their observance of the festival. He would also introduce into his address some topical comments and explanatory notes in order to arouse the interest of his audience.

When Shabat Hagadol occurs on Erev Pesach, this address is usually given on the preceding Shabat so that the congregation can learn the necessary laws before they prepare for the festival for all the preparations will have been completed by Shabat Hagadol.

> *It is an ancient custom, on the eve of Shabat Hagadol, to bake a small quantity of bread from the flour which has been reserved for baking the matzot. This bread is called 'the 'chalah' of the poor' or 'the 'chalah' of the synagogue' and is distributed to the poor. Each person carries out this practice according to his means. Rabi Aharon of Lunil said; 'Since people have begun to neglect this custom, a curse has come upon the crops.'*

Maharshal of Lublin taught; 'Before Pesach every-one should eat a small amount of food made from the 'flour for Pesach,' so that if there is the slightest suspicion that there is some chametz in this flour, then it will be as if he had eaten the part which is chametz before the festival, and the food he eats on Pesach itself will be completely free of any trace of chametz.'

Rabi Yeshaya Horowitz ('Shelah') has said that this teaching of Maharshal is the reason for baking the 'chalah' of the poor,' that is to say, that by doing this, one can be completely sure that no chametz remains in the flour with which he bakes his matzot. This chalah is distributed to the poor so that by virtue of fulfilling the mitzvah of feeding the hungry, a person may be saved from the sin of eating chametz on Pesach.

THE TENTH OF NISAN

Although the greatness of the tenth of Nisan and the memory of its miracles and wonders have been transfered from that day to the Shabat before Pesach, as we have already explained, nevertheless some of the importance of that day still remains. Some other events which took place on that day are forever associated with the tenth of Nisan.

After thirty-nine years in the wilderness, the virtuous Miriam died on the tenth of Nisan and the Israelites were deprived of one of their three benefactors. Why were these three benefactors, Moshe, Aharon and Miriam, so called? Because it was due to them that three gifts were given to the Israelites. The Manna was given because of Moshe, the clouds-of-glory were given because of Aharon and the miraculous well because of Miriam.

When Miriam died the well ceased. 'And the children of Israel, the whole congregation, came to the wilderness of Tzin in first month and the people camped in Kadesh,

157

and Miriam died there and was buried there. And there was no water for the congregation and they assembled against Moshe and Aharon' (Bamidbar 20). That day has been established as a fast for the righteous for all generations, in memory of that virtuous woman.

A year after this event, this day was again marked out for another incident, but this time a joyous one. On the tenth of Nisan the Jordan was divided for the Israelites and its waters rose up as a heap. The people crossed the river and as they emerged from the Jordan to take possession of the chosen land, the feet of our ancestors trod for the first time on the holy soil. Among these people there were many who had come out from Egypt, the whole tribe of Levi, the children, the old men and some of the women, for the decree 'In this wilderness they shall perish' did not apply to them.

We read in the Book of Yehoshua; 'And the people went up from the Jordan on the tenth day of the first month and they encamped in Gilgal at the eastern edge of Jericho.' Our Sages have said: 'The mitzvah of taking the Pesach lamb became applicable to them when they were in the Jordan,' for we read in Shmot; 'On the tenth of this month each man shall take a lamb for his household; and we read there 'And the people went up from the Jordan on the tenth of the month' (Yalkut).

TOPICAL EVENTS WHICH ARE REMEMBERED FOREVER

Despite the great joy of the people over this event, it was not allowed to overshadow completely the memory of Miriam, and the fast to mark her death was not annulled. For the three benefactors, Moshe, Aharon and Miriam, who looked after the Israelites from the time they became a nation, were benefactors for all generations. In each age we think of these great people as if they were actually with us and we mourn their death as if it had just taken place.

We find many similar events which although they happened to that generation, are nevertheless remembered in all future generations, for example, the day on which the *Mishkan* was erected and the day on which the last of those who were prohibited from entering the Land of Israel died. However this does not apply to the various festivals for it explicitly states in the Torah that these were to be celebrated in every age.

We often find that people and incidents leave behind them an impression which lasts for all time, so that we always remember the event on the day on which it happened. On the other hand there are many great events and important people which, although they are remembered for all time, are not associated with any particular day. For these people and these deeds influenced the general course of events rather than one special day.

Only the Sages, who understand the times, are able to distinguish between those events which leave a marked impression upon the actual days of their anniversaries, and those whose influence is spread equally throughout the year: In the former case, a festival or a fast is established; in the latter, the anniversary has no special memorial.

This applies to the tenth of Nisan. Even though many incidents occurred on that day, the death of Miriam, the withdrawing of the well and the crossing of the Jordan, it is only the first of these that is permanently recalled by the fast, whereas there is no memorial for the others.

There are some who say that it is for this very reason that we remember the miracles that took place in Egypt on the tenth of Nisan, not on that day but on Shabat Hagadol, so that people should not think that we are celebrating the dividing of the Jordan and its crossing.

If Shabat is appointed as the day on which to remember these miracles, then everyone will know that it is those which happened in Egypt that are being recalled, because the crossing of the Jordan did not take place on Shabat. Furthermore since the tenth of Nisan, when it is a weekday, was

159

fixed as a fast in memory of Miriam, the joyous events are recalled on Shabat, whether or not this is the tenth of Nisan.

SOME MIDRASHIM ABOUT THE VIRTUOUS MIRIAM

'Why was she named Miriam ? Because from the moment that she was born, the Egyptians embittered the lives of the Israelites. (*Mar* — bitter).

'And the midwives feared God.' Who were these midwives? Yocheved and Miriam. Our Rabis said that although Miriam was only five years old, nevertheless she would go with her mother and nimbly assist the women in childbirth.

'And his sister stood at a distance.' Why did Miriam stand at a distance ? Rav Amram in the name of Rav said; Because Miriam used to prophesy saying, 'My mother will bear a child who will save the Israelites.' When Moshe was born the whole house became full of light. Her father arose and kissed her on the head saying, 'My daughter, your prophecy has been fulfilled.' That is why the verse refers to 'Miriam the prophetess, the sister of Aharon.' Was she only the sister of Aharon and not of Moshe too ? She uttered this prophecy when she was the sister of Aharon, before Moshe was born. When Moshe was put into the river, her mother rebuked her. 'My daughter, what has become of your prophecy ? That is why the verse says, 'His sister stood at the distance to know...' that is, to know how great would be the distance until her prophecy would come true.

'His sister stood at a distance.' This teaches us that a person is repaid exactly in the way he acts. Miriam waited by Moshe for one hour, and the Omnipresent delayed everything in the wilderness for her sake, the Ark, the Divine Presence, the cohanim, the Levites, and the seven clouds of glory. 'The people did not journey until Miriam had been gathered in.'

'The tribes never marched in their ranks, with their banners, unless Miriam went in front of them.

'Rabi Eliezer said: Miriam also died with 'the kiss' (of God).

'Rav Ami said; Why is the chapter on Miriam near to the chapter on the red heifer ? To teach us that just as the red heifer brings atonement, so does the death of a righteous person.

'There were three good benefactors of the Israelites, Moshe, Aharon, and Miriam. In their merit three gifts were granted to the people, the manna, the cloud and the well. The well was given by virtue of Miriam and when she died it was withdrawn. As it is said, 'And Miriam died there' and immediately afterwards, 'And there was no water for the congregation to drink.' (Tr. Ta'anit 9).

THE WELL OF MIRIAM

'How was this well made ? It was in the shape of a sieve-like rock out of which water gushes forth as from a spout. It travelled with them in all their wanderings, up hill and down dale, and wherever they halted, it halted too, and it settled opposite the entrance to the Ohel Mo'ed. Then the leaders of Israel would appear and walk around it, each with his staff, chanting the words of this song; 'Spring up, o well, sing to it, spring up, o well.' Then the water would gush forth from the depths of the well and shoot up high as a pillar. Each of the Princes would draw the water towards himself with his stick, each man for his tribe and each for his family. Any woman who needed to visit a friend in another tribe would travel there by a boat. The water overflowed beyond the encampment where it surrounded a great plain in which grew every conceivable kind of plant and tree' (Tanchuma Bamidbar).

'The well was at the entrance of the courtyard, near to the tent of Moshe. It would inform the people how they should encamp. As soon as the curtains of the Mishkan were in position, the twelve leaders of the tribes would stand by the well and chant the song, '... the well which the princes have dug.' Then the waters of the well would separate into different rivers. One river would surround the camp where the Divine Presence dwelt and from there other rivers would branch out into the four corners of the courtyard, each extending to the furthest point. From these, other rivers would branch out to form boundaries between each tribe and even between each family, so that everyone knew his own position' (Yalkut Pikudey).

'If you wish to see the well of Miriam, go up to the top of the Carmel and look into the distance. There you will notice a sieve-like rock in the sea. That is the well of Miriam' (Tr. Shabat 35).

'There is said to be a custom to draw water from a well at the end of Shabat, for at that time, the water of the well of Miriam fills every other well and whoever comes in contact with it, or drinks it, is cured of all his ailments' (Kol-Bo).

Nisan CHAMETZ AND MATZAH

CHAPTER SEVEN

The laws of Pesach are more stringent than those of any other festival. The mitzvot which belong to the other holy days are applicable only during the festival itself. They cannot be carried out either before the festival or after it. For Pesach however, there is one mitzvah which must be done beforehand and its effect is noticeable even afterwards. This is the mitzvah of removing the chametz.

Even if a person fulfilled all the requirements of Pesach meticulously, if he brought his Pesach-sacrifice to the *Beit Hamikdash* on the fourteenth of Nisan and ate it together with *matzot* and bitter herbs, if he related the story of the going out from Egypt and praised God and thanked Him for the redemption, if he carefully abstained from eating *chametz* all the seven days of the festival, if he did no work on the first and on the seventh' day and carried out all the other laws of Pesach, nevertheless he would have commited many transgressions that are explicitly stated in the Torah if he did not remove the chametz from his house before Pesach or retained it in his possession, and his punishment will be very grave.

Although we may begin to remove the chametz thirty days before Pesach, this can be done at any time before the festival. But in order that the mitzvah may assume greater importance in our eyes, our Sages have given us a fixed time, namely the eve of the fourteenth of Nisan. Half an hour before the stars appear at the end of the thirteenth of Nisan, one is forbidden to work or to transact any business, or even to learn Torah, until he has searched his house for chametz for the purpose of removing it. (See below, page 170).

'It shall neither be seen nor shall it be found in one's possession.' The prohibition of chametz on Pesach does not only apply to eating it or deriving benefit from it. The Torah demands that every Jew shall neither see, nor possess any chametz at all on Pesach. 'For seven days no leaven shall be found in your houses' (Shmot 12). 'No leaven bread shall be seen by you, nor shall any leaven be seen by you in all your borders' (ibid.). Here we find two 'mitzvot lo ta'aseh' (commandments not-to-do) concerning the removal of 'chametz,' in addition to the 'mitzvat aseh' (commandment to-do), 'By the first day you shall cause all leaven to cease from your house' (ibid.).

Therefore before midday of the fourteenth of Nisan, every Jew must put away all leaven that is in his house or that is in his possession elsewhere. If he does not do so by this time, then he transgresses a 'mitzvat aseh.' If he does not do so from midday of the fourteenth of Nisan until the end of Pesach, then at each moment he is guilty of transgressing the 'mitzvat aseh' to cause all leaven to cease, and the two 'mitzvot lo ta'aseh,' not to see it or to possess it.

However many legal authorities maintain that if he does not remove the chametz by the correct time, he is not guilty of the two negative commands until the eve of the fifteenth of Nisan, whereas he becomes guilty of the positive command by midday of the fourteenth.

SEARCHING AND NULLIFYING THE CHAMETZ

It is a 'mitzvat aseh' of the Torah to cause the leaven to cease, even before the time when it is prohibited to eat it. *For it is said, 'By the first day you shall cause the leaven to cease...' According to our tradition this word 'first' refers to the fourteenth of Nisan, the first day to which the laws of Pesach apply. As a proof of this we have the phrase 'You shall not slaughter the Pesach sacrifice while there is still chametz.' As the Pesach offering took place on the fourteenth of Nisan, we know that the chametz must be removed before this time.*

What does the Torah mean by the expression 'to cause the leaven to cease?' It means that a person must nullify it in his mind, he must think of it as dust and discount it from his possession, — or to put it differently, any chametz which he possesses is, in his eyes, as useless as dust.

The Scribes interpret this phrase as meaning that one must search in every hidden nook and cranny in order to remove it from the boundaries of his house.

The Scribes also tell us that we must search for the chametz and cause it to cease at the beginning of nightfall on the fourteenth of Nisan, by the light of a candle. No learning is arranged for this time, lest the study be extended and a person be prevented from carrying out the search for chametz at the right time.

We have already remarked that if a person nullifies in his mind any chametz which is in his possession and considers it as the dust which has no owner then he has fulfilled the mitzvah of 'causing the chametz to cease.' Thus he cannot be guilty of transgressing the commands which forbid him to see it or to possess it, since these mitzvot only apply to chametz which he owns. For our Sages have explained the words, 'There shall not be seen by you' to mean 'You shall not see what is yours,' but that which belongs

167

to others or is ownerless, you may see. If this is the case, why is it necessary to conduct such a thorough search for the chametz?

There are two reasons for this. The first is that the act of nullifying the chametz and declaring it ownerless depends on a person's thoughts. He must do this meaningfully and with complete sincerity. Since not all people think in the same way and some may treat the matter more lightly and not renounce their ownership of it in all honesty, our Sages have decreed that a person cannot nullify the chametz or declare it ownerless until he has actually removed it.

The second reason is that since a person is accustomed to eat chametz throughout the year, he may forget the prohibition if he sees it in his house. It is therefore necessary to search for it and to remove it before the time from which it is prohibited to eat of it.

Even though the Sages have insisted that we search for the chametz thoroughly and remove it from our possession, we are still not absolved from renouncing ownership of it completely. This must be done after the search for one might not have looked properly and a choice morsel which is left in the house may be a cause for sin on Pesach. Or he may have left some chametz for a certain purpose and then forgotten to remove it. We are also afraid of finding chametz on Shabat or on the first or last days of Pesach when we cannot burn it. Even if we find it on the intermediary days of Pesach, we may delay removing it for some reason, and meanwhile we would be guilty of transgressing the commands not to see it or to possess it.

Although we have said that the search and the removal must actually be carried out — by decree of the Rabis — and that one may not rely on re-

nouncing it in his heart as required by the Torah, nevertheless there are circumstances, even according to the Torah, when this mental renunciation, even if done with complete sincerity, is not effective. If he was under compulsion or if he forgot to declare the chametz ownerless until after the correct time, then such a renunciation is entirely useless. For from that time onwards, it is forbidden to derive any benefit from it and it is as if it no longer belongs to him. How then can a person renounce and nullify that which is not his? However it is only where nullifying is concerned that the chametz is not considered his property, but the Torah still reckons it as his where the prohibition 'it shall not be seen...' applies. Now, he has no other method of fulfilling the command to 'cause the leaven to cease' and to refrain from transgressing the commands 'not to see it or to possess it,' than actually to search for it and to burn it completely.

THE TIME FOR SEARCHING

Our Sages have decreed that the time for searching for the chametz is the eve of the fourteenth of Nisan, because in the evening everyone is at home, and also because it would not be possible to search in every corner and crevice by ordinary daylight. It is necessary to use a candle for this, and since candle-light does not show up so well by day, the time for this search was fixed for the night. The correct time is when the stars appear so that the candle-light shines brightly. Although it is usual for zealous people to carry out the mitzvot as early as possible, this mitzvah may not be performed before the stars appear. Nevertheless a person should prepare himself in advance so that he is ready to begin searching for the chametz at the correct time without any delay.

For half an hour before the stars appear, near to the setting of the sun at the end of the thirteenth of Nisan, one should be careful not to start any work, nor should one eat until he has searched for the chametz. Even if he has a fixed time for learning he should postpone this until afterwards. If he began to learn or to do any other work at a time when it was still permissible to do so, as soon as the time for searching for the chametz arrives, he must interrupt whatever he is doing.

The congregation should recite 'ma'ariv' earlier than usual lest it be impossible to gather people together afterwards. Prayer is a mitzvah that is frequently performed, whereas searching for the chametz is done only once during the year, and a frequent mitzvah always takes precedence over an occasional one. But a person who normally says ma'ariv alone, should carry out the search first, for there is no danger of him forgetting to say ma'ariv since it is his normal practice to pray alone.

If he did not search for the chametz on the eve of the fourteenth, he should do so on the day itself, but by candle-light and not by the light of the sun. If the natural light is very strong, as for example in a covered place in front of the house where one side is completely open, then he may search for the chametz by the light of the sun. This was also applied to other rooms or buildings which have much natural light or where the windows are not glassed in.

If he did not search for the chametz by the time it becomes prohibited, that is midday, he should do so afterwards, and if he did not do it even then, he should search for it with a candle on Pesach itself. As soon as he finds any he must dispose of it completely.

If he did not search either before Pesach, or on Pesach itself, he should do so after Pesach. He must burn any chametz which has remained in his house from before Pesach, or dispose of it in such a way that no one can derive any benefit from it.

If a person sets out on a long journey by sea or by land with the intention of not returning home until after Pesach, and if there is no one at home to search for the chametz at the correct time, he must carry out the search by the light of a candle on the night before he leaves home, that is, if he begins his travels within thirty days before Pesach. If however, he leaves home before then, he does not need to search. If he leaves home more than thirty days before Pesach and intends returning home before the festival, he must search before he goes, for he might come back at the last moment and have no time to dispose of the chametz. If he does not intend to return he does not need to search, but if he knows that there is some chametz in his house, some authorities maintain that he must dispose of it in any case.

If a person moves out of his house within thirty days before Pesach, he must remove the chametz before he goes, unless he knows that another Jew will move in during that period and dispose of the chametz himself.

Why was the limit fixed for thirty days? Because of the ruling; 'Thirty days before Pesach one should enquire deeply into the laws of the festival.' The duty of searching for chametz therefore becomes operative from then.

If the eve of Pesach occurs on Shabat, the search is undertaken on the night of the thirteenth of Nisan, that is, on the previous Thursday night, and sufficient food is left for the Shabat meals.

171

THE CANDLE

We do not search by the light of a torch, but by the light of a single small candle, because one cannot hold a torch to a crevice or a hole. There is also the danger of setting fire to the house and if a person is worried about this danger he will not concentrate on the task in hand. If he did use a torch, he must repeat the search with a candle, but not say the blessing again.

We do not use a candle made of tallow, lest it drip onto 'kasher' vessels, nor of meat fat, lest it drip on to milk dishes, nor of oil lest it drip onto clothes and soil them. All these fears would prevent a person from searching properly. One should use a candle which gives a bright light, and if it should drip, it neither stains nor renders 'trefah.' However if he did use a candle made of one of these other substances, he need not repeat the search. If he has no wax candle, he should search with whatever type he has, as long as it is not a torch. A candle with two wicks is considered a torch. Even if two wax candles are melted together and made into one, it is still considered to be a torch since it has two wicks, and the search is not valid.

The initials of the Hebrew words for tallow, meat fat, oil and torch spell out the word 'afraid,' that is we are afraid of not performing the mitzvah properly if we use any of these.

THE BLESSING FOR THE SEARCH

Before beginning to search for chametz one must say a blessing, just as one does before performing any other mitzvah. Some people are particular to wash their hands before saying this blessing.

If he forgot to say the blessing before beginning to search, he should say it before he finishes.

How is the blessing worded ? 'Blessed are You, O Lord our God, King of the world, Who has made us holy with His commandments and commanded us to remove the chametz.' This search is the first stage in the process of removing the chametz, although at the time of searching, he cannot remove all the chametz in his possession. He must not only leave some food to be eaten the next morning, but even the chametz he finds has to be placed on one side for burning on the following day. Immediately after the search he nullifies and renounces ownership of any chametz which, unknown to him, still remains in his possession. Since this act of nullifying is part of the act of removing the chametz, the blessing said before the search, covers all aspects of it, even its burning on the morrow when he again nullifies any chametz that may still remain.

Why do we not thank God for having kept us alive to perform this mitzvah as we do for any other mitzvah carried out for the first time in the year ? It is because the search is part of the preparations for the festival, and when we thank God with the blessing 'shehecheyanu' during the kidush on the first night, this blessing covers all the mitzvot connected with Pesach, (Tur). Furthermore this blessing is only said at a time of joy when we derive physical benefit from the action, but when we search for the chametz we are full of regret at having to destroy any which still remains (Abudraham).

Just as one may not speak between saying a blessing and performing the action, so one must proceed immediately from this blessing to the task of searching for the chametz, without any interruption. If he did interrupt to speak of something connected with searching for the chametz, he does not need to repeat the blessing. But if his talk was of other matters, he

173

must say the blessing again. He must also be careful not to speak until he has completed the search. If he spoke after beginning to look for the chametz, even on an unrelated subject, he need not repeat the blessing.

If the members of his household assist him in the search, they must stand by him and listen while he says the blessing and then say 'Amen,' so that they are included in his blessing. The person saying the blessing must intentionally act on their behalf in this matter. However, if they did not hear his blessing, they do not need to say it for themselves, because the actual duty of searching for the chametz devolves on the head of the household, although others may assist him.

Should the head of the household not carry out the search himself but nominate someone to do it, this other person represents him and must say the blessing. This applies whether the representative is a member of the household or a stranger.

If someone possesses property in various places, he must look for chametz in all of them, shop, office or house. He says the blessing in one of these only and this covers the search in all of them. Similarly if he sends other people to search for him in these other places, he must say the blessing in one place while the others listen with full intent. They then go to their various places to look for the chametz, relying on the blessing said by the head of the household.

The blessing must be said whether the search takes place on the eve of the fourteenth of Nisan, on the morning of that day, after midday or during the festival itself. But if one starts out on a journey, by land or by sea, or leaves his house empty, within thirty days before Pesach, he does not say the blessing although he must search for the chametz. Nor does he say it if he makes the search after Pesach.

THE MANNER OF SEARCHING

Every place which is to be searched must be thoroughly cleaned before the search begins. Even if he knows there is no chametz in any particular place, he must still search there.

Where does a person have to search for chametz? Every place into which there is a possibility of bringing chametz must be searched. even those rooms in which it is not usual to eat for the chametz may have been brought in accidentally. In fact, every room in the house including the attics, requires searching, for he might have gone into a room with food in his hand.

Crevices high up on the walls and out of reach, or low down, less than three hand-breadths from the floor, do not require searching. But if he knows that he has used these for any purpose, then he must look there for chametz. In a house where there are small children, one must certainly look in the holes near the floor for youngsters could easily have put some chametz there. The tops of flat cupboards which are sometimes used for storage must be searched.

If chametz has been brought into a cattle stall or chicken run within thirty days before Pesach, these must be searched. Even though it is possible that the food has already been eaten by the animals this possibility does not outweigh the certainty that chametz has been present there. However, if no chametz has been taken there within this period, these places do not require searching for we are now faced with two possibilities: the animals may already have consumed the chumetz or it may have gone bad and be unfit even for a dog to eat. If one finds chametz while

175

searching a cattle stall or chicken run and wants the animals to eat it, he must stand there until they have done so and watch they do not drag it from place to place, for it could lie hidden in some corner until Pesach, thus making him transgress the command forbidding him to possess any chametz.

Synagogues and houses of study require searching. The beadle says the blessing and carries out the search, but he does not need to renounce ownership afterwards since the chametz is not his property.

If there has been a landslide and the stones and rubble are more than threebreadths above some chametz which is buried there, he does not need to remove the chametz. It is sufficient if he nullifies it. If there is merely a small heap of stones above the chametz he must remove the stones and dispose of the chametz. He must search under the beds, in the cupboards and in all the household utensils, lest some chametz has found its way into any of these.

If he has set aside a place to store chametz which he has sold to a non-Jew or is about to sell him on the morrow, he need not search there.

A person should be very careful to search his own pockets and those of his children, and shake them out for sometimes one puts chametz into a pocket. It is better to do this on the fourteenth, by day, when he is disposing of the chametz, rather than on the previous evening, for he may forget and put some chametz in his pocket again after the search. Some say that he should examine his pockets while searching for chametz in the evening and repeat the operation the next morning when he disposes of it.

One should be careful not to starch garments within thirty days before Pesach. It is the searching itself which constitutes the mitzvah and not the finding of any chametz. If he searched and found nothing he *has fulfilled the mitzvah. Nevertheless it is an old custom to put some pieces of chametz in various places in the house, which he gathers up as he searches. These should be hard and not easy to scatter. They should be placed out of reach of small children who do not understand, and also of mice who may drag them about. He should know exactly how many pieces have been put in the house so that he can check that he has collected all of them. According to the 'Ari' (Rabi Itzchak Luria) one should put ten pieces in the house.*

It is a good practice to use some feathers or a knife to make it easier to get into holes and crevices.

AFTER THE SEARCH

Immediately after the search, he must declare as null and void any chametz which, unknown to him, remains in his possession. This declaration is in Aramaic but if he does not know the language, he may say it in whichever one he understands:

'Any leavened bread or leaven which is in my possession and which I have not seen, nor disposed of, nor did I know of it, may it be considered as null and as ownerless like the dust of the earth.'

A person who searched for chametz on behalf of someone else should use the third person in his declaration, 'Any leavened bread ... which is in the possession of so-and-so ...'. If a housewife searches on behalf of her husband she should say, '... which is in the possession of my husband.' These people have been appointed as representatives only to fulfill the mitzvah but it is the owner who actually possesses the chametz and he alone would be guilty of transgressing the prohibition if he allowed it to remain in his possession. Legally a house and its contents belong to the husband so that if a woman carries out the search

177

for the chametz, she cannot afterwards declare it ownerless, since it is not hers. She is only acting on behalf of her husband.

Any chametz which is found during the search, or which is left to be eaten the following morning, should be hidden in a carefully guarded place where it cannot be found either by children or by mice. By the fifth hour of the following day he must burn whatever is left.

When we say the 'fifth hour' we are not referring to the ordinary times of the clock. The hours of daylight are divided into twelve equal 'hours.' According to whether the fourteenth of Nisan occurs early or late in the year, these 'hours' will have either less or more than sixty minutes. Only by knowing the precise moment of sunrise and sunset, is it possible to calculate the exact time before which the chametz must be burned. One should therefore consult a calendar specially prepared for this purpose rather than relying on one's own judgment and unwittingly committing a transgression.

Even though he has declared the chametz as null after his search, he does so again when he burns it on the morrow by the fifth 'hour.' The reason for this repetition is that his declaration of the previous night only referred to the chametz of whose existence he was unaware, but it did not cover the chametz which he left to be eaten in the morning. It is possible that some of this may have found its way into a hidden corner and be discovered on Pesach, thus making him guilty of seeing and possessing chametz. He therefore repeats his declaration renouncing ownership. In this second declaration there is a slight change of wording. '... which I have seen and which I have not seen, which I have disposed of and which

*I have not disposed of . . . ,' because now he refers to
all the chametz in his possession.*

*He burns the chametz first and then declares it
null and void so that he may fulfill the mitzvah of
burning it with his own chametz.*

*If one did not search for the chametz or nullify
it by the beginning of the sixth 'hour' of the fourteenth of Nisan because he forgot or was under compulsion, he should now search for it and dispose of
it, but he cannot renounce ownership of it since it
is forbidden to derive benefit from it after this time
and it is no longer considered as his. One cannot
renounce ownership of something one does not possess.*

*One should rinse the mouth well after eating the
last chametz on the morning of the fourteenth.*

SELLING THE CHAMETZ

A person who possesses a large quantity of chametz and
is loath to dispose of it because of the great loss he would
incur, may sell it to a non-Jew. After writing a bill of sale
he may then leave the chametz in his own house without
transgressing the prohibition neither to see it nor to possess it,
for the chametz no longer belongs to him but to the non-
Jew. However, he must set this chametz aside in a special
place which he then rents to the non-Jew so that it becomes
the property of the latter until after Pesach, as we shall
explain in detail.

The place in which this chametz is kept should be inacces-
sible so that neither he nor the members of his household are
likely, from force of habit, to take anything out of there
during the Pesach. He puts in writing for the non-Jew that
he sells him his chametz at a certain price. The non-Jew
gives him a token sum of money, or something of monetary
value, to signify that he takes possession of the chametz from
that moment. An agreement is made that if the non-Jew does

179

not pay the full amount stipulated, by the end of Pesach, all the chametz will then revert to the seller, but the sale is not invalidated retrospectively. This means that throughout Pesach the chametz actually belongs to the non-Jew, and the Jew is not guilty of transgressing the command neither to see nor to possess it.

Although he is fully aware that the non-Jew will not carry out the terms of the sale and pay the full amount and that the chametz will thus revert to the original ownership, nevertheless when he sells it, he must consider it as if properly sold and no longer his own.

For a sale to be valid, certain conditions must be fulfilled. Firstly there is the conscious intention of the vendor to sell. Secondly there is the payment of money and/or the nominal transfer of the goods to the buyers. If these conditions are fulfilled, then the chametz may remain in the house of the Jew because it is no longer his property. However if the price of the goods rises during Pesach, the non-Jew had a perfect legal right to complete the purchase and the Jew cannot prevent him from doing so.

The sale of chametz to a non-Jew may be effected through a delegate. Nowadays it is customary for the people to sell their chametz through the offices of the 'Beit Din' (Rabbinic court). Any individual who possesses chametz may transfer it to the 'Beit Din' who will sell it to a non-Jew on his behalf by a legal and valid bill of sale.

Only chametz which is visible to the eye needs to be sold to a non-Jew. As for the chametz which is absorbed into household utensils, it is sufficient to wash them well and lock them away. Some people take a stricter view and include all their chametz dishes in the bill of sale to the non-Jew. However, when those dishes revert to Jewish ownership after Pesach, they do not require 'tevilah' as is normal when buying vessels from a non-Jew, since it is only the chametz in them which has been sold and not the actual dishes.

As long as it is permitted to derive benefit from chametz, (that is, until the end of the fifth 'hour' of the fourteenth of Nisan) it is permitted to sell it to a non-Jew. After this time it is forbidden since it is no longer his and one cannot sell something which one does not possess. If he does sell it after this time, the sale is not valid. He had no alternative except to burn it, however great the loss he incurs.

SOME PROHIBITIONS CONCERNING CHAMETZ

What do we actually mean by the word 'chametz ?' Any flour made of wheat, spelt, barley, rye or oats, which is mixed with water and allowed to ferment before being baked comes under the definition of chametz according to the Torah.

The time necessary for this fermentation process to take place has been established by our Sages as eighteen minutes, so that if eighteen minutes have elapsed from the time of adding the water to the flour and nothing further has been done to the mixture, then it is definitely chametz. The time taken for kneading, rolling and other processes is not included in these eighteen minutes, but once the dough has become warm through being handled, we are careful not to leave it even for a moment. If the flour was mixed with fruit juice or with eggs, or if it was mixed with water and put straight into the oven without leaving it to ferment, it does not become chametz. However we are careful not to do this for Pesach, lest some water be mixed with this dough. Then if the dough, or part of it, has to be left, it may ferment and the owner will have transgressed the prohibition of seeing and possessing it.

Since it is forbidden to eat chametz on Pesach, or

181

to dissolve it in water and drink it, or to derive any benefit from it, the only course open is to burn it or to completely dispose of it in some other way.

Even the smallest particle of chametz is forbidden on Pesach. If a minute quantity was mixed with an amount one thousand times greater, the whole quantity is still forbidden. But if this minute quantity was mixed in the food before Pesach at a time when chametz is still permitted, then it is neutralized because it is less than one sixtieth of the total amount, providing that the chametz is completely dissolved and no longer discernible.

It is forbidden to eat chametz beyond midday on the fourteenth of Nisan, that is, from the beginning of the seventh 'hour.' Whoever infringes on this prohibition is liable to punishment according to the Torah. We read there 'You shall not eat any chametz with it,' that is, with the Pesach offering, and our traditional interpretation of this is, 'You shall not eat chametz from the time when it is permitted to slaughter the Pesach sacrifice,' namely from midday. Our Sages have forbidden us to eat chametz from the beginning of the sixth 'hour' so that we should not inadvertently overstep the exact limit. From then onwards, it is forbidden both to eat chametz and to have any benefit from it. During the sixth 'hour,' the prohibition is derived from our 'Sofrim,' (the Scribes), but from the seventh 'hour' onwards, the prohibition is from the Torah itself.

There is a further decree not to eat chametz during the fifth 'hour' lest the day be cloudy and it be difficult to tell the exact time, but it is not forbidden to have benefit from it during the fifth 'hour.' We can summarize these rules by saying that it is permitted to eat chametz on the fourteenth of Nisan until the end of the fourth 'hour.' During the fifth *'hour' we do not eat it but we may benefit from it. (Rambam, Hilchot Chametz and Matzah, Chap. 1).*

We have already pointed out above that these 'hours' are not the hours of the normal clock, but divisions of the day depending on its length.

Anyone who willfully eats a morsel of chametz, the size of an olive, from the eve of the fifteenth of Nisan until the end of the twenty-first of Nisan, incurs the penalty of 'karet' (premature death), as it says, 'For whoever eats chametz, that soul shall be cut off from its people.'

One is permanently forbidden to derive any benefit from chametz which has been allowed to remain over Pesach. This prohibition is in the nature of a fine imposed by the 'Sofrim.' If a person transgressed the command neither to see nor to possess any chametz, then this chametz is forbidden to him. This ruling applies whether he left it by mistake or acted under duress. It was introduced so that one should not leave chametz in his possession on Pesach in order to benefit from it afterwards (Rambam, ibid.).

THE GREAT CARE AND STRICTNESS REGARDING
THE PROHIBITION OF CHAMETZ

The Torah is more strict about chametz than about other forbidden foods. We must cause it to cease before Pesach, we are warned neither to see it nor to possess it, nor to derive benefit from it. The punishment for eating it is the very grave one of *karet* and the Sages have forbidden even the smallest particle of it. Because of this, sin-fearing Jews who are eager to observe the mitzvot, have taken further stringencies upon themselves, so that there should not be the slightest possible doubt regarding chametz. We must on no account belittle any custom of this type which may be practised in one community more than in another, for a custom has the force of the Torah in any field of Jewish life, and especially so when it concerns Pesach. If a single individual is accustomed to carry out one of the laws of Pesach most meticulously, one should not rebuke him, but should rather copy him, even if the chance of infringing the mitzvot of Pesach is very remote.

See how great is the virtue of loving one's fellow-man. Our Sages have said that drinking together fosters friendship and whoever derives benefit from his friend loves him, and whoever denies benefit to his friend displeases the Sages. Nevertheless on Pesach many worthy people are accustomed not to eat in one another's house. They do not borrow or lend dishes even though it is well-known that each in his way is a God fearing man, scrupulous in his observance of the mitzvot.

Our Sages tell us that one should not object to this practice, nor should it be considered as pride. It is due only to the extra strictness regarding the laws of Pesach. The Ari (Rabi Itzchak Luria) said that whoever is careful to avoid even the most minute particle of chametz on Pesach can be assured that he will not sin throughout the whole year.

THE PURGING OF VESSELS

Household utensils which are used throughout the year must not be used during Pesach because as they are used, they absorb and discharge chametz. Even though the amount of chametz discharged is minute, we still cannot use the dishes because as we have already explained, even the smallest quantity of chametz is forbidden.

If one wishes to render his chametz dishes fit to use on Pesach, he purges them with boiling water. How is this done? He cleans and scours them thoroughly to remove any dirt or rust. He must be especially careful to clean round the handles and other projections where chametz is likely to accumulate. Then he puts them into a cauldron of boiling water so that they are completely immersed, while maintaining the water at boiling point. When he takes them out they are fit for use on Pesach. This process is known as 'purging.'

Receptacles such as saucepans or pots may be purged as follows; he cleans each one in the manner described and fills it to the brim with boiling water. He heats an iron rod or stones until they are glowing hot and throws them into the boiling water so that it overflows. By this method the vessels become fit for use on Pesach since any chametz which may be discharged in use would have been brought out into the boiling water. It is usual to wash the vessels in cold water immediately after they have been purged.

The boiling water used for this process must be clean. If many vessels are purged one after the other, the water in the cauldron must be changed as it becomes dirty. Neither the cauldron nor the dishes should be used for twenty four hours before being purged.

One should be careful to purge the dishes before midday on the fourteenth of Nisan. If it is necessary to do so after this time, one should consult a scholar.

If many utensils are placed in the cauldron for purging at the same time, there should be space between them so that the boiling water can cover each dish separately. For the same reason they should not be held tightly with tongs.

Any chametz utensils which have been purged for Pesach must be used as before, that is to say, dishes formerly used for milk foods can only be used for milk foods on Pesach, and likewise dishes formerly used for meat can only be used for meat on Pesach. However some people who do not allow the use of dishes to be changed during the year after purging, do permit it for Pesach.

Glassware with a smooth surface may be used on Pesach if it is soaked in water for three days. The water must be changed every twenty four hours.

The process of purging cannot be applied to utensils made of china or of earthenware, nor can it be used for utensils which are made of many parts and cannot be taken to pieces such as mincing machines for meat or fish, kettles with spouts or necks too narrow to clean properly, vessels which have been patched or have holes or dents which are difficult to clean, graters, sieves, woven baskets, etc. For these there are special processes of glowing, but these should be carried out only on the instructions of a scholar. This ruling also applies to a mortar or other appliance used for sharp spices.

Purging by the method described is of no avail for appliances used during the year for frying, roasting or baking, nor for the burners on primus stoves or ovens. They must be heated in fire until they are glowing red. However as there are many different varieties of these, it is better to ask the advice of a scholar.

Hot saucepans and plates containing hot food should not be placed on working surfaces or kitchen tables until these have been covered with sheets of metal or with boards of wood. For a dining table it is sufficient to cover it with cardboard, and then a tablecloth.

GUARDED MATZAH (Shmurah) AND ORDINARY MATZAH

All matzah which is eaten on Pesach must be guarded against anything likely to make it chametz. Matzah which is not guarded in this way may not be eaten throughout Pesach. There is another mitzvah concerning the matzot, namely that these must be made specifically for the purpose of fulfilling the mitzvah of eating matzah on Pesach, as we read in the

Torah, 'You shall guard the matzot.' Many authorities maintain that we can only carry out the mitzvah of eating matzah on Pesach with 'shmurah' matzah.

How do we guard this matzah which is to be eaten on Pesach ? From the moment when the wheat is brought to the mill to be ground, it is guarded from contact with any water or other moisture, so that it (the wheat) is clean and whole rather than split and that all processes of grinding, packing and transporting the flour to the bakery are done with clean and dry appliances. The flour is guarded against being used for baking on the same day on which it was ground, for it is still warm and therefore liable to ferment easily. It is guarded while being kneaded to ensure that this is not done near an oven nor near an open window exposed to the sun, lest it become hot and ferment quickly. The water with which the flour is mixed is also specially guarded. (See below 'Water that has stood overnight'). The entire array of utensils and machinery used from the moment of sieving the flour until the completion of the baking, must be smooth, clean and polished (i.e. rubbed down) every hour, so that no crumbs of dough roll from one batch to the next. There are many other precautions to be observed until the dough is put into the oven and also while it is being baked. The sole purpose of all these measures is to fulfill the Mitzvah of the Matzot.

In what way does ordinary matzah differ from the matzah which is called 'shmurah' ? Ordinary matzah is guarded, in the way we have just described, from the time of grinding the wheat, whereas the title 'shmurah' is applied when the wheat for the matzah is guarded from the time of harvesting.

There is a difference of opinion among our great authorities as to the exact nature of the 'guarding' that is involved in this matzah. The majority maintain that it is sufficient to guard the wheat from the time it is ground until the end of the baking process. If this is done it is perfectly *kasher* and

187

one can fulfill the mitzvah of matzah on Pesach with a matzah prepared in this way. This is the accepted practice among the Jewish people. However there are a few authorities who dispute this, claiming that this mitzvah has not been properly observed unless the wheat has been guarded from the time when it was reaped. Therefore, those who observe the mitzvot very strictly — and on Pesach more people do so than during the rest of the year — accept the ruling of this minority and eat matzah shmurah, that is, matzah baked from flour which has been specially guarded from the time of its being reaped.

Many people make a point of eating this type of matzah at least on the first night of Pesach (in the Diaspora, on the second night too,) when the eating of matzah is a positive command ordained in the Torah and is accompanied by a special blessing (see below). A piece of matzah shmurah, the size of an olive, is shared out to all who take part in the Seder that they may say the appropriate blessing. The mitzvah of eating matzah on Pesach is fulfilled by eating this first piece at the Seder, but there is no obligation to eat matzah during the rest of Pesach.

How do we carry out the extra precautions required for matzah shmurah? People go out to the fields to cut the wheat before the ears are fully ripe and are still slightly green. For once the wheat is completely dry and has become white, it no longer absorbs moisture from the ground. If it were to rain, the wheat would be liable to ferment even though it is still attached to the ground. It is carefully examined to make sure that there are no grains that have split or are sprouting. It is then guarded with all the necessary precautions until it is taken to the mill for grinding.

WATER THAT HAS STOOD OVERNIGHT

The water used for making the dough, both for matzah shmurah and for ordinary matzah, must have stood overnight after being drawn from a river or well. This water must stand in a vessel that is not attached to the river or well for at least twelve hours. This is because the water may be slightly warm as it is being drawn and would thus cause the dough to ferment quickly.

The water is drawn at twilight, that is, between the setting of the sun and the appearance of the stars. The Sephardim do this shortly before sunset. After sieving, it is put into covered barrels and kept in a cool place near the bakery. The water must remain like this overnight for a period of twelve hours before being used. If there are less than twelve hours in the night, we must wait until twelve full hours have elapsed before commencing the baking.

It is permitted to draw a large quantity of water at one go to use for several days. As the water is being drawn, one should mouth the words, 'For the purpose of carrying out the mitzvah of the matzah.' This water must be drawn into vessels that are both nice and clean in order to fulfill the mitzvah in a handsome way, and it must be done by a Jew. We do not use old vessels, even Pesach ones, for this purpose but we buy new earthenware ones so that we may show our love for this mitzvah.

HAND-BAKED MATZAH AND MACHINE-BAKED MATZAH

Throughout all the generations people have zealously carried out all the fine details concerned with the baking of the matzah, that we have been commanded to eat on Pesach. The method of baking has remained unchanged. Nimble hands have performed each process from making the dough until the baking was complete.

About one hundred and thirty years ago, a machine was invented for baking matzot. Most, or all, of the processes were done by this machine and the matzot were untouched by human hands. The Rabbinical authorities at that time, and ever since, have been divided in their opinions as to whether matzot baked by machinery should be permitted on Pesach. Those who allow it say that such matzah is to be preferred, for it is baked more quickly and there is less danger of it becoming chametz than when the work is done by hand, providing of course, that special care is exercised to ensure that the parts of the machinery are kept clean and that no pieces of dough remain which could be transferred from one batch to the next.

Those who forbid it say that when baking matzah, we must be fully conscious of the fact that we are performing a mitzvah. A machine can have no such intentions. They also claim that the intricacy of the machinery makes it impossible to ensure that no pieces of dough remain in the grooves or in the wheels, thus rendering the matzah chametz. Furthermore since the various parts of the machine are made of metal and move very quickly, they generate heat which may cause the dough to ferment slightly. An additional argument used is that the time limit (eighteen minutes) for the process of making dough by hand has come down to us by tradition, whereas we have no tradition concerning the time limit for making matzah by machinery. As there exists the possibility that the time for this method is different, we have to take the stricter view and retain the original method.

Those who forbid machine-baked matzot also claim that it would harm the poor people. Many poor families look forward at this time of the year to earning a livelihood several weeks before Pesach and thus providing their needs for the festival. Baking matzot by machinery would deprive them of this opportunity.

Those who permit this type of matzah — and they are in the majority — have produced counter-arguments to all these points so that their opinion has finally been generally accepted by many who fulfill the mitzvah on Pesach by eating matzah that has been baked by machinery.

However, there are many people who take great pains at the *Seder* to eat a piece of matzah, the size of an olive, baked by hand and on this they say the special blessing. There are also some who are even more particular and eat hand-baked matzot throughout the festival.

LEGUMES

All Ashkenazi Jews strictly abstain from eating all kinds of beans, rice, millet, maize, ground-nuts and seeds on Pesach. The reason is that some of these are ground into a type of flour which is used for baking. If one were to see confections made of these kinds of flour being eaten on Pesach, he might think they were chametz and belittle all the many prohibitions of chametz. Our Sages therefore forbade the use of all these species on Pesach, and their decree has been accepted throughout Ashkenazi Jewry. This rule is not relaxed, except for an invalid or at a time of emergency, and then only on the instructions of a scholar.

Among Sephardi Jews this prohibition was not accepted, but they take special precautions to ensure that these are clean and sorted out before Pesach to ensure that no forbidden grain is mixed with them.

Sun flower seeds which have been salted are forbidden because the salt used is often processed with flour.

If one's parents and ancestors generally, have always accepted this custom, then one may not relax it.

SOAKING MATZAH IN WATER

Many pious people do not eat any matzah that has been soaked or dipped in water or soup. They eat it only in its natural form, or they soak it in milk or in fruit juice which definitely contain no water. In the Diaspora where Pesach lasts for eight days, these people will eat matzah in water or soup on the last day of the festival.

Many people have tried, in vain, to find in the *Halachah*, the source of this custom. After matzah has been properly baked, it is impossible to make it chametz even by soaking it in all the water in the world. Nevertheless those who do keep this custom, are very strict about it and will not even use Pesach dishes in which matzah has been soaked.

191

This practice belongs to that group of Jewish customs which have been adhered to for so long that one may not abolish them. If a person finds that he can no longer keep this up, he must consult a scholar, for every Jewish custom which has been observed by faithful Jews is sacred even if the reason for it is not known.

It is said that a certain great *tzadik* (pious man) once asked a scholarly pupil to search the whole Torah to find the origin of this custom. When the pupil admitted that he was unable to find the source, his teacher exclaimed, 'What an important custom this must be for it requires no foundation to support it !'

The Ravan mentions this custom of not eating matzah soaked in water on the first night of Pesach. He says this is not because of the fear that it may become chametz, but to enhance the mitzvah in our eyes. We want the taste of the matzah to remain in our mouths during the whole of the first night because it is a positive command of the Torah to eat matzah on that night. If one eats matzah soaked in water, he is merely eating some mixture, but he does not have the proper taste of matzah.

CHAMETZ AND MATZAH, SOME HIDDEN MEANINGS

The practical rules for disposing of the chametz on the fourteenth of Nisan and the many other laws of Pesach have been invested by our great Sages with deep and ennobling ideas, of which we present a small selection.

The difference between chametz and matzah is minute. We use the same flour, the same water and the same oven for both of them. It is only by waiting and doing nothing that they become different. The dough ferments, its volume increases, its shape changes and its taste is soured. These changes have come about by themselves with no effort on the part of the maker. In order to produce matzah which is suitable for fulfilling an important mitzvah, we have to work hard, to take pains and to make an effort.

Chametz and leavening agents are symbols of pride, and haughtiness and therefore even the most minute particles are forbidden on Pesach, for these qualities, in whatever small degree they are present, harm a person's character.

It is the addition of a minute amount of no import that forms the difference between matzah and chametz — merely waiting and doing nothing. Even in writing the Hebrew words, the addition of a minute stroke of the pen is all that differentiates chametz from matzah. We simply lengthen one part of one letter of the word matzah, and we find we have the letters of the word chametz.

This is the greatness of our sacred tongue. The words and the letters of which they are composed, did not come about by chance, but by the wisdom of the Creator. For every word, and every letter in it, and even the shape of the letters and the order in which they occur are symbolic of a deeper meaning. Some of these we are able to comprehend, but to understand them all, we must wait until 'the whole earth is full of the knowledge of God.'

Chametz is a symbol of the evil inclination. The search for chametz and its removal becomes a symbol of the struggle against this evil inclination. Chametz is more pleasant to the taste than matzah. It is more beautiful in appearance and more blown up in size. So is the evil inclination. It attracts a person to the pleasures of this world; it makes him more beautiful in his own eyes and boosts him in the eyes of others who think he is greater than he really is. It is a mitzvah to get rid of this chametz completely. When this commandment was first given to the Israelites, it became like a shield which defended them from the punishment that was imminent.

The sinfulness of the Egyptians, based on pride in their riches and their might, had reached its climax. These riches and this power were their gods. They worshipped the sheep which enriched their owners. (The Hebrew word for a 'flock of sheep' is *ashtarot* from the word *ashir* meaning rich.) Egypt

193

— that great sea monster that straddled the Nile and that
boasted 'My Nile is my own and I have made myself' —
was a nation of overlords. All other nations were subject to
Egypt. Even among themselves, anyone who was bigger than
his neighbor was lord and master over him. Every firstborn
was singled out as a favourite over those younger than he.
In every Egyptian household there was a firstborn who was
favoured in this way. Even the servant who worked at the
millstones was not too lowly to abstain from scorning someone who was even lower, thus becoming more important in
his own estimation. The enslaved and the subjugated in Egypt
did not seek freedom for themselves. All they sought was
mastery over those who were lower than themselves. The
entire territory of Egypt was a land of evil pride and haughtiness so that when Pharaoh spoke the words, 'Who is God
that I should listen to Him ?' he was voicing the sentiments
of the whole population, free men and slaves alike.

They would rather let the whole nation and the whole land
be destroyed by the plagues that followed one another than
consent to give up their mastery and let the slaves go free.
Could the one who said 'My Nile is mine and I have made
myself' ever admit that there was One greater than he ?

When God passed over the land of Egypt to smite it and
to make it the lowliest of nations where formerly it had been
the greatest 'so that Egypt may know that I am God,' then
whoever was still able to breathe exclaimed, 'God is righteous
and there is none beside Him.'

Into every single house and into every single place where
there was a trace of pride, the plague penetrated. As there
was no house without its firstborn so there was no house
without its dead. Then came the moment for all boastfullness
and conceit and false pride to disappear from the world, the
moment when the glory of the kingdom of God was about to
be revealed and exalted over all His kingdom.

At that moment the firstborn of Israel and the great ones
among them were also in danger of invoking God's anger,

for they too might have been influenced by the bestiality of Egypt in the same way that the other slaves there had been affected by it, even down to the humblest servant who sat by the millstones. If among the Israelites there were any who once had said, 'I am greater than you,' would they now be spared when justice was about to be done to all the first-born and the true greatness was to be restored to the King of Glory alone ?

'Then God spoke to Moshe and Aharon in the Land of Egypt... Speak to all the congregation of Israel saying... each man shall take a lamb for a father's house, a lamb for a household... and all the congregation of Israel shall slaughter it... and they shall take of the blood and put it on the two door-posts... and they shall eat the flesh on that night roasted in fire (in the manner of slaves), with matzot (in the manner of those who are branched) and with bitter herbs (in the manner of those who are crushed) they shall eat it.'

All this was to tell us that even though the whole House of Israel still dwelt in Egypt among the filth and bestiality of that country, they could testify that they had purified themselves from this uncleanliness. This goddess of besti-ality lay slain before them with its blood on the doorposts and lintels of their houses. The chametz, swollen and blown up, was gone from their midst and all their food, the lamb, once the symbol of idol-worship, the matzah prepared in great haste and the bitter herbs eaten in a humbled mood, all pointed to one idea — 'we are free men. We are no longer slaves of Pharaoh but servants to the King of all the world.'

'And I shall pass over the land of Egypt in that night and I shall smite all the firstborn in the land of Egypt... and the blood shall be as a sign for you on the houses... and I shall pass over you so that there will be no plague to destroy you when I smite in the land of Egypt.'

The removal of the chametz like the slaying of the Pesach lamb and putting its blood on the doorposts of their houses, shielded the Israelites from punishment in Egypt. In every

195

generation we reap the reward of these acts, for by them we testify that there is one God, that all greatness is His, that everything comes from Him and all that we eat is given by Him as a reward for the effort we invest into keeping the mitzvot of our King.

Rabi Chaim Vital, in his book Hakavanot, compares the first thirteen days of the month of Nisan to the first thirteen years of a person's life. Each day represents a year. On the 'eve of the fourteenth' when he is obliged to carry out the mitzvot, he 'searches for the chametz.' At that moment the good inclination enters into his being and undertakes to fulfill the mitzvot, so that he is equipped with the strength to fight the evil inclination, to search it out and to destroy it wherever it may be found.

'THERE IS NO MAN SO RIGHTEOUS IN THIS WORLD WHO DOES ONLY GOOD AND NEVER SINS'

The search for the chametz is a warning against the evil inclination. It teaches us to seek for it in hidden places and get rid of it so that we may enjoy freedom from its fetters and appreciate that freedom as if we had only now come out from Egypt. For this reason we put down pieces of bread while searching for the chametz to indicate that even if a person has cleansed himself from sin and iniquity, as far as lies within his power, he should not boast, 'I am purged of all sins' for if he were to continue his search, he would surely find some more chametz which is the symbol of pride. 'For there is no man so righteous in this world who does only good and never sins.' He who prides himself that he has already corrected all his faults, can be certain that he has not even begun to serve God properly.

IN PREPARATION FOR THE HAGADAH

Throughout the year it is considered a virtue to speak as little as possible, 'to say little and do much,' whereas on Pesach it is a virtue to speak as much as possible of the great deeds we are commemorating. 'Whoever tells of the story of the coming out from Egypt at great length is to be praised.' Our Sages tell us that recounting this story is a vital aspect of Pesach and indeed, we can see in the Hebrew name itself the words 'Peh sach,' 'the mouth speaks.'

As long as there is chametz in the house, you cannot celebrate Pesach. If you wish to observe the festival you must first cause all leaven to cease from your house and from your property.

The heart of a man and his inward thoughts are his house and his property. As long as there is chametz, the symbol of pride, in a person's heart, he considers himself handsome and important. He boasts of himself, he ascribes to himself virtues which he does not possess so that his tongue and his heart are not in harmony. He pretends to be fine when he is not so, he pretends to be great when he is not so, he talks heroically but he is weak-hearted.

Such a man is not ready to celebrate Pesach. When he tells his children the story of Pesach, they will not listen to him. When he praises God, his words are not acceptable. He merely pours out words for his own self-aggrandizement but he cannot praise God as befits Him. He is swollen with pride like the dough itself. There is chametz in his heart and there is no sincerity in his praise.

But if a person wishes, in all sincerity, to praise God, the living God, the God of truth, for His miracles, His wonders and His mighty deeds that He has performed for us and for our ancestors, to praise Him in such a manner that his praise will be acceptable to God, he must cause all leaven to cease from his heart. He must purify his tongue from all deceit. His heart must be pure and truthful and his speech must be decent. Then he can fulfill the command, 'You shall tell your son on that day' and his son will listen.

When he sings praises to the name of God, the angels above together with all who dwell on earth, will listen to his song, a song of truth that wells from a true heart and a refined tongue. Whoever tells of the coming out from Egypt in this manner, he is indeed praise-worthy.

Now we can understand that the search for chametz, the symbol of pride, on the eve of the fourteenth of Nisan, is an indispensable preparation for Pesach, for 'Peh Sach,' for the mouth that speaks of the great deeds of God on the fifteenth of Nisan.

That this matter of searching for chametz before Pesach is symbolic of purifying the heart and tongue before praising God, we can see from the Talmud itself. Usually the language of the Talmud is concise and to the point; in Tractate Pesachim however there is a very lengthy discussion on the exact meaning of the phrase, 'on the eve of the fourteenth we search for chametz.' The Hebrew word used is 'the light of the fourteenth' and our great Sages appear to be divided in their opinions as to whether this word 'light' is a euphemism for 'night' or is to be understood literally. Difficulties are raised, arguments produced and quotations cited from the Bible and other sacred sources in support of one side or the other, until finally we see that in reality there is no disagreement. The word 'or' — light, in this context means night.

How many pens have been worn out, how much ink has been spilt, how many children have wearied their brains to explain and to understand all these discussions and arguments — and then we find that there is no argument at all !

Our Sages wanted to emphasize the importance of refined speech. If a person's speech is pure and refined when he is carrying out the mitzvah of searching for the chametz, the mitzvah of matzah and the mitzvah of singing God's praises, it is a sure sign that he will always speak in purity and with refinement. Instead of using the word for 'night' which symbolizes spiritual as well as physical darkness, he will refer to 'light' in all its implications.

How important it is for a person's speech always to be pure and refined, for him to weigh his words carefully before giving utterance to them, to avoid speech that is vulgar and coarse and to choose language that is decent and wholesome. Our Sages have symbolized this great idea by dwelling at length on the subject of searching for chametz and disposing of it completely before we come to celebrate the Pesach. The detailed discussion on this search for chametz comes at the very beginning of Tractate Pesachim. The inside and the outside of chametz, when baked, are different in appearance but matzah looks the same from all angles. Only when one's mouth has been searched for chametz so that his words and his thoughts are in harmony, does he become like the matzah in which there is no guile. Only then will every word that comes from his mouth be pure and acceptable to God. Only then can he praise and glorify God on the festival of Pesach.

Nisan EREV PESACH

CHAPTER EIGHT

The fourteenth of Nisan is a day of endless activity, a day full of mitzvot. Some of these are concerned with the day itself and some are in preparation for Pesach on the following day.

Were it not that the Jewish people loved the mitzvot so dearly, they would be unable to carry out the manifold duties of this day. Not only do they love to perform these mitzvot, but they even yearn for more mitzvot, like a rich man who is eager to increase his wealth. The verse in Kohelet, 'He who loves money is never satisfied with money' prompted Rabi Itzchak to remark, 'He who loves mitzvot is never satiated with mitzvot.'

Such is the nature of the Jewish people — because they are so eager to do mitzvot, they can always find time to do more mitzvot, and it is this characteristic which enables them to do all that is required on the fourteenth of Nisan.

What special features are associated with this day ?

The fast of the firstborn;

the first day of the three-day fast of Esther and Mordechai;

the fast of pious people;

the cessation from work;

the removal and declaration of *ma'asrot* in the Land of Israel;

the day on which Ya'akov was blessed;

the disposing of the chametz and the end of the time limit for purging utensils;

consideration of the food that is permitted and the food that is forbidden on this day;

in our time — reading the chapter on the order of the Pesach offering;

in the times of the Beit Hamikdash — the Pesach offering itself;

the special *chagigah* offering of the fourteenth of Nisan;

baking the matzah to be used for the mitzvah;

preparing the *eruv chatzerot* (common ownership of a courtyard) and the *eruv tavshilin* (for cooking food on Yom Tov to be eaten on Shabat).

immersing in the *mikvah*, and

preparations for the *Seder* on the eve of the fifteenth. Each of these will be explained and discussed in the following pages.

SHACHARIT ON EREV PESACH

On Erev Pesach we rise earlier than usual for *shacharit* so that we can finish eating chametz before the time limit expires, that is, by the end of the fourth 'hour' of the day. We omit *mizmor le-todah* (Tehilim 100) from *shacharit* because it refers to the offering of a thanksgiving sacrifice. This type of sacrifice was not brought on the fourteenth of Nisan since it had to be offered with chametz and there was a possibility that it would not be completely eaten in time. In Sephardi communities this Psalm is not omitted. If Erev Pesach occurs on a Monday night, we do not say '*El erech apaim*' and Psalm 20 in *shacharit*.

It was customary for the elders of the community to visit the local prisons on the fourteenth of Nisan to see if there were any Jewish captives. They would use every possible endeavour to obtain their release — at least for the duration of Pesach. Even if the prisoner was a proven criminal, they would try to free him, bearing in mind that when the Holy One, Blessed be He, brought us out from Egypt we too were not worthy of being redeemed. If their efforts were in vain they would try to induce the prison officers to allow special food to be brought in so that the prisoner would not have to eat chametz. They would also make special efforts to see that Jewish soldiers serving in foreign armies be supplied with Pesach food, however costly this may be.

The Ramah writes that one should bathe, shave and wear good clothes on the fourteenth of Nisan just as one does on Shabat.

THE FAST OF THE FIRSTBORN

It is an ancient and widespread custom for the firstborn to fast on Erev Pesach in memory of the miracle which saved the Jews from the plague that slew the firstborn of the Egyptians. This fast should really be held on the actual anniversary of the event, namely the fifteenth of the month, but by then the festival of Pesach has already begun and we do not fast on a festival.

There is another reason for fasting on the fourteenth. The Israelites humbled themselves before God and praised Him, declaring that greatness, power and sovereignty are His alone, that their firstborn were saved from death — unlike the Egyptians who proclaimed in their unlimited pride, 'I am, and apart from me there is none other.' The fast of the firstborn on the fourteenth of Nisan is a reminder of the fact that the firstborn of Israel humbled themselves before God and accepted the yoke of God's Sovereignty. The abstention from food and drink, is a sign of a heart subdued before God.

There are different customs associated with this fast. Some say that every firstborn, male or female, whether from the father or from the mother, must fast on that day. If there is no firstborn, then the oldest in the house must fast, since there was a person who died in every Egyptian household. If it happened that there was no firstborn in the house, then the oldest one there died. In contrast to this, there was no Israelite's household in which a miracle did not take place and this fact should be remembered forever.

However others say that only firstborn males need to fast

and this is the generally accepted custom. A child who is born after a miscarriage is considered as the firstborn and fasts on this day. It is usual for a father to fast for a first-born son who is too young to do so himself. If the father is himself a firstborn, then his fasting includes him and his son. Some authorities take a stricter view and maintain that in such a case the mother has to fast for her young son.

If the first child was born after midnight on the fourteenth, the father does not need to fast, since any child born in Egypt after midnight on that day did not die in the plague. When Moshe said, 'Thus says God: At midnight I will go out in the midst of Egypt and every firstborn will die,' he was speaking of midnight of the fourteenth, and referred only to those who were already born by that time.

There are some who say that a father does not need to fast for a first child born less than thirty days before the fourteenth of Nisan. This opinion is based on the fact that this fast, which is only a custom, should not be considered more important than the law concerning the redemption of the firstborn which is a specific mitzvah of the Torah and does not take place until the child is thirty days old.

If Erev Pesach occurs on Shabat, the fast is observed on the previous Thursday for if a fast is suspended it may not be held on a Friday. But if Erev Pesach is actually on Friday, then the fast takes place on that day, although some people take a more lenient view and do not fast on Erev Shabat.

This fast is generally treated with leniency so that if there is a meal connected with a mitzvah, such as a *brit milah* (ceremony of circumcision) or a *siyum* (completion of the study of a Talmudical tractate) the firstborn participates in this. It has therefore become the usual practice to arrange for a *siyum* to take place in the Synagogue after shacharit. The firstborn who are present partake of this and having broken their fast for a mitzvah, are then allowed to eat during the day.

If the firstborn who are fasting pray together, the *chazan* (cantor) adds *anenu* to the blessing of *shmah kolenu*. However some are of the opinion that there should be no public mention of the fast, since it is the month of Nisan, which, as we have already explained, is a month of rejoicing.

THE FAST OF THE PIOUS

Pious people are accustomed to fast on Erev Pesach even if they are not firstborn sons. We read in the Talmud of Rav Sheshet who used to fast all day on Erev Pesach because he was a delicate person. If he ate anything in the morning then his evening meal was tasteless. Since it is a mitzvah to eat matzah at the *Seder* with relish, he would abstain from food all day on Erev Pesach. The pious people who are in the habit of fasting frequently have taken an example from Rav Sheshet and refrain from eating on that day so that they may enjoy the taste of the matzah at the Seder.

Rav Ya'akov Emden has given another reason for this fast. 'It was on this day that Haman sent out the decree that all Jews were to be killed.'

WORK ON EREV PESACH

Erev Pesach is unlike Erev Shabat or the eve of any other festival since work is forbidden from noon onwards. Some are of the opinion that it is forbidden even before noon. Rashi gives the reason for this in his commentary on Pesachim, 50. 'So that one should not be occcupied with work and forget to dispose of the chametz, to slaughter the Pesach lamb and to prepare the matzah for the Seder. It is a mitzvah to be busy with these things from early in the day so that there should be no delay in observing the Seder.'

Rav Mordechai Yafe gives another reason. 'When the Beit Hamikdash was in existence the day on which anyone brought a sacrifice was considered by him as a festival on which all work was forbidden, for on that day all his sins were forgiven. Everyone had to offer the Pesach lamb on Erev Pesach, making the day like a festival for all Israel. As the time for this offering was from noon onwards...it became the custom to cease work from then.'

Tosfot on Pesachim 50 declares that even nowadays when this sacrifice can no longer be brought, the prohibition still remains.

This prohibition applies to work from which one derives profit or which is a complete task in itself; for example, one may not make a new garment but one may repair a garment to be worn on Yom Tov.

Work that is allowed on *chol hamo'ed* is also allowed on Erev Pesach.

Cutting the hair and trimming the nails should be done before midday. If this was not possible the nails may be trimmed after noon but the hair may be cut only by a non-Jew. This may not be done by a fellow Jew, even without charge.

Our Sages have said that a person will never succeed in any work he does on Erev Pesach.

THE REMOVAL OF CHAMETZ AND ITS NULLIFICATION

We have already explained above that chametz may not be eaten after the end of the fourth 'hour' of the fourteenth of Nisan. All chametz which then remains in the house and has not been sold to a non-Jew in the proper manner, must be removed and burnt during the fifth 'hour.' While burning the chametz one must renounce ownership, both verbally and with full intent, of any chametz which he still possesses. The purging of utensils can only be effected during the time that it is still permitted to eat chametz. (See above p. 185).

BI'UR MA'ASROT

In the Land of Israel, where the laws of *trumah* and *ma'-asrot* (heave-offering and tithes) are obligatory, one usually allocates the part of the harvest intended for the cohen, the Levite or the poor man and puts it aside, and then he is allowed to use his own part, even before the actual giving away of the tithes. He may put off the actual giving until some later date (within a prescribed period).

However, the Torah prescribes to dispose of any accumulated *trumot* and *ma'asrot* on two special days each seven-year *shmitah*-cycle : On Erev Pesach of the fourth *shmitah* year. and on Erev Pesach of the *shmitah* (seventh) year itself.

The 'disposal' should be done by giving the cohanim, the Levites and the poor the tithes due them, or, if these are not available, by taking the tithes out of the house and destroying them. This mitzvah is called *bi'ur ma'asrot* (disposal of tithes).

After all gifts and tithes have been duly distributed on Erev Pesach of the said years, one is bidden by the Torah to declare before God: 'I have cleared out that which is holy from the house, and I have also given it to the Levite, to the stranger, to the orphan and the widow according to all Your commandments which You have commanded me. I have not transgressed any of Your commandments nor have I forgotten any of them. I have not eaten of it while mourning and I have not used up any of it in a state of impurity. I have listened to the voice of God, my Lord, I have done everything which you have commanded me. Look down from Your holy dwelling place and bless Your People, Israel, and the Land which You have given us as You have sworn to our fathers, a land flowing with milk and honey.'

It is told in the Midrash :

'There was once a man who used to tithe his produce properly each year. His field produced a thousand measures and he would give away a hundred for ma'aser. With the remainder he would sustain himself and his family for the whole year. When his time came to die, he called his son and said to him, 'Look well to the field for it produces a thousand measures each year. Of this I give a hundred as ma'aser and with the rest I support all my family.' The son copied his father's example during the first year but in the second year he did not give the full quantity of ma'aser, and the field produced less. So it went on; as he decreased the amount of ma'aser that was due, so the field yielded less and less, until eventually he harvested only a hundred measures. When his relations heard of this, they dressed themselves in white and came to visit him. 'I have been rejected by God,' he said to them, 'Why do you come to make merry?' 'Far be it from us to gloat over you,' they answered, 'We have come to rejoice with you. Hitherto you were the owner of the field and God was, as it were, the cohen, for He had a hundred measures as against your thousand measures. But now God has become owner and you are His cohen seeing that now you have only a hundred measures' (Yalkut Re'eh 892).

A DAY DESTINED FOR BLESSINGS

The fourteenth of Nisan — Erev Pesach — was destined from the time of creation to be a day of blessings. Long before the children of Israel were born, before they were enslaved and before they were redeemed on that night, our ancestors already knew that this was to be a night of song and praise. All the storehouses of goodness and light are opened then and whoever receives a blessing on this day from a worthy person, is privileged to enjoy all these treasures.

It is thus told in Pirkey d'Rabi Eliezer:

'When the eve of Pesach approached, Itzchak called his eldest son, Esav, and said to him, 'My son, on this night all the world recites God's praises and the storehouses of dew are opened. Make me tasty dishes and I will bless you while I still live.' But the spirit of God warned 'Do not eat the bread of a wicked man and do not desire his tasty dishes' (Mishley).

'While Esav was delayed in bringing this for his father, Rivkah said to Ya'akov, 'My son, on this night the treasures of dew are opened and the angels above sing. On this night

your children will be redeemed and they will sing God's
praises. Make a tasty meal for your father that he may bless
you while he yet lives.' However, Ya'akov knew that it is
more important to obey one's father than one's mother and
feared lest he incur his father's curse, but his mother said,
'My son, the blessings are for you and for your children.
If there are to be curses, let them fall upon me' (Bereishit
27), so Ya'akov went and fetched two young goats. Itzchak
surely did not require so much to eat, 'A righteous man
eats to satisfy his soul' (Mishley 13), but one corresponded
to the Pesach sacrifice and one was to make a tasty dish.

'Then Ya'akov came into his father's room and said, 'Arise
and sit up and eat of my food so that your soul may bless
me.' When Itzchak heard the voice of his son he said, 'The
voice is the voice of Ya'akov, speaking of the Unity of God.
I can hear him accepting the yoke of God's Sovereignty with
this voice. The voice is the voice of Ya'akov studying the
Torah. With this voice I hear him occupying himself with
the Torah.' Furthermore whenever the descendants of Ya'-
akov loudly declare. 'Hear, O Israel, the Lord our God, the
Lord is One' or when they raise their voices in study of the
Torah, the heavens above tremble.

'Rabi Yehudah said, 'Itzchak gave ten blessings to Ya'akov
to correspond to the ten sayings with which the world was
created. May God grant you, 1. from the dew of heaven
2. and from the fat of the land, 3. and much corn, 4. and
wine, 5. nations will serve you, 6. peoples will bow down
to you, 7. be a master to your brethren, 8. the sons of your
mother will bow down to you, 9. those who curse you will
be cursed, 10. and those who bless you will be blessed.'

A BLESSING AND NOT A CURSE

We learn that King David never went out to war on Erev
Pesach because, this day was destined from the time of the
Creation, to be a day of dew that gives new life, a day rich
in blessings. As the night follows that day, all creatures above

211

sing songs of praise. It was therefore not fitting to make war and slay on the day leading up to this night of praise — even for King David who fought for God's cause. For on this night no human creature is permitted to destroy any of the works of the creation, the Creator alone has this right.

'I will pass through the land of Egypt in the night and I will smite all the firstborn of Egypt, from man to beast, and I will execute judgement against all the gods of the Egyptians, I am God.'

'I will pass through the land of Egypt,' I, and not an angel. 'I will smite all the firstborn of Egypt,' I, and not a *saraf*. 'I will execute judgment against all the gods of the Egyptians, I am God,' I am He, and not a messenger, I am He and there is no other. Not an angel and not a *saraf*, not Moshe the messenger of God nor King David, nor any other creature. None is allowed to pass judgment on that night except God alone. He may disrupt the order of creation to redeem Israel, His people.

WHAT MAY WE EAT ON THIS DAY ?

We may eat chametz on Erev Pesach during the first four 'hours' (an 'hour' is a twelfth part of daylight duration) of the day. For the rest of the day we may eat 'rich' matzah, (that is, matzah made with fruit juice or with eggs, so that one cannot fulfill the mitzvah of eating matzah with it at the Seder). From the beginning of the tenth hour we may not eat even this, so that the piece of matzah eaten at the Seder will be even tastier. However we may eat fruit, vegetables, meat and fish, as long as we do not fill ourselves with these and still have an appetite for the matzah in the evening. If a person is ailing, so that whatever little he eats during the day takes away his appetite for the evening, he may not eat anything at all throughout the whole day. We have already mentioned Rav Sheshet who used to fast all day on Erev Pesach for this reason.

The type of matzah with which one performs the mitzvah at the Seder may not be eaten all day, but it may be fed to a child who is too young to understand the significance of the miracle of Pesach. Eating matzah before the Seder would be a sign of greed and lack of self-control. Many people do not eat matzah from Rosh Chodesh Nisan so as to enhance the mitzvah of eating it on this night. There are some who do not eat fruit on Erev Pesach so as to enhance the mitzvah of eating 'charoset' which is made from fruit, or horse-radish because of the mitzvah of the bitter herbs; but most people do not follow these customs.

Matzah which has been correctly baked and afterwards ground and made into dough with wine or with oil, is not classified a 'rich' matzah and may not be eaten on Erev Pesach.

BAKING THE MATZAH FOR THE MITZVAH

Even though we have prepared sufficient matzah for all the days of Pesach and have ensured that it has been baked with the utmost care and concern for all the details of the law, nevertheless, because of our love for the mitzvot, we go to great lengths to bake additional matzot on Erev Pesach for the special purpose of fulfilling the mitzvah of eating matzah on Seder night. This is baked after the sixth 'hour' of the day, (some say after six and a half 'hours' of the day have passed) by which time it is forbidden to derive any benefit from chametz. This baking is carried out in trembling anxiety lest something go wrong with the dough and possibly make it chametz. This matzah, is baked specially at this time to remind us of the Pesach offering which was slaughtered and prepared after midday on the fourteenth of Nisan.

Meticulous care is exercised over the baking of this matzah.

213

The process begins on the previous night when water is drawn for the morrow (see page 188). The water is sieved well and stored in a cool place to be used the next day.

Kav Hayashar records that he saw many great men who used to draw water with a small vessel and pour it into a large barrel. While doing so they would count Aleph, Beth, Gimmel to the end of the alphabet. This was done in order to invest the water with the sanctity of the letters of the Torah. When they carried the water home, they would lift up the pitchers on their shoulders as they neared their houses and carry them in this manner. On their way to draw the water, and also on their return home, they would speak only in the sacred Hebrew language, for they were engaged in performing a holy task.

As midday approaches on the fourteenth of Nisan, the oven is heated to half-strength. The flour made from the wheat that has been watched from the moment of reaping is brought in and a sufficient quantity is kneaded to obligate the taking of chalah, (although some people knead less than this amount). One person adds the water, one person mixes it, one rolls the dough and cuts it in pieces, one perforates these and takes them to the oven, and another looks after the baking. There should not be less than three people working together in a team.

None of these processes may be done by anyone who is not required by the Torah to keep the mitzvot. At every stage of the preparation, from the drawing of the water onwards, everyone who is engaged in these tasks says aloud, 'We are doing this in order to make the matzah for the mitzvah.'

Most of what we have described here applies to all matzah that is made especially for Pesach and not only that which is baked on Erev Pesach, but we have mentioned it here because the latter has special significance.

While the dough is being kneaded one should say, 'Any crumbs that may fall from this dough or that stick to the

utensils are declared ownerless.' This is said in case the
crumbs become chametz while they are still in his possession.
As soon as one batch of dough is finished the tables and all
the utensils used are scoured and cleaned. All the crumbs
which have fallen are gathered and thrown outside before
the next dough is started. This procedure is repeated until
the required amount has been baked.

A bowl of cold water is kept available so that the baker
can cool his hands in it from time to time. This water is
changed frequently so that it does not become warm and
so that it does not become mixed with the particles of dough
from his hands.

It is the custom to sing Halel during the baking to remind
us that the Pesach offering used to be brought to the accompaniment of Halel.

Because of the special importance of this matzah one
should not delegate the task of baking it to another person.

Rabenu Asher Ben Yechiel himself used to put great effort
into baking this matzah. He would urge on the workers and
assist them in rolling the dough. Rokeach says that everyone
must prepare these matzot himself. We learn this from the
verse, '... their kneading troughs bound up in their garments.' Rav Natan asks, 'Did they have no beasts to carry
their burdens?' But the Israelites loved the mitzvot so much
that they wanted to perform them by themselves. According
to the effort put into them, so they were rewarded.

Rabi Moshe Ben Machir, the author of Seder Hayom says
that each person should mix the dough himself, or at the
very least, he should add the water. Rabi Itzchak Luria in his
Sefer Hakavanot writes that one should exert oneself over
this mitzvah to such an extent that he becomes hot and
perspires.

Maharil used to kindle the fire for baking the matzot with
the branches of the lulav (used on Sukot) and some people
use the covering of the Sukah.

The early scholars (Rishonim) maintain that the three

matzot used for the mitzvah at the Seder, should be large and made of 1680 grams of flour, which is the measure of an *Omer.* (i.e. one tenth of an *ephah*). Most communities do not follow this ruling but take great care to ensure that the matzot are very thin and baked as quickly as possible. To use such a large quantity of flour would mean baking a thick cake.

When the baking is completed all the matzot are placed together, covered with a cloth, and *chalah* is separated with the appropriate blessing; 'Blessed are You, O Lord, our God, King of the Universe, Who has made us holy with His commandments and commanded us to separate the chalah.' The Sephardi version is slightly different: 'To separate the chalah for *trumah*.'

As the mitzvah of separating the chalah belongs to the woman of the house, the matzot should be brought home for the housewife to fulfill her special duty. Our Sages have said that if the husband separates the chalah himself without her permission, he should pay her ten gold coins.

The chalah should be burned as soon as it is separated.

A CUSTOM BASED ON LAW

The custom of baking the matzot for the mitzvah on Erev Pesach after midday is not simply due to piety. It is based on a legal ruling, the origin of which is to be found in the Jerusalem Talmud.

'The Torah compares the matzot to the Pesach offering. As this sacrifice was brought after the sixth 'hour' of the day, so the matzot should be baked at that time. Other authorities allow us to use matzah that has been baked earlier, as long as it was made specifically for Pesach. Nevertheless because of this statement in the Jerusalem Talmud, it is proper to take a strict view and endeavour to bake the matzot for the Seder after midday on the fourteenth of Nisan.

If Erev Pesach occurs on Shabat, this matzah should be baked on the previous Friday after midday.

216

In former generations there were some outstandingly pious people who, when Erev Pesach occurred on Shabat, would bake the matzah for the mitzvah after nightfall on Pesach itself. They would choose as their assistants God-fearing men who were skilled in their craft and they would station overseers there to ensure that not even the smallest particle of chametz was present. Any crumbs which might possibly become chametz were destroyed before this could happen. While they worked, they would pray continuously that their work be successful and acceptable before God. They took such great pains because of their desire to perform the mitzvah at its proper time.

Nowadays we refrain from baking at this time lest we are unsuccessful in our work, for not everyone is worthy of being helped by God in such a way that all his efforts will prosper. At a time of great emergency however, during a famine, for example, when the flour is not available beforehand, our Sages have permitted the matzah for the mitzvah to be baked on Pesach itself.

A WARNING

Since we take such infinite care to carry out every detail of this important mitzvah at the correct time, there is a danger that in our anxiety we will become angry and raise our voices against others engaged in the same mitzvah. We might shout at a fellow-worker who is not nimble enough at his task. We must remember that there is no mitzvah so important that it overrides the prohibition against exhibiting anger and offending our fellow-man.

Our Sages have warned all who bake matzah after midday on Erev Pesach to refrain from bitterness and anger, not to introduce the sin of anger into the matzot for this is as serious as introducing chametz into the matzot.

A certain *tzadik* has pointed out that the verse in the Torah, 'You shall keep the festival of the matzot' is immediately preceded by the words. 'You shall not make for

217

yourselves gods of molten metal.' This juxtaposition of verses warns us against becoming angry while baking the matzot. Anger is compared to idolatry, so when we are about to fulfill the mitzvah of keeping the festival of Pesach, we are first adjured not to make gods of molten metal. We must steer clear of any form of idolatry — including anger.

Further support for this idea is contained in the ruling that, although five kinds of grain are suitable for matzot, we use only wheat. The Hebrew word for wheat is *chitah* which is similar to the word *chet* meaning 'sin.' We are reminded of the sin of Adam, for our Sages tell us that the Tree of Knowledge whose fruit was forbidden to man, was of wheat. They compare the evil in man to wheat. On Pesach we celebrate the true freedom of the soul, which means our evil inclination and purifying ourselves from sin. We take wheat, *chitah*, grind it well and perform in purity and out of love all the intricate details of this mitzvah. It is therefore unseemly to mix into this mitzvah any element of sin such as anger.

There is also a simple explanation for our preferring wheat to any other kind of grain. It is the choicest variety and when we perform a mitzvah we always try to do so in the best possible manner.

A TALE

A story is told of the great Rav Shmelke of Nickolsburg who was willing to forfeit his life for the sake of any mitzvah, great or small. Every mitzvah was performed in the handsomest manner possible. When it came to baking the matzot for Pesach he gathered all his energy to ensure that they were baked with scrupulous care and that there was not the slightest shadow of doubt that they were completely kasher. Yet his soul would almost leave his body out of the terrible fear that he had not done everything possible in preparing the matzah.

Having carried out all the complicated processes with great

exactness, Rav Shmelke would then sort out all the matzot he had baked, rejecting one after another, until he selected the three finest to grace his Seder table. All the while he would shed tears of prayer blessing his Maker, to prosper all these efforts; his heart was filled with anxiety lest he had somehow failed in his duty towards Him.

As he returned from the bakery one Erev Pesach bearing in his hands the three prized matzot, carefully wrapped, his face betrayed its usual concern. Perhaps after all there was something amiss. Perhaps the matzot were not properly baked according to the Torah. As he walked, one of his pupils came alongside of him, he too carrying the matzot which he had just baked, his face suffused with joy. The *tzadik* knew that such happiness comes only from performing a mitzvah and asked the pupil what he had done to make him rejoice. 'I am happy,' he answered, 'that I have been so successful in baking these matzot.' The tzadik, envious of his pupil's happiness, asked if he would exchange his matzot for those that he himself had baked. The pupil was delighted to accede to this request. For the first time, the joy of Rav Shmelke was complete as he performed the mitzvah of the matzot at the Seder.

The pupil rejoiced sevenfold at being privileged to eat matzot baked by the great tzadik himself, for these were surely ten times more *kasher* than his own.

Now why did the tzadik rejoice over his pupil's matzot more than his own? 'All the time that I was baking my matzot' he said, 'my heart was troubled and I was beset with doubts, for I could not be absolutely sure they were perfect. But these matzot have been baked by a man who is upright and he testifies of their being baked properly; in such a case there is no place for doubt.'

From this episode we can derive three lessons. 1. That the Torah was not given to the angels in heaven, but every Israelite is capable of performing the mitzvot properly. For if there had been anything amiss with the pupil's matzot,

God would have prevented them from coming into the possession of the tzadik. 2. The love of their fellow-Israelites and their confidence in them is more important to the tzadikim than all the effort and energy they exert in learning Torah and practicing the mitzvot. 3. The happiness derived from a mitzvah is so great that because of it a pupil was privileged to eat of the matzot over which the great tzadik had toiled and labored.

RECITING THE ORDER OF THE PESACH OFFERING

After *minchah* on Erev Pesach, or after saying the *ketoret* and before *shmoneh esreh*, it is the custom to read about the sacrifice of the Pesach lamb. We read the relevant verses from the Torah, the Nevi'im and the Ketuvim and also a description of the sacrifice as it was actually performed in the Beit Hamikdash.

This recital is in accordance with the verse 'We will give the offerings of our lips in place of the bullocks.' We yearn to fulfill the mitzvah of the Pesach sacrifice as we were enjoined, in the holy place and in company with all the pilgrims. But as we have not been found worthy to do so, we bring the offerings of our lips instead of the offerings of the bullocks and we read those chapters which tell us of the Pesach offering and its special mitzvot.

These readings were preceded by a prayer;

'O Master of the World, You have commanded us to bring the Pesach offering at its proper time on the fourteenth of the first month, with the cohanim carrying out the *avodah*, the Levites standing on their platform and the Israelites in their correct positions, all singing Your praise. But now, because of our sins, the Beit Hamikdash has been destroyed, the Pesach offering has been annulled, we have no cohen to perform the *avodah*, no Levite to stand on his platform and no Israelite to take up his position. We can only render the offerings of our lips in place of the sacrifices. May it therefore be Your will, O our God and God of our fathers,

that You may consider these prayers as if we had brought
the Pesach offering at its right time, as if we had stood in
our places and as if the Levites had sung praises and thanksgiving to God. And may You establish Your Sanctuary in
its place so that we may come up and offer before You
the Pesach offering at its proper time, as You have written
in Your Torah.'

Then we read the chapters and verses relevant to the
subject. In Jerusalem it is the custom to recite this at the
Western Wall. With tears and subdued hearts they pray
that God speedily allow us to enjoy the festivals, rejoicing
over the rebuilding of His city and exulting in His service,
so that we may eat there of the sacrifices and of the Pesach
offerings, carrying out the mitzvot which our Maker has
commanded us.'

THE PESACH-OFFERING IN THE SANCTUARY

The number of people who went up to Jerusalem on Pesach
was far greater than on any other festival. On each of the
three *Regalim* (pilgrim festivals), three mitzvot had to be
performed: Appearing in Jerusalem, the festival sacrifice
and rejoicing. On Pesach there is the additional mitzvah
of the special offering. This mitzvah consists of many other
mitzvot, both *aseh* and *lo-ta'aseh* (positive commandments
and prohibitions).

The Torah does not tell us of the punishment that befalls
a person who does not go up to Jerusalem on the other
pilgrim festivals, just as it does not mention the punishment
for infringing any of the positive commands (with the exception of circumcision). But if one purposely disobeys the
positive command to offer the Pesach sacrifice at the right
time, the punishment is explicit and severe — *karet*, being
cut off from his people.

The only one of the pilgrim festivals on which women
have to appear in Jerusalem is Pesach, although normally

they are exempt from those mitzvot whose observance depends on a fixed time.

For all these reasons, the crowds which thronged to Jerusalem were greater on Pesach than on any other occasion of the year.

People seeing Jerusalem today are filled with wonder at the thought that it would have absorbed so many millions of pilgrims, cohanim and Levites in addition to its normal population. How could this small city have accommodated them all ? How could they all have celebrated the festival in its midst ? How could they all have entered the courtyard while the Pesach offering was being slaughtered ?

When Israel dwelt in its own land and the Holy One, Blessed be He, caused His Divine Presence to dwell in Jerusalem, no man ever said, 'There is no room for me to spend the night in Jerusalem,' or 'There is no room for me to come into the courtyard of the Beit Hamikdash.' Our Sages do not list this fact among those miracles which took place in the Sanctuary, for this is a natural characteristic of the city — there is space within it for all her children who come from far and near, there is room for all who come into the courtyard of the Beit Hamikdash. But if they should cease to come, then Jerusalem shrinks and the Beit Hamikdash seems too small to contain them, so that strangers should not come there and feel at home.

King Agrippa once wished to know the number of people in Jerusalem. He asked one of the cohanim to set aside for him one kidney from each Pesach offering and the number came to one million and two hundred thousand, double the number of males who came out of Egypt. But this was not the full number, for there was not a single Pesach lamb that was shared by less than ten people. Rav Chiya said there were forty or fifty to each offering and Bar Kapara said perhaps even a hundred. This number did not include those who were ritually unclean and could not bring the offering, or those Jews who were in distant lands at the time.

Every Jew, whether he was in the Land of Israel or abroad, provided that he was not more than thirty days journey from the city (about 900 miles), had to go up to Jerusalem and offer his Pesach sacrifice. Even the poorest person who had no donkey to ride on and who lived far from the city had to do everything in his power to arrive in time for Pesach. He would begin to make arrangements thirty days before, when people began to discuss and to learn the laws of the festival.

Four days before Pesach there were already large numbers of pilgrims in the city. Each group of people who shared one lamb would send one of its members to examine the animal for blemishes at least four days before it was due to be slaughtered.

'On the tenth of this month each man shall take for himself a lamb for a father's household, a lamb for a house and it shall be kept by you until the fourteenth day of this month' (Shmot 12). Our Sages tell us that they used to examine this lamb four days before it was slaughtered to see if it had any blemish. This applied not only to the Pesach celebrated in Egypt but to Pesach every year. (It does not apply to *Pesach Sheni.*'

By the time the fourteenth of Nisan arrived, the population of Jerusalem was as numerous as the sands on the sea shore. The noise of man and beast that filled the air of the city could be heard far off. Each person provided himself with animals for the various sacrifices. There were five of these; three of them common to all the Pilgrim festivals and two were additional ones specially for Pesach. The sacrifices were:

1. The *chagigah* offering of the fourteenth of Nisan — a *Shlamim* (peace-offering). Although not compulsory, everyone used to bring this offering voluntarily. As the Pesach offering had to be eaten when one was already satisfied (so

that people would know they were eating it because of the mitzvah and not because they were hungry) the *chagigah* offering was eaten beforehand to ensure this.

2. The Pesach offering itself, which consisted of a perfect male lamb or goat.

3. The burnt-offering which accompanied the appearance in the Sanctuary on a *Regel* (pilgrim festival). This offering had to be brought by everyone who came up to Jerusalem in fulfillment of the verse, 'They shall not appear before Me empty-handed.' This was consumed on the altar and the owner had no share in it.

4. The peace-offering of the festival was also obligatory for the Torah tells us 'You shall celebrate three festivals a year for Me.' The word 'celebrate' means that one must sacrifice a peace-offering in honor of the festival. The meat was eaten by the owner.

5. The peace-offering of rejoicing was likewise compulsory, according to the verse 'You shall rejoice on your festivals.' Rejoicing is expressed by feasting on meat and therefore the Torah commanded us to bring peace offerings in addition to those required by the festival.

EREV PESACH IN THE PRECINCTS OF THE BEIT HAMIKDASH

The *avodah* of the Pesach sacrifice reached its climax on the fourteenth of Nisan. The pilgrims who had gathered from all parts of the country would prepare themselves for the sacrifice. If Pesach came on a weekday they would also offer up the festive offering of the fourteenth of Nisan. They were extremely careful to remove all chametz from their possession, not only because of the general prohibition of chametz, but also to comply with the law that forbids the Pesach sacrifice to be offered while there is still some chametz in existence. They would hasten to make themselves ritually pure before the festival began.

Everyone's eyes would be directed towards the roof of a balcony on *Har-Habayit* (the Temple-Mount) where two

'Thanksgiving' loaves, unfit for use, were lying. As long as these loaves lay there the people could eat chametz. At the beginning of the fifth 'hour' a messenger sent by the *Beit Din* would remove one of them. Then the people would stop eating chametz, although they did not yet burn whatever remained. When the people saw that both loaves had been taken away, they immediately lit bonfires everywhere and burned their chametz.

Aba Shaul said that the people were kept informed by means of two oxen that ploughed on the Mount of Olives. As long as both the oxen were ploughing, the people could still eat chametz. When one was withdrawn they stopped eating it and when the second was withdrawn, all the people burned their chametz.

After seven and a half 'hours' of the day had passed, the daily offering was slaughtered and after eight and a half 'hours' it was offered up. Immediately after this they would begin offering the Pesach sacrifice. If Erev Pesach came on a Friday, all this would take place an hour earlier.

A SELECTION OF THE LAWS CONCERNING
THE PESACH OFFERING

It is a positive mitzvah to slaughter the Pesach offering on the fourteenth of Nisan after midday. The offering consists of a male sheep or goat in its first year, and the law applies to everyone, male and female.

A person who willfully failed to keep this mitzvah, not because he was ritually 'unclean' or because he was on a distant journey, incurred the penalty of *karet*.

The Pesach offering, like the other *kodashim* could only be slaughtered in the courtyard of the Beit Hamikdash. The slaughtering had to be carried out after midday. If it was done before then, the sacrifice was ineffective. Only after the *Tamid* and the incense of the afternoon had been offered and the lamps prepared, could the Pesach offering be brought.

If one slaughtered the Pesach offering while still in posses-

sion of chametz the bulk of an olive in size, he was liable to
the punishment of flogging. This applied to the person who
actually slaughtered, the one who sprinkled the blood, and
the one who burnt the portions of the sacrifice on the altar.
Any of these people or any of the group which ate the
offering who possessed such a quantity of chametz at the
time of the sacrifice, was liable to be flogged, although
the Pesach offering itself was Kasher.

THREE GROUPS

'The slaughtering of the Pesach offering took place in
three groups in accordance with the verse 'All the assembly
of the congregation of Israel shall slaughter it.' Our Sages
refer each word 'assembly,' 'congregation' and 'Israel' to a
different group. How was this carried out ?

'When the first group had filled the courtyard to capacity,
the doors were closed and the slaughter of the animals began.
Throughout the slaughtering and the offering up, the Levites
would sing the Halel. If the first group of people had not
yet finished their tasks, the Levites would repeat the Halel
a second time and even a third time if necessary, although
this never happened' (Rambam Hilchot Korban Pesach).

Each time that Halel was sung, the trumpets were sounded
three times, teki'ah, tru'ah, teki'ah. The cohanim stood
row after row with dishes of silver and dishes of gold in
their hands. The whole of one row had silver dishes and
the whole of another row had golden ones and they remained
separate so that it would appear even more beautiful. These
vessels were wide at the top and pointed at the bottom so
that they could not be put down on the ground, for the blood
in them might congeal and be unsuitable to sprinkle on the
altar.

When the animal had been slaughtered, the cohen would
receive the blood in the vessels and hand it on to his fellow
and he to the next one so that many people should have
a share in the mitzvah. When it reached the cohen who

was nearest to the altar he would toss it, in one swift motion, against the base. As he received a full vessel, with one hand, he would pass an empty one to his fellow with the other hand.

The lamb was then suspended and skinned, the carcass was opened and cleansed. The portions which belonged to the altar were set aside, put into a dish, salted and offered up by the cohen on the altar.

How did they suspend and flay the animals? Hooks of iron were fixed into the walls and into the pillars and on these the animals were hung and skinned. If a person had no place to suspend his offering, there were thin smooth staves which he placed on his shoulder and on that of his fellow and thus he would hang it up and skin it.

When the first group had finished the doors of the court-yard were opened and the people would go out to allow the second group to come in. They, in turn, would be fol-lowed by the third group, and the procedure for each would be exactly the same. When all were finished the courtyard would be washed. Each person would take his animal with the skin and bring it to wherever he was staying in Jeru-salem.

If the fourteenth of Nisan was on Shabat, the ceremony took place exactly as it did on a weekday. The courtyard too was washed, for the prohibition did not apply to the Sanctuary. As they could not carry on Shabat the first group would take its Pesach offerings and stay on the Temple Mount, the second would stay in the *chil* (the area on the Temple Mount around the walls of the Sanctuary's courtyards) and the third group would remain in the courtyard itself. All remained in these specific places until after Shabat.

Pesach offering could be slaughtered by those who joined together to share one animal. We are told in the Torah 'You shall make your count for the lamb' which infers that this must be done while the animal is still lamb, that is, a living creature. Those who share in it are known as 'members of the group.'

How many members could be included in each group ? As many as could be provided with a piece of meat the size of an olive, if one of the members of the group was a drunkard and a glutton, the others could give him his share and send him away to eat by himself, but if he was only a drunkard and not a glutton, they could not do so.

ROASTING THE MEAT AND EATING IT

> It is a positive command to eat the meat of the Pesach offering on the night of the fifteenth of Nisan. 'They shall eat the meat on that night roasted in fire. They shall eat it with matzot and with bitter herbs.'

> To carry out this mitzvah properly one should feel satisfied after eating this meat. Therefore one who brought a festive offering for the fourteenth of Nisan should eat of this first and then finish off with the meat of the Pesach sacrifice, so that he is full. However, his duty has been fulfilled by eating a piece the size of an olive. This meat can only be eaten if it is roasted in fire.

> If, on Seder night, one eats a piece the size of an olive either underdone or cooked, he incurs the punishment of flogging. 'You shall not eat of it raw (i.e. underdone) nor boiled but roast with fire.' One who eats of it completely raw has transgressed a positive command.

> The word 'raw' in the Torah refers to meat which as been slightly roasted but is not yet fit to eat. The word 'cooked' refers to meat which has been boiled in water, fruit juice or any other liquid.

> Roasting the Pesach lamb on stone or metal is forbidden for we are commanded to 'roast it in fire,' on fire itself and not on anything else. One may use

*a utensil with holes that allows the fire to penetrate,
but one may not use a spit made of metal which
becomes hot, since the meat is roasted by the heated
metal and not from the fire itself.*

*How is the Pesach offering roasted? A spit or
skewer of pomegranate wood is thrust through it from
its mouth to its buttocks and it is hung like this in
an oven over a fire. The knees and the entrails are
hung separately on the spit but not placed inside
the animal, for there they would not be roasted, but
rather cooked by the juices of the animal. The pomegranate tree was specially chosen for this purpose
for it does not exude moisture like other trees. This
moisture when heated might cook the flesh.*

*Any portion of the meat that touched the earthen-
ware part of the oven must be scraped off. If any of
its juice dripped down on the earthenware and came
back on the carcass that part must be removed, for
this part would then have been cooked by the juice
and not roasted by the fire.*

*Two offerings are not roasted together on one spit,
lest they become mixed up and one group might
eat of the lamb that belongs to another group.*

*Although the Torah allows the Pesach offering to
be eaten throughout the night until dawn, the law
is that it is not eaten after midnight. This is to prevent
anyone overstepping the time limit and thus transgressing a commandment.*

*If the members of the group fell asleep while eating
the Pesach offering, even at the beginning of the
night, they do not eat of it again. But if only some
of them slept during the meal they may continue to
eat when they awake.*

*We were commanded to eat this meat roasted be-
cause this is how kings and princes eat meat, for it
is more tasty when roasted. Ordinary people who can*

only afford a little meat, eat it boiled (for it does not shrink so much when cooked like this). When we eat the Pesach offering we are reminded that we were delivered from Egypt in order to be a free people, a kingdom of cohanim and a holy nation. It is therefore fitting to eat in the manner of free and noble people.

Another reason is that this is a quicker method of cooking and the Israelites were not able to tarry while the meat was being boiled in a pot. (Sefer Hachinuch).

After the matzah and bitter herbs are eaten, a blessing is said, '...Who made us holy with His commandments and commanded us to eat of the sacrifice' and then the meat of the festive offering of the fourteenth of Nisan is eaten.

Then another blessing is said, '... and commanded us to eat of the Pesach offering' and the meat of this is eaten. The Pesach offering is eaten only after one is already satisfied with other food. One reason for this has already been mentioned, to impress upon a person that he is eating this in order to fulfill a mitzvah and not simply because he is hungry.

Another reason is that this meal is like a royal banquet where roast meat is a special delicacy served at the end of a meal. A further reason is that the Torah forbids any bone of the Pesach lamb to be broken. If one is very hungry he will want even to break the bones in order to eat the marrow.

While eating the Pesach offering Halel would be sung, in accordance with the verse in Yeshayahu, (30): *'The song shall be for you as on the night when the festival is celebrated.'*

Certain people do not eat of the Pesach lamb; 1. Those who are ritually unclean. However, if the majority of the population are unclean because of contact with a dead body, they celebrate Pesach and eat the lamb in this state. 2. One who is uncircumcised, even if this is because of danger to his health. 3. One whose sons or slaves are uncircumcised, that is, for instance, if after slaughtering the Pesach lamb, he had bought a servant, or if a son had been born to him and it was not yet time to circumcise him. 4. One who has converted to idolatry 5. A resident non-Jew, that is, a non-Jew who has undertaken not to worship idols. 6. A hired servant in the sense of a proselyte who has been circumcised but has not as yet immersed in the mikvah.

EATING IN A HOUSE

'One may only eat of the Pesach lamb in a group, and no one who has joined a group may be excluded from it. Anyone who takes a morsel of this meat from one group to another on the night prior to the fifteenth, incurs the penalty of flogging. The Torah tells us, 'You shall not take any of the meat outside.' Any meat that has been taken outside the house, whether purposely or in error, may not be eaten for it is like the meat of 'Kodshei Kodashim' (most holy sacrifices) which could not be taken out of the courtyard of the Beit Hamikdash. It is also compared to the meat of 'Kodashim Kalim' (sacrifices of minor sanctity) which could not be taken outside the walls of Jerusalem. Such meat is 'trefah' and those who eat it incur the penalty of flogging.

'If a small portion of a limb of the Pesach offering protruded outside the house where it was being eaten, one must cut through the flesh until he reaches the bone and then pare off the meat. The meat that was inside the house must be eaten but the meat that was outside must be burnt. As it is forbidden to break any of the bones, he pares the meat as far as the

231

joint, detaches the bone that has protruded outside and throws it away.

'*If two groups are eating in the house, there must be a partition between them, for the word 'outside' means outside the group with which one is eating. One group turns to one side, and one to the other so that they remain as two separate groups.*

'*If the water used for mixing the wine was in the middle of the house, then when the server stands up to pour out the wine he must close his mouth and turn away his face until he reaches his own group. This is done if he is eating the meat of one group while it becomes necessary for him to serve the other group, for it is forbidden to eat the Pesach lamb with two groups of people*' (*Rambam, Hilchot Korban Pesach*).

'*When a king makes a banquet everything is served to him and to his invited guests in the royal palace, but when a poor person makes a big feast he sends out portions to his friends, for he is not used to sitting with so many people at his table. On this night we are like kings and therefore we do not take the meat of the Pesach offering outside the house*' (*Sefer Hachinuch*).

It is not usual to slaughter a lamb for an individual even if he is able to consume the whole of it alone, but he should rather join together with other people to form a group.

THE LEFTOVER OF THE MEAT AND THE BONES

'*One should endeavor not to leave any meat from the Pesach offering until the morning. 'You shall not leave of it till morning.' If he did do so he has transgressed 'a mitzvat lo ta'aseh' a prohibition command, but he is not flogged for this prohibition should be corrected by the mitzvah to burn the leftover, and so it is considered a positive command' (Rambam, Hilchot Pesach).*

'The reason for this is that on this night, we imitate the actions of kings and princes who have no need to leave any food from one meal until the next. We burn anything that remains just as kings do, to re-mind us and to impress on our minds that when God brought us out of slavery to freedom, we were privileged to become a royal nation' (Sefer Ha-chinuch).

'If one who is ritually pure breaks a bone of the Pesach lamb, he is punishable by flogging. However, if he did so while he was unclean (i.e. the majority of people were in a similar state and were therefore permitted to bring the sacrifice) then he does not incur this penalty. This punishment applies whether the bone was broken on the night of the fifteenth or on the fourteenth or several days later. For this reason, the bones, together with the meat that is left over, are burned so as to avoid the possibility of breaking them. The punishment applies only to one who breaks a bone on which there is some meat the size of an olive, or in which there is some marrow. If one breaks a bone after it has already been broken, he is punishable.

One should not eat the fragile bones of a tender young goat. If he does so, he is liable to be punished, for it is immaterial whether the bones are hard or soft' (Rambam, Hilchot Korban Pesach).

SOURCES OF MERIT

Sefer Hachinuch dwells at length on the subject of the many mitzvot surrounding the Pesach sacrifice:

'The basic reason for all these mitzvot is to remind us of the miracles of Egypt. It is not good manners for princes and statesmen to scrape the bones and break them as dogs

233

do. Only poor people who are starving act like this. From
the moment that we became a special nation, 'a kingdom
of cohanim and a holy people,' we had to behave in a way
that demonstrates by our actions the high status to which
we were raised. Every year, on the anniversary of that occasion, we repeat these actions so that the idea is implanted
in our minds forever.

'You may ask, 'Why does God command us to do so many
things to remind us of this miracle ? Surely one deed would
suffice to fix the matter in our minds and to ensure that
our children after us remember it ?' Only a childish way
of thinking could have induced you to pose such a question.
Now listen, my son, and endeavor to understand. I will teach
you how to profit by the Torah and the mitzvot.

'Know that a man is influenced by his deeds. His heart
and his thoughts always follow the actions with which he is
occupied, be they good or bad. Consider a man who is
thoroughly wicked at heart and whose thoughts are bent on
evil throughout the day. If such a man were to attempt to
study Torah and mitzvot, even if not for the true goal, he
would immediately tend to become a better person. Although
his original intention had not been for the sake of the Torah
itself, he would eventually do it for the right purpose and
would destroy the evil inclination within him. For the heart
follows the actions. Now consider a man who was completely
righteous, honest and upright, and whose sole desire was to
keep the Torah and the mitzvot. If such a man were to
engage in shameful deeds — for example, the king might
compel him to undertake some evil task — if his whole
day were occupied with that evil, in time he would inevitably
change from being a righteous man and become completely
wicked. For it is well known, as I have already remarked,
that a person's character is influenced by his actions.

'Therefore our Sages have said, 'The Holy One, Blessed
be He, wanted to make Israel worthy, accordingly He gave
them many mitzvot to perform.' By these actions our thoughts

234

will be influenced and our lives will be improved. Through doing good deeds we will come to live better lives and will be worthy of everlasting life.

'Our Sages hinted at this idea when they said (Menachot 43), 'Whoever has a *mezuzah* at the entrance to his house, *tzitzit* on his garments and *tefilin* on his head is assured that he will not sin.' For these are recurring mitzvot which exert a continuous influence.

'Therefore look well to your work and to your deeds for you will be influenced by them, but you will not be able to exert an influence on them. Do not let yourself be tempted to think, 'Since I have complete faith in God, how can it affect me if I occasionally idulge in the pleasures of other people, or sit in their company in public places, or jest with them, or do other things which are not actually classified as sins? I am as strong-willed as they are, in fact, 'my little finger is thicker than their loins,' so how can they drag me down after them?' No, my son! Guard yourself against them. Many have drunk from their cup of poison, but you rather save your soul. And now that you know this, do not think of the numerous mitzvot as a burdensome way of remembering the miracles of Egypt. For it is a basic principle of the Torah that as we increase our good actions, so we will be influenced to the good.'

THE CHAGIGAH OFFERING OF THE FOURTEENTH OF NISAN

'When the Pesach lamb is offered on the fourteenth of Nisan, peace offerings are also sacrificed on the same day. These can be either sheep or cattle, large or small, male or female, like all the peace offerings. These sacrifices are given the special title of the 'Chagigah Offering of the Fourteenth.'

'This 'chagigah' is brought when the fourteenth of Nisan is on a weekday, when the majority of the people are ritually pure and when the Pesach lambs are in short supply. But if the fourteenth is on a

Shabat, or if the Pesach lamb is eaten when the majority are in a state of ritual impurity, or the Pesach lambs are numerous, then this chagigah offering is not brought. It is a voluntary sacrifice, and like others of this category, may be eaten for two days and one night. But if the meat of this 'chagigah' is put on the table together with the meat of the Pesach offering, then it may not be eaten after midnight and anything that remains of it must be burned, The reason for this is that the different kinds of meat may be mixed up and there is danger that the Pesach offering might be eaten after the time limit' (*Rambam, Hilchot Korban Pesach*).

EYEWITNESS REPORT BY A ROMAN COMMISSIONER

In the book Shevet Yehudah, mentioned by Rav Ya'akov Emden in his Sidur, there is an eyewitness description of the ceremony of the Pesach sacrifice, written by a Roman official who was stationed in Jerusalem during the period shortly before the destruction of the second Beit Hamikdash. His account corresponds to all the details laid down in the Torah and elaborated by our Sages. He describes the beauty of the ceremony and the impression it made on him. This description makes us realize how great is our loss in the destruction of the Sanctuary, so that we should pray to God with all our heart to restore the Service to His Sanctuary, speedily in our days.

'When the beginning of the month, which they call Nisan, arrives, couriers and messengers are sent out by order of the king and the judges, to all the area surrounding Jerusalem that whoever possesses sheep and cattle should hurry to bring them to the capital so that there be a sufficient supply for the pilgrims, both for their sacrifices and for their food. If anyone did not obey this order, his money would be confiscated for the use of the Sanctuary. All owners of cattle would hurry to obey and, on the way to Jerusalem they would bring their herds through a river to cleanse them of any dirt. When they reach the mountains round Jerusalem, they are so numerous that the grass cannot be seen. It appears to have become completely white because of the many sheep there. The sacrifice is offered on the fourteenth, so when the tenth of the month comes, everyone goes to buy his sacrifice which they call the 'Pesach.' It is a rule among them that no one asks another to let him go first, even if it were King David or King Shlomo. When I suggested to one of the cohanim that this was not polite, he told me that before the Omnipresent there is no greatness and in His service all are equal.

'When the fourteenth of the month arrives they go up a high tower of the Beit Hamikdash which they call *Lul* — it has a platform made like our 'canapario' — and blow on three silver trumpets. Then they make a proclamation, 'O, people of God, hearken ! The time has come to slaughter the Pesach offering for the One Who causes His Presence to dwell in this great holy House.' When the people hear this announcement, they put on their festive attire for, from midday onwards, it is a festival for the Jews, since that is the time for the sacrifice.

'At the entrance to the great courtyard twelve Levites stand outside with silver sticks in their hands. Inside stand another twelve with golden sticks. Those outside are to keep the pilgrims in order that they do not harm one another in their great haste, and so that they do not enter in confusion and cause quarrels. It once happened on Pesach that an old man and his offering were crushed by the pressure of the crowd. The Levites who stand inside have to keep order among those who are leaving the courtyard. These also used to close the gates of the courtyard when enough people had entered.

'At the place where the offerings are slaughtered there are several rows of cohanim, some with silver spoons and some with golden spoons in their hands. The cohanim in one row all have silver spoons and those in another row all have golden ones, so that it looks most beautiful. The cohen at the head of each row receives a spoon of blood from the slaughtered animal and passes it to his neighbor and he to his neighbor until it reaches the altar. The one standing nearest the altar would send back the spoon empty and this would be passed from hand to hand until it reached the other end of the row. This was done in such a way that each cohen received a full vessel with one hand and an empty one with the other. There was no delay in this procedure. The men were so nimble that it seemed as if the vessels were flying like arrows from the bow of a trained marksman. They used to practice this for thirty days before the required time so that there should be no mistakes and they would know their task perfectly.

'At the same place there are two high platforms on which stand two cohanim with trumpets of silver. These are sounded whenever a new group of pilgrims begins to bring sacrifices so that the Levites who are standing on their platforms should know that they must now sing the *Halel* with joy and thanksgiving, accompanied by all the musical instruments which they possess. The owner of the offering also says Halel and if all the offerings have not yet been slaughtered, then Halel is repeated. After the slaughtering the pilgrims go to the courtyards. Here all the walls have iron teeth and prongs so that the offerings can be hung up and skinned. There are also bundles of sticks so that if there is no hook vacant, a person will suspend a stick from his shoulder to that of his friend and skin the lamb on it. The parts that are to be offered on the altar are given, and then the owner goes away joyfully, like a victorious warrior returning from battle. For it is considered a great disgrace among the Jews if one does not bring the Pesach offering at the correct time.

'While the cohanim are engaged on this task they wear

short red tunics reaching to the thighs. These are red so
that any blood which is spilt does not show. They stand bare-
foot and their sleeves reach only to the elbow so that they
should not be hampered while they work. On their heads
they wear a small hat with three cubits of cloth wound
round it into a turban. People have told me that the Cohen
Gadol has a white turban made of forty folds of cloth.

'The ovens on which they roasted their sacrifices were
at the entrance to their houses, and they told me that this
was to demonstrate their faith and also to rejoice even more.
They sing joyfully while they eat and their voices can be
heard from afar. No one locks his door that night in Jerusalem out of respect for the many strangers passing through
the streets.'

'When King Alphonso the Great of Spain read this description he said, 'The Jews deserve to be honored for their
great past.'

'Another writer has recorded, 'I, Shlomo, was sent to Ma-
laga to ransom prisoners. There in the king's court, the non-
Jews arranged a Pesach sacrifice. They actually made an
altar, the priests stood in rows with silver soons in their
hands and a choir sang the Halel. Both the king and the
people were greatly impressed with this sight and the king
said 'If this was how the Jews once lived, how can they
possibly go on living, now that all this is lost ?'

THE SANCTITY OF PESACH TODAY

'One should be very careful not to set aside meat specially
for Pesach, that is to say, a person should not declare that a
certain animal, whether alive or after it has been slaughtered,
is for Pesach, for it might seem that he was dedicating
this as a Pesach sacrifice and then he would be guilty of
eating something sacred outside the proper place. He should
rather say, 'This meat is for the festival.' Some people extend
this prohibition to fowls and fish as well.

239

ERUV CHATZEROT — COMMON PROPERTY

The Torah prohibits carrying things on Shabat from a private to a public domain or vice-versa.

The definition of 'public domain' or 'private domain' is based on the structure of the given space rather than on the ownership thereof. A public street, for instance, is considered a 'private domain' if it is covered by a roof or surrounded by walls; an open lot is considered a 'public domain' if it is open to a wide street, even though it is owned by a single person.

Courtyards, hallways, roofs, and the like, of buildings where many people have apartments, although owned and used by all tenants, are nevertheless considered private domain. Hence it is permitted by the Torah to carry from a private apartment to the common courtyard and other parts of the general premises.

However, since people might err and not always distinguish between courtyards and real public domain,' it was enacted by the 'Beit Din' of 'King Shlomo' to avoid carrying even from house to courtyard or vice-versa unless an 'eruv chatzerot' is done to symbolize the 'mixture' of all private premises around the courtyard (or adjacent to it) with the courtyard itself, to be recognized as one single domain. (same goes for hallways, roofs, etc.)

This 'eruv' is done by taking some food before the Shabat, 'transferring' it to the possession of all 'partners' in the common courtyard and then putting it in one of the private places. The private place and the other similar places are thus given a symbolic status of 'mixed ownership' as the courtyard.

It is customary in many Jewish communities to collect a small quantity of flour from everyone in town before Pesach. This is made into one large matzah, the volume of eight, or at the very least, six eggs. This is brought to the Synagogue and used for the mitzvah of 'eruv chatzerot.'

As nightfall approaches, but before ma'ariv the Rav or one of the important citizens, takes the matzah in his hand and says, 'Blessed are You, O Lord our God, King of the Universe, Who has made us holy with His commandments and commanded us concerning the mitzvah of the Eruv.'

Then he recites from the 'sidur' (prayerbook), or in any language that he understands; 'By means of this Eruv, may it be permitted for us to carry from house to house, from yard to yard, from roof to roof, from house to yard and from yard to house, wherever it is necessary, on every Shabat and festival of the year, for us and for all the Jews who dwell in this town.'

Then he puts the matzah in a carefully guarded place where it remains until Erev Pesach of the following year.

Even if the flour is not collected from all the inhabitants, the eruv chatzerot can still be declared. One person makes a matzah of his own flour, of the required size, on behalf of everyone, even a thousand people or more, and the eruv includes them all. This is the usual practice today.

The person who provides the flour hands it to someone else, not a member of his own household, and says to him; 'Take possession of this flour as a representative for all the people of the town (or district).' He then takes it back again and says the appropriate blessing followed by the statement, as mentioned.

The reason for making this eruv on Erev Pesach goes back to the times when the flour used to be collected from each individual. On Erev Pesach, the flour would be abundant in every household in preparation for baking, and it would be easier to collect. Furthermore the matzah baked at this time could be kept over Pesach since there was no chametz in it.

In some places an eruv chatzerot is prepared every week before Shabat, lest the matzah go bad and become unfit to eat. If this happened, then it could not serve the purpose.

Only a complete matzah can be used for the eruv. A section, however large, is unsuitable for this mitzvah. Several whole matzot can be placed together to form the required quantity, namely, the volume of eight eggs.

ERUV TAVSHILIN

An 'eruv tavshilin' is always prepared on Erev Yom Tov when the festival is immediately followed by Shabat. The details of this subject are to be found in Vol. 1 page 58. Here it only remains to be mentioned that Jews living in the Land of Israel never need to make 'eruv tavshilin' for Pesach since the first day of this festival can never fall on a Friday. Jews living in the Diaspora do so when the first two days of Pesach are Thursday and Friday.

IMMERSING IN THE MIKVAH

Our Sages have said, 'A person must purify himself for the Regel (pilgrim festival). (Tr. Rosh Hashanah 16).

Why did our Sages require ritual purity on pilgrim festival rather than on Shabat which is more important ? It is because on a pilgrim festival every Jew had to go up to Jerusalem to appear in the Beit Hamikdash and to eat of the holy sacrifices. This mitzvah could only be fulfilled if a person was in a state of ritual purity.

Why did our Sages command us to purify ourselves now-

adays before a festival, when we can no longer bring sacrifices ? It is because a Jew should always imagine that the
Beit Hamikdash still exists. He should keep himself in a
state of purity as if he were going to eat of the sacrifices
and of the Pesach offering, just as the Torah has commanded
us.

The greater our faith in God and the firmer our belief
that He will renew our days as of old, and the more we
wait in anticipation to fulfill His word, so God will hasten
our redemption and our eyes will behold the building of
His Glorious House — may it come speedily in our days.

This purification that our Sages speak of consists of
immersing the whole body in natural water; sea water or river
water, or the water of a proper *mikvah* (ritual bath), but
not in tap water. If one does use tap water, then he does
not immerse himself but approximately thirteen litres of this
water are poured over him at one time. We can summarize
these rules by saying that if he uses natural water he immerses and if he uses tap water it is poured over him. The
former is to be preferred, especially on Erev Pesach.

Utensils are prepared for use on Pesach by purging, by
intense heat and by rinsing in water. A man too, prepares
himself for Pesach. He is no longer a slave to the evil inclination which is symbolized by the chametz, but he has achieved
spiritual freedom. His body is hot with perspiration because
of the many mitzvot with which he has been busy for the
festival. The tears flow from his eyes when he confesses
his sins. Then be immerses in the Mikvah and emerges purified in body and in soul, ready to receive the sanctity of
Pesach.

This immersing on Erev Pesach completes the process of
spiritual purification. One begins preparing for the festival,
both physically and spiritually, thirty days before Pesach
begins. On each day God removes a little of the evil in us,
so that by the time Erev Pesach arrives we are completely

243

cleansed of all our sins. 'One who wants to become pure is helped from Above.'

PREPARING FOR THE SEDER

It is a person's duty to show respect for and delight in this festival by having his hair trimmed, by wearing fine new clothes and by eating the best possible food. He must also make a great effort to adorn his table on this night in the most lavish manner. He must banish modesty and simplicity and let every kind of decoration and adornment appear on his table. The pillows on which he leans, and the dishes from which he eats, should remind him of a king's palace in which poverty and austerity are unknown. Even though the demands of Erev Pesach are very numerous. nevertheless one should use every endeavor to ensure that all the preparations are completed in good time, that the table is set, the pillows prepared, the food cooked and that everything necessary for the Seder is ready. Immediately on his return from the Synagogue the master of the house can commence the Seder without delay, together with all the members of his household, including even the smallest children. It is the special mitzvah of this night to arouse the curiosity of the youngsters by means of various unusual activities and to encourage them to ask questions so that one can fulfill the mitzvah of the Torah, 'You shall tell your child...'

Nisan THE SEDER NIGHT

CHAPTER NINE

On *Seder* night many complicated questions arise in connection with the detailed procedure of the evening. It was therefore the custom for many rabbis to delay commencing their own Seder until the rest of the people had almost concluded theirs. A rabbi is not allowed to answer questions of this nature if he has just drunk a quarter of a *log* of wine (approx. 86 gr.). If the rabbi were to start his own Seder at the same time as the other people, he would not be able to advise them, where necessary, on the various difficulties of the Seder service. Rabi Shmuel Salant, the Rabbi of Jerusalem, had his own special method of coping with this problem. He would quickly gather ten men in his own house for the ma'ariv prayer which was said as soon as possible. He would then sit down immediately to celebrate the Seder. After bringing this to a speedy conclusion, he would lie down to sleep for half an hour. By the time the rest of the people were ready to begin their own Seder, Rav Salant would be refreshed by his sleep, and all influence of the wine would have worn off. He was alert to answer any questions of ritual and to deal with problems arising out of the Seder celebrations. If any difficulties arose earlier, before Rav Salant had awoken from his sleep, the other rabbis who had not yet commenced their own Seder, were still available to deal with them.

Concerning this custom one can truly say that whether one hurried or whether one delayed, all that mattered was that one's intentions should be to serve God.

There are many people who normally spend much time

in making preparations for carrying out a mitzvah to ensure that it is done properly, but on Seder night they complete their preparations in good time and hurry to begin the Seder without delay.

THE CORRECT TIME FOR THE SEDER

On Shabat and festivals it is permitted to 'lengthen' the day (and thereby add to its holiness) by commencing earlier, but Pesach is different in this respect. The mitzvah of eating matzah belongs essentially to the night for it was closely connected with the Pesach sacrifice which was also eaten at night. 'They shall eat the meat on that night... They shall eat matzah and bitter herbs.'

Other mitzvot of the Seder, of Torah or Rabbinic origin, are closely related with the mitzvah of matzah and should also be performed after nightfall.

However, since it is a special mitzvah of the Seder, to tell the story of Pesach to the children, it is required to start the Seder as early as possible (after nightfall), so as to ensure that the children do not fall asleep before this mitzvah is performed.

WHILE IT IS STILL DAY

There are certain things which should be prepared for the Seder while it is yet day — the wine for the four cups, the matzah, the Seder dish containing the bone, egg, bitter herbs, charoset, karpas and chazeret, also salt water, candles ready for lighting, a wine goblet for each person at the table, and an additional large goblet for Eliyahu.

T h e w i n e used for the mitzvah of the four cups should be the best that one can afford, but not of such a type that induces drunkenness and sleep. Unless the white wine is of superior quality, one should rather choose red wine.

T h e m a t z o t should be of the shmurah type, that is to say, guarded from the moment the wheat is harvested, and if possible, baked after midday on Erev Pesach. If chalah has not been separated, this should be done before nightfall. All the matzot are wrapped in a cloth and the appropriate blessing is said before the chalah is separated. If less than 1,680 gram has been used in making the total quantity of matzot, no blessing is said when setting aside the chalah. After this, the three matzot wrapped in a special covering, are placed in position on the table.

T h e S e d e r d i s h should be large enough to contain the six items necessary for the Seder arranged in the correct manner.

T h e b o n e , with some meat on it, should be roasted while it is yet day. This is most important for on this night we may not eat roast meat, since it might seem as if we are eating of the Pesach sacrifice. Just as one may not eat roast meat on this night, so one may not actually roast it on this night, unless the intention is to eat it on the following day. This bone is placed at the upper right side of the dish.

T h e e g g is either boiled or roasted, or roasted after being boiled. It is placed at the upper left side of the dish opposite the bone. The bone and the egg represent respectively the Pesach sacrifice and the festival *chagigah* offering which, in olden days, were among the most important mitzvot of this night.

T h e m a r o r (bitter herbs), consists of leaves and stalks, (but not roots) of leaf lettuce. Some people use the leaves for the mitzvah of *maror*, and the stalk for the mitzvah of *korech*. Horse-radish or any other bitter vegetable may be used.

These vegetables are carefully examined to ensure that they are free from insects, rinsed well and placed on the Seder dish between the bone and the egg, but slightly lower, for the bitter herbs are essential to the Pesach sacrifice which is symbolized by the bone. 'You shall eat it (i.e. the Pesach sacrifice) with matzot and bitter herbs.'

C h a r o s e t is a compound of ground apples, almonds and other nuts, blended together with cinnamon and ginger, and mixed with wine. Some people also use dates and date honey. It is similar in appearance to clay which is made of stubble and water. The *charoset* should be prepared during the day, but if one forgot, it may be done after nightfall. The charoset is usually made as a thick mixture and after nightfall more wine is added to thin it down so that one can easily dip the bitter herbs into it. It is placed further to the right side of the Seder dish than the bone but below the bitter herbs. The word 'charoset' is Aramaic, denoting this type of food. It is also similar to the Hebrew word for 'clay' (charoset) of which the bricks were made during the period of slavery in Egypt.

K a r p a s means parsley, but one may use potato or cooked carrot or raw radish or any other vegetable which is not bitter to the palate. It is placed further to the left side of the dish than the egg, on the same level as the charoset.

As both the charoset and the karpas are needed by the bitter herbs — as will shortly be explained — they are placed in the same row, below the latter.

C h a z e r e t consists of the leaves of lettuce, horse-radish, or any other vegetable which is suitable for use as bitter herbs. It can be the same type that has been used for the bitter herbs or a different one and is placed at the bottom of the Seder dish, between the charoset and the karpas. (We call these by different names only to distinguish between the bitter herbs placed higher on the Seder dish, which it is a mitzvah to eat, and the chazeret which is placed only as a reminder, as we shall explain.)

We now have six items arranged on the Seder dish in the form of two triangles, each with its base uppermost, like the Hebrew vowel *segol*. The upper triangle contains the bone, egg and bitter herbs which are essential mitzvot of this night, while the lower triangle contains the charoset, karpas and chazeret which are used only in conjunction with the former items.

When the Seder dish is properly arranged, it is placed

above the three matzot, which are covered by a special cloth. Today, only the eating of the matzot is a positive command of the Torah, whereas the other objects on the Seder dish are either mitzvot ordained by the Sages, or customs to remind us of something. It is therefore the custom to place the matzot in a special position on the table and not to put them together with the other objects. Some people, however, do place the matzot on the Seder dish.

The salt water, into which the karpas is dipped, is prepared while it is yet day. If the Seder night occurs on Shabat and one forgot to prepare the salt water in advance, it should be made of weaker strength than usual, for on Shabat, one may not prepare salt water consisting of more than two-thirds salt to one-third water.

All the goblets should be rinsed before nightfall and placed on the table in readiness.

When all is ready for the Seder, we go to the Synagogue for the minchah and ma'ariv prayers. Some people recite the minchah prayer earlier in the day on Erev Pesach so that the order of the Pesach sacrifice can be read afterwards, and so that there should be no undue delay because of the many duties of the day.

MA'ARIV IN THE SYNAGOGUE

The ma'ariv prayer on this night of Pesach is in no way different from the ma'ariv of the other Pilgrim Festivals, for the special mitzvot of this night are carried out at one's own table. Nevertheless, the special status of this night is discernible even in the Synagogue.

If the first day of Pesach coincides with Shabat, we omit *magen avot* from ma'ariv. This prayer is especially intended for those who work late and have to travel far to reach the Synagogue. The ma'ariv prayer is extended so that those who come late should not find the building empty. On Erev Pesach however, everyone is home from his work by midday and can arrive at the Synagogue in good time. Another reason for this omission is so that we can begin the Seder as early as possible for the sake of the young children.

In some communities the ma'ariv prayer is prolonged by the inclusion of the Halel. In many places there is no variation at all from the other festivals of the year, and *magen avot is* included when Erev Pesach coincides with Erev Shabat.

It is the custom in some Synagogues to recite *kidush* over wine after ma'ariv is concluded every Shabat and festival, but this is not done on Erev Pesach. The wine used for kidush is also the first of the four cups which must be drunk on Seder night, and these must all be drunk in the same place, namely at home. Furthermore, the main reason for reciting kidush in the Synagogue is for the sake of strangers who have nowhere to eat. On Seder night, however, every stranger eats at someone's table and not in the Synagogue.

Another reason for reciting kidush in the Synagogue is that the people, after hearing it, should be able to say it more fluently and correctly in their own homes. But this does not apply to the Seder night when everyone recites kidush from the Hagaḍah.

The main variation in the ma'ariv of Erev Pesach lies in the recital of Halel in the Synagogue. In the Diaspora this is also said in the Synagogue on the second night of the festival. Normally Halel is only said by day, but this first night of Pesach heralds the light of a new era, so we recite the complete Halel with the appropriate blessing. This custom is mentioned in Tractate Sofrim (Chap. 20). Halel is sung with great rejoicing to the accompaniment of a beautiful tune so that we may, quite literally, 'exalt His Name together.' Even though several authorities dispute this custom, it has already become common practice to sing Halel in public, with a blessing, on the eve of this sacred festival.

Halel is also recited at home during the Seder, and indeed this recital is more important than the one in the Synagogue.

Yet there is no blessing for Halel said at home; it is included by the one said in the Synagogue. One reason for this is that the Halel said during the Seder is in integral part of the Hagadah, a chapter as it were, in the glorious tale of the Exodus from Egypt. The telling of this story requires no blessing.

This answer, however, poses another question. The performance of every mitzvah is preceded by a blessing, and yet our Sages have not ordained that we say any blessing before carrying out the mitzvah of telling the story of our departure from Egypt.

On this night every Jew is aware of his freedom and his redemption and his soul is full of praise for his Maker, so that the entire Hagadah is in the nature of a blessing and thanksgiving to God. When the saying of the blessing constitutes an actual mitzvah in itself (as for example, the blessing after food, 'You shall eat and be satisfied and bless...') then we say no blessing before it.

There are several other reasons for saying no blessing before Halel: 1. The kidush itself, which is also in the nature of a blessing, makes mention of the departure from Egypt; 2. The blessing '...Who has redeemed us...' is considered part of the Halel; 3. The recital of Halel is not consecutive, part of it is said before the meal and part of it afterwards.

NIGHT OF SONG

The Holy One, Blessed be He, wanted to gladden the hearts of the Jewish people, to inspire them with hope for the days to come, and to acquaint them with a knowledge of the greatness of ancient days. 'The song shall be for you like the night of the holy festival' (Yeshayahu 30). That is to say, that the song of the future shall be like this night of Pesach. This does not refer simply to the night on which the Israelites came out of Egypt, nor to the moment when they crossed the Red Sea and burst into song, for there was no sacred festival as yet. Even the duties of the festival of which they had been informed in Egypt were only given to them as sacred mitzvot later in the wilderness.

'The night of the holy festival' refers to such a time, in each generation, year after year when in every single Jewish home, people talk of the mighty deeds of God and speak in praise of all that He did for them when they came out of Egypt. On such a night everyone sings the praise of the living God, those who dwell above and those who dwell on earth. The very walls of the houses and all that they contain, the vault of the heavens and the depths of the earth, the sea and all its waves, all combine in song and praise on this night of the holy festival.

The song of this night, the song in which the entire creation joins, is not always heard by the human ear. There are times when the ear is not attuned to this music. There are times when the ear hears but does not comprehend what it hears. A veil of forgetfulness intervenes and lustful desires confuse the mind. If a person could achieve complete purity of heart and quiet repose of the soul, then his ear would absorb that song, which, rising up from his innermost being and from all that is around him, fills all the world. 'Praise, O you servants of God, praise His Name.' At such a moment the very soul must echo, 'May the Name of God be blessed from now and for evermore. O, would that my heart might feel like this forever, that no veil might intervene nor any cares confuse me, that I could always see how 'the Name of God is praised, from the rising of the sun unto its setting.'

And then, when the earth will be filled with the knowledge of God in the days to come, and every mouth will declare God's praises in song, that song will be no more glorious than the song which is sung on this holy festival — but the heart of mankind will be open to receive it and the ears of mankind will be alert to accept it.

It is therefore the duty of each individual to attempt to purify his heart before he celebrates the sacred Seder. When his heart is free of all evil thoughts, then his ears will hear

the song of this night and his body and soul will join together in extolling the Living God.

Rav Yeshayah Horwitz (Hash'lah Hakadosh) wrote: 'On
returning home after ma'ariv, one should conduct oneself as
a prince. there should be an abundance of silver and gold,
together with garments of silk and tapestry — to demonstrate
to all how one's heart rejoices at the great kindness of God.
This night and all the laws connected with it are of the utmost
holiness, for it was then that God chose us from all the
nations and sanctified us with His commandments. It is therefore unseemly for anyone to indulge in idle talk on this
night, so that the bond between each Jew and the Almighty
should not be broken. Everyone should devote himself solely
to the mitzvot of the night, to telling of the miracles of Egypt
and teaching them to the members of his household.'

It is told of Maharil that non-Jews would often deposit
with him, as pledges, gold and silver ornaments. Throughout
the year he would not touch these but on Seder night he
would lay them out in array on a special table so as to delight
the eye with their beauty. His purpose in doing this was that
one should sit down to the Seder in a happy mood, for the
soul is uplifted and the heart sings only when one is in a
good frame of mind.

A WHITE GARMENT FOR THE SEDER

*Although it is a mitzvah to adorn oneself on this
night with brightly colored, costly garments of silk
and tapestry, nevertheless, it is customary for the
head of the household to wear a plain white garment.*

*One of the reasons for this is that the dead are
clothed in white before burial. This reminder will
prevent a person from becoming too full of pride.
Similarly the eggs which many people eat at the Seder
are also a symbol of mourning and thus a warning
against pride. In addition, the ninth of Av, the anniversary of the destruction of the Beit Hamikdash,*

always occurs on the same day of the week as the first day of Pesach, so a symbol of mourning is appropriate. However, other authorities interpret this quite differently. They maintain that there is nothing finer than a plain white garment for it was thus that the Cohen Gadol entered the innermost sanctuary. On this night each Jew who celebrates the sacred Seder is like the Cohen Gadol performing the Avodah.

This custom of wearing a white garment at the Seder is not observed among Sephardi Jews.

LIGHTING THE CANDLES

Before kidush, the woman of the household lights candles and recites two blessings, '. . . to kindle the lights of the festival' and 'shehecheyanu.'

If Yom Tov occurs on a weekday she lights the candles after, or as soon as, it gets dark. She says the blessing first and then kindles the lights. If Yom Tov occurs on Shabat, she lights the candles while it is still day, before Shabat begins, reversing the order of her actions. She lights the candles first and then says the blessings. In her blessing, she makes mention of Shabat as well, '. . . to kindle the lights of Shabat and of the festival.'

When she recites the blessing 'shehecheyanu' she should bear in mind that this also refers to all the other mitzvot of the evening, just as the head of the household has this thought in mind when he includes this same blessing in the kidush.

THE ORDER OF THE NIGHT

The mitzvot of this night are manifold. There are positive mitzvot and mitzvot *lo ta'aseh* (prohibitions), mitzvot ordained by the Sages, decrees, ordinances, important laws and sacred customs — and all of them are carried out at our own table. We have been taught that we must not perform the mitzvot 'bundle-wise,' but each must be carried out singly at its right time, and in its right place and in the correct order. Our Sages have therefore laid down the order in which the mitzvot must be performed on this night, and this order is immutable for all the generations of the Jewish people.

Because of our many sins the Beit Hamikdash has been destroyed so that we have neither Pesach sacrifice nor festive *chagigah* offering and the mitzvot associated with these cannot be effected. Nevertheless, there are still many mitzvot which are performed at our tables on Seder night, and our Sages have instituted many additional ones to remind us of those we would have been keeping had the Beit Hamikdash still been in existence.

Even if our order of the Seder night inevitably differs from that which pertained in the days of the Beit Hamikdash, our present arrangement is unchangeable — and will remain so until the Beit Hamikdash is rebuilt and we will return to the original order.

'Therefore let each person be filled with fear and trembling as he comes to fulfill the commandments which the Sages have ordained concerning the Seder and the Hagadah. Let no one lightly esteem this order. Even if some items appear to him insignificant, he should carry them out in the knowledge that none of these is a trivial matter and unworthy of consideration' (Maharil).

The Zohar speaks of the mitzvah of telling the story of the departure from Egypt in these terms: 'The next mitzvah is to speak in praise of the departure from Egypt, for a person must always praise this event. It has been said that whoever speaks of the exodus from Egypt with rejoicing and gladness will assuredly rejoice with the *Shechinah* (Divine Presence) in the world-to-come. This is the greatest joy of all — the privilege of rejoicing with God. The Holy One, Blessed be He, also rejoices at this story. He gathers around Him His heavenly Hosts and says to them, 'Listen to my children praising My greatness and rejoicing at the redemption which I have wrought.' Then all of them assemble together and join themselves with the Jewish people and listen to their tale of praise and happiness at the redemption brought about by God. They give thanks to God for all these miracles and mighty deeds and praise His heavenly company on earth, the Jewish nation, which rejoices at its redemption, thus magnifying God's greatness and power.

'The Jewish people too glorify their Master by telling this story, similar to an earthly king whose power and strength appear greater when his subjects laud his mighty deeds, acknowledge him, and tremble before his greatness.'

Each separate custom of this night and the order in which the various events take place, and even the variations practiced in certain communities have been invested by our Sages with deep and hidden meanings and with sublime and lofty interpretations. Our approach to these great ideas is on a simple level, but since we obey the teachings of our Sages, follow their actions and desire to perform all the mitzvot of this night with the lofty intentions of the deep and hidden meanings, then we will be privileged to rise to the highest pinnacle of holiness. For this pinnacle is reached by means of a pure and joyful heart rather than by the exercise of the intellect.

It is for this reason that our teachers give abundant praise to the Jewish people who sanctify themselves and purify themselves by means of the mitzvot which they carry out at their tables on this night. 'The Holy One, Blessed be He, leaves all His heavenly company and all His righteous ones in Gan Eden and comes to see how the Jewish people on earth rejoice in the mitzvot of this night and declare His praise.'

Although we cannot delve into the hidden meaning of each separate part of the Seder, we will be rewarded for our faith in the high purpose of each of these and for our desire to know all the explanations of those facets within our realm of understanding.

The very name 'Seder' — 'order' is explained by Maharal of Prague as a symbol of the miracles and wonders which the Holy One, Blessed be He, did for us in Egypt. They are the source of the miracles in every generation and of the miracles promised for the future. For each of these miracles was done with forethought in a purposeful order and no miracle takes place outside of this scheme.

Even the long process of exile and slavery was pre-ordained by the One Who causes all things to happen, so that the name 'Seder' given to this night has an added significance. The name is also an indication of all the festivals and appointed days of the year which, as we shall explain, are fixed according to the days of Pesach.

THE MITZVOT OF SEDER NIGHT WHICH APPLY TODAY

There are two positive mitzvot of the Torah applicable today. The first is the eating of the matzot. 'On the first day, on the fourteenth day of the month, in the evening, you shall eat matzot' (Shmot 12). The second is telling the story of the departure from Egypt — Hagadah. 'You shall tell your son on that day saying, 'Because of this did God act for me when I came forth out of Egypt' (Shmot 13).

Although this mitzvah mentions 'on that day,' our Sages have referred it to the eve of the fifteenth of Nisan when the mitzvah of eating matzah is put into effect, for the phrase 'because of this' refers to the moment when the matzah (and at the time of the Beit Hamikdash, the Pesach offering and the bitter herbs) is present on the table before us. The celebrant points to it and says to his son, 'Because of this — so that I can fulfill this mitzvah, has God acted for me.'

Our Sages have taught us that the phrase 'You shall tell your son' is to be understood quite literally. Everyone who has a son is in duty bound to tell him of the exodus from

259

Egypt. If he has no son then he must tell all who sit with him. Even if he sits alone, he must recite this great event to himself.

Since we have no altar on which to offer up our sacrifices, all the other mitzvot of the Torah concerning the Pesach lamb and the festive offering (chagigah) are not applicable today. The bitter herbs mentioned in the Torah were eaten only together with the Pesach lamb, so the mitzvah of eating this nowadays was instituted by the Sofrim.

The Sages have also ordained another mitzvah especially for this night — the drinking of four cups of wine. We now have four mitzvot for this night, two from the Torah, matzah and Hagadah, and two from the Sages, the four cups and the bitter herbs.

In addition there are the mitzvot of kidush and the blessing of shehecheyanu, both of which precede the other mitzvot. These, however, are not exclusive to the Seder night but are said on the eve of every festival. (According to some authorities the kidush for Yom Tov is a mitzvah of the Torah in the same way that the kidush for Shabat is.)

In order to carry out all these mitzvot and in order that we may also remember all the other mitzvot which are not applicable today, our Sages have ordained many customs and practices, each to be performed in a prescribed order, as follows: Leaning at the table, dipping the karpas in salt water and eating it after washing the hands, dividing one matzah and hiding part of it for the end of the meal, telling the story of the exodus from Egypt according to the established version which ends with the blessing '... Who has redeemed Israel,' the special blessing for eating this after the appropriate blessing, (for some people, also eating eggs in salt water), eating the afikoman, singing praises to God.

All the mitzvot and customs practiced on this night remind us in some way of the slavery which preceded the redemption and of the redemption itself. The Hagadah too 'begins with dishonor and ends with praise,' for it tells us first of the slavery in Egypt and what caused it, and concludes with telling us of the redemption and how we became worthy of it.

RULES FOR CONDUCTING THE SEDER

The Seder service must begin with the recital of kidush and the blessing 'shehecheyanu,' for without this we can neither eat nor drink those things which are compulsory for this night.

Three blessings are included in the kidush; '...Who has created the fruit of the vine;' '...Who has sanctified Israel and the appointed seasons;' and 'shehecheyanu.' (If this night coincides with the end of Shabat, two further blessings are added. See below). The wine that is drunk after saying this kidush constitutes the first of the four cups of the Seder.

The second rule is that we may not perform the mitzvot 'bundle-wise.' We therefore do not drink all the four cups at one time but spread them out through the evening. This mitzvah of the four cups is very dear to us for it reminds us of the four ways in which the redemption is described in the Torah, each expression representing a different aspect of that redemption. Because of this, each cup of wine must be given its own special importance. No greater honor can be accorded to these four cups than to ascribe each one to a special place and to drink it only after a group of blessings or praises to God for the kindness which He has shown to us.

When the heart is full of these blessings and of these praises, then the moment is ripe to drink the cup of redemption.

In the procedure of this night we find two groups each of blessings and praises and each of the four cups is drunk at the end of one of these. The first cup is taken at the end of the blessings of the kidush; the second after the Hagadah and the 'Egyptian Halel' (Tehilim 113 and 114) and the blessing which concludes this, '...Who has redeemed us...' The third cup is drunk following the blessing after food, and the fourth after the conclusion of the Halel and the prayers which follow it, namely 'The soul of all living' (*Nishmat*) and Tehilim 118 with its final paragraph.

The third rule is that the mitzvah of Hagadah — telling the story of Pesach to the inquiring child — must be given priority because of its importance. Since it is a mitzvah of the Torah we should say it immediately after kidush, but we purposely delay it in order to prompt the children to ask questions. We let them see various surprising and strange ceremonies which arouse their curiosity so that when they hear the Hagadah they will more readily absorb its meaning. It is for this reason that we eat the karpas, divide the matzah and raise the Seder plate before we begin to relate the story of Pesach.

The fourth rule is that the eating of the matzah must precede the eating of the bitter herbs. Even in the times of the Beit Hamikdash they were eaten in this order and in the Torah, matzah is mentioned first, 'They shall eat it with matzah and with bitter herbs.' Nowadays it is especially important to keep to this order since matzah is a mitzvah of the Torah and the eating of bitter herbs is ordained by the Sages.

The fifth rule concerns the *afikoman*. This is eaten at the very end of the meal so that the taste of the matzah — the most precious of all the mitzvot — should remain with us. We may neither eat nor drink after this, apart from water. The only exception is the third and fourth cups of wine which are drunk after the afikoman, since their place in the Seder ceremony is fixed by other considerations which we have already explained.

A BRIEF SUMMARY OF THE SEDER

Bearing in mind these five rules it is easy to understand the order of the Seder.

1. The kidush, which is the first of the cups of wine, and its blessings.

2. Washing the hands for karpas, dipping it in salt water and eating it with its accompanying blessing, dividing one of the matzot in half. All these are intended to arouse the curiosity of the child.

Even though these practices are closely linked with the eating of the bitter herbs, as we shall shortly explain, we perform them early, to follow immediately after kidush, so that they act as an introduction to the commandment 'You shall tell your son.' (The rules for washing the hands for karpas are exactly the same as washing the hands before a meal, except that no blessing is said).

3. The recital of the Hagadah together with the Egyptian Halel and its concluding blessing, is the principal mitzvah of this night and must no longer be delayed.

It precedes even the mitzvah of eating matzah which is also from the Torah. The mitzvah of Hagadah requires the children to participate with the adults, whereas the mitzvah of matzah applies only to adults.

4. The second cup of wine is now drunk at a specially honored point in the Seder — as a climax to the Hagadah and the first part of the Halel which ends with the blessing for redemption.

5. The hands are washed, as is usual before any meal, and the correct blessing is said. The matzah of the mitzvah is then eaten, preceded by two blessings, '... Who brings forth bread from the land' and '... Who has commanded us to eat matzah.'

6. Eating the bitter herbs is one of the main features of the Seder and follows immediately the eating of the matzah. The blessing which precedes it is '... Who has commanded us to eat bitter herbs.' The blessing on vegetables is not said, since this blessing was already said on karpas and it includes the bitter herbs.

7. *Korech.* Although matzah and bitter herbs have both been eaten separately, they are now eaten together in a sandwich. This is in accordance with the opinion of Hillel

263

the Elder who maintained that they should be eaten together.

8. An egg is eaten in salt water. There is no basis in Halachah for this but it is an old-established custom among many people, some of whom eat it at the end of the meal. In some Sephardi communities it is the custom to eat this on two occasions during the recital of the Hagadah. Others, in particular first-born sons who have been fasting, are accustomed to eat it immediately after the kidush.

9. The festive meal is now partaken of so that all eating and drinking can be finished before the afikoman.

10. The afikoman is eaten at the end of the meal.

11. The meal is followed by the usual blessings after food.

12. The third cup of wine is drunk at a noteworthy stage in the Seder — following the blessings after food.

13. Halel is completed together with Tehilim 117 and the prayer *nishmat kol chai*, ('The soul of all living...,' as far as the words '...King Who is lauded with praise'), so that the Seder should close on this note of praise, giving added importance to the fourth cup of wine.

14. The fourth and last cup of wine is now drunk.

15. The blessing after wine is said, followed by various songs and the reading of *Shir Hashirim* (the Song of Songs).

SYMBOLS FOR THE SEDER

So that people may conduct their Seder in an orderly manner and easily remember the unalterable arrangement of the various ceremonies, many of our great teachers (e.g. Rabi Meir of Rottenburg, Rabi Yosef Tov Elem and others who are anonymous) have composed symbols to help us. Some are brief and others are lengthy. Some consist of a few words composed of the initial letters of each separate part of the Seder. In whatever form these symbols appear, they have all acquired a certain degree of sanctity by being incorporated into the Hagadah, each community having adopted its own method for remembering the details of the Seder.

As the Hagadah is sacred, so everything connected with it is equally holy and these symbols, just like other sacred writings, have become the subject of many explanations literal, symbolic, homiletical and mystical.

The most common memory aid is the one ascribed to Rashi, or possibly to Rabi Shmuel of Plecy, one of the Tosafists. This consists of sixteen words, which, in a concise rhyme, give the complete order of the Seder:

Kadesh, urchatz   *Maror, korech*
Karpas, yachatz   *Shulchan orech*
Magid, rochtza   *Halel, nirtzah.*
Motzi, Matzah   *Tzafun, barech*

These symbols allude to the fifteen main features of the Seder (according to the order explained above) as follows:

1. *kadesh* — the recitation of the *kidush*;
2. *urchatz* — washing of the hands without a brachah;
3. *karpas* — eating of a vegetable;
4. *yachatz* — breaking of a matzah and hiding its bigger part for the *afikoman*.
5. *magid* — recitation of the main part of the Hagadah, telling the story of the exodus from Egypt;
6. *roctzah* — washing of the hands for the meal (with a brachah);
7. *motzi* — the brachah *hamotzi* over the matzah;
8. *matzah* — performing the mitzvah of the matzah;
9. *maror* — eating of the bitter-herbs;
10. *korech* — eating of bitter-herbs with matzah;
11. *shulchan orech* — the Yom Tov dinner;
12. *tzafun* — eating of the *afikoman*;
13. *barech* — recitation of *birkat hamazon* (grace after the meal);
14. *Halel* — the second part of the Halel.
15. *nirtzah* — additional songs of praise.

THE KIDUSH

As on all festivals, the Seder begins with kidush. If the first night is on a weekday, three blessings are included; '...Who creates the fruit of the vine,' 'Who sanctifies Israel and the appointed seasons' and 'shehecheyanu.' This last blessing applies also to all those mitzvot which are performed anew on this night, for example, Hagadah, matzah, maror and the four cups of wine.

If the night of Pesach occurs on the eve of Shabat, the kidush begins, as is usual on Friday night, with the quotation, 'The heavens and the earth were finished...' Then the blessing on wine is said followed by a slight variation of the second blessing, '...Who sanctifies Israel, the Shabat and the appointed seasons.'

If the first night occurs at the end of Shabat, the kidush contains five blessings in the following order; 1. '...Who creates the fruit of the vine,' 2. '...Who sanctifies Israel and the appointed seasons,' 3. '...Who creates the lights of the fire,' 4. '...Who makes a distinction between the holiness of the Shabat and the holiness of the festival' and 5. 'shehecheyanu.'

The goblet used for kidush must be whole and contain not less than 86 grams. According to Chazon Ish the goblet should contain 150 grams as with each of the four cups. The greater part of the contents should be drunk at one time while reclining on the left side. The last of the four cups should be completely finished.

SOME REASONS FOR THE MITZVOT

1. Reclining

When partaking of the four cups, of the matzah, of the korech and of the afikoman one must recline on a couch, or on an armchair or on a chair with cushions. This is how kings and noblemen used to eat, and on this night every Israelite conducts himself as a king.

Rambam describes it thus: Every individual must regard himself as if he personally had just come out from the slavery of Egypt. Therefore when he feasts on this night, he must do so in a reclining position in the manner of free men.

Me'iri remarks: This reclining symbolizes freedom and redemption and rouses us to praise the One Who granted us this freedom and redemption from abject slavery.

The celebrant reclines on the left side and eats and drinks with the right hand. Even if he is left-handed he still follows this practice.

A son, eating at his father's table, reclines in the same way. Although normally a son would not act in such a lordly way before his father, on an occasion like this the father will readily permit it. A pupil eating at the table of his teacher does not recline, except with the express permission of the latter. It is not usual for women to recline except among the Sephardim.

One does not recline while eating the maror or the karpas for these remind us of the days when 'they embittered their lives.'

If a person who is in duty bound to recline, eats or drinks without doing so, he must eat or drink again, but without repeating the appropriate blessing. There are some authorities who maintain that this does not apply to the third and fourth cups of wine, and this view is generally accepted. A person who forgot to recline while eating the afikoman does not eat this again, since the afikoman cannot be eaten twice.

The Hebrew word 'to lean' is very similar to the word 'to go round,' and our Sages deduce from this that just as God made all the people go a roundabout way when He brought them from Egypt, so all the people, even the poorest among them, must lean at the Seder.

One who reclines throughout the whole of the Seder is indeed to be praised, although it is compulsory to do this only for the four cups of wine, the matzah and the afikoman.

Nowadays it is not usual to recline at a meal, but our Sages have retained this custom to remind us more forcibly of the great miracle of our redemption from slavery to freedom.

We pay special honor to this occasion by celebrating the Seder in the company of many guests, for the original Pesach lamb was eaten in large groups. When noble and distinguished men hold a banquet, they do so with much ceremony and in the presence of a large number of visitors. Some people maintain that celebrating the Seder in company with many others is also part of the mitzvah of reclining.

It is customary for the head of the household not to **pour** the wine for himself, nor to go out to wash his hands before eating karpas or matzah. Instead, the water is brought to him at the table, since in this, as in all his actions during the Seder, he must conduct himself as a nobleman.

2. The Four Cups

On this night of Pesach it is the duty of each person to drink four cups of wine: One for kidush, one for the mitzvah of Hagadah, one at the end of the blessing after food, and one to mark the end of the Halel. If he drank them one after the other he has not fulfilled the mitzvah.

In the Talmud it is said: The mitzvah of drinking these four cups applies equally to men, women and children (in order to cause them joy and to keep them wakeful), for everyone was redeemed from Egypt' (Tr. Pesachim 108).

Even a poor person, who is supported by charity must make every possible effort to carry out this mitzvah.

If someone has no wine (or grape-juice which is also considered as wine), or if he is ailing and fears lest the wine have a harmful effect on his state of health, he must ask the opinion of a learned Rabbi.

In common with all the other practices of this night, the four cups of wine symbolize various phases of the going down to Egypt and the exodus from there. These four cups also symbolize four other periods of subjugation which the

Israelites endured after their slavery. Their subjugators will eventually be judged and punished by God Who will bring comfort to the Jewish people.

In the Jerusalem Talmud our Sages have explained this subject. 'Why do we have four cups of wine?' Rabi Yochanan said in the name of Rabi Benayah, this refers to four stages in the redemption. 'Therefore say to the Children of Israel, *I am God, I bring you out* from the burdens of Egypt. (Even if He had left us in Egypt to be slaves, He would have ceased the burdensome yoke. For this alone we would have been grateful to Him and therefore we drink the first cup). *I will deliver you* from their slavery. (We drink the cup of salvation for He delivered us completely from serving them). *I will redeem you* with an outstetched arm and with great judgments. (Because He confused them and crushed them on our behalf so that they could no longer afflict us, we drink the third cup). *I will take you* unto Me for a people and I will be your God.' (The greatest aspect of the redemption is that He brought us near to Him and granted us also spiritual redemption. For this we raise the fourth cup).

'The phrase '*I will bring you to the land*...' which follows, is not included, for this gives good tidings about the land which is to be given to them but does not refer to the redemption as such.

'Rabi Yehoshua Ben Levi said: 'The four cups of wine on Seder night remind us of the four occasions on which Pharaoh's cup is mentioned in the book of Bereishit, (Chap. 40). 'The *cup* was in my hand.' (This was said by the chief butler when relating his dream to Yosef, who in turn interpreted it); 'And I squeezed them into the *cup* of Pharaoh;' 'And I put the *cup* into the hand of Pharaoh;' 'And you shall put the *cup* of Pharaoh into his hand.' (The phrase at the end of the chapter 'And he put the *cup* into the hand of Pharaoh' is not included, for it merely tells how Yosef's interpretation came true).

Both Yosef and the chief butler were slaves to Pharaoh

who ruled over them. It was as if a hint were being given to Yosef, 'The slavery is now beginning as the 'cup' is being put into the hand of Pharaoh, but your children are destined to take it out of his hand and they will thank God with the cup of salvation four times over.'

'Rabi Levy said that the four cups of wine refer to the four kingdoms which subjugated Israel after Egypt — Babylon, Persia, Greece and Rome. Our Sages also taught that they refer to the four measures of punishment that the Holy one, Blessed be He, is destined to mete out to the nations of the world:

'For thus said the Lord, God of Israel, take the wine cup of fury from My hand and make all the nations, to which I send you, drink it' (Irmeyahu 25).

'Babylon has been a golden cup in the hand of God, making all the earth drunk. The nations have drunk of her wine, therefore they have become mad' (ibid. 51).

'For there is a cup in the hand of God and the wine is red, it is full of the mixture. And He pours out from this, but its dregs, all the wicked of the earth shall squeeze them out and drink them' (Tehilim 75).

'Upon the wicked He will rain snares; fire and brimstone and tempestuous winds shall be the portion of their cup' (ibid. 11).

'In contrast to these, the Holy One, Blessed be He, is destined to give Israel four cups of comfort to drink. 'O Lord, the portion of my inheritance and of my cup, You maintain my lot' (ibid. 16).

'You anoint my head with oil, my cup is overflowing' (ibid. 23).

'I lift up the cup of salvation and call on the name of the Lord.' (ibid. 116. The Hebrew word 'salvation' appears here in the plural form and therefore refers to two cups).

Abarbanel refers the four cups to four redemptions spread over various periods of history. 'Israel has four different redemptions; the first redemption took place when the Holy

One, Blessed be He, chose Avraham our father and his off-spring to be the forerunners of the people of Israel. The second redemption was from Egypt. The third redemption is seen in the fact that God preserves us during the long years of exile and delivers us from all our enemies who seek to destroy every memory of Israel. The fourth redemption awaits us in the future.'

The Gaon of Vilna said that the four cups of wine indicate four worlds: this world, the days of the Messiah, the revival of the dead and the world-to-come. This means that if a person carries out all the requirements of the Seder in the proper way, he is assured of all these worlds. He can already give praise and thanksgiving for this to the One Who has done, and will do, such great kindness for him.

Maharal connects the idea of the four cups with our four Matriarchs: Sarah, Rivkah, Rachel and Leah, for it was because of their virtues, and the virtues of Avraham, Itzchak and Ya'akov that Israel was redeemed. Our Sages have taught that the three principal mitzvot of this night, Pesach, matzah and maror, were given to us because of our three forefathers, and we find in the Yalkut that their names together with the names of our great mothers, were engraved on the rod with which Moshe performed the signs and miracles.

Beney Yessachar writes that Israel was given the privilege of the mitzvah of the four cups as a reward for the four virtuous acts which they carried out in Egypt. They did not adopt heathen names, they retained their own language, they did not commit acts of immorality and there were no talebearers among them. Great is the value of such precautions, for even though the Israelites defiled themselves with all the evils of Egypt, the fact that they preserved these barriers against total assimilation, earned for them the title of 'Distinguished' and made them worthy of being redeemed.

The Israelites are praised by the prophet, Irmeyahu, for having gone into the wilderness at God's bequest, without querying His commands. Because they set aside their own

271

ideas and accepted His, they were known as the 'generation
of wisdom.' Anyone who is capable of overriding his own
opinion and deferring to that of God, is granted true wisdom
— for the highest form of wisdom is to realize that, after all
our learning, in the final analysis we really do not know.

It is because of this that we drink four glasses of wine.
Normally wine causes the drinker to become confused, but
we want to demonstrate that we know nothing except 'that
which You, O God, have taught us.' By acknowledging this
we achieve the highest form of knowledge.

What a world of difference there is between the Israelites
and other nations. Usually when a man becomes drunk the
whole world shrinks before him. He forgets all that he has
ever known, and nothing exists for him except his drink.
Not only does he forget that which he knew well in the past
but he certainly cannot see what the future holds in store
for him. But the Children of Israel are different. When the
night of Pesach arrives they eat and drink, and even though
they drink to excess, they can review their entire history, back
to the time when God brought a new light to the world
through Avraham, and forward to the future redemption.

They are able to see before them their own destiny and
the destiny of each nation, as clearly as if it had already
come to pass, and for this they praise and thank God. This
is possible only because they have suppressed their own desires
before the will of their King in Heaven and every deed
of theirs is performed only at the request of Him Who has
exalted them and sanctified them through His commandments.

The wine they drink on this night is not the wine of
merrymaking and drunkenness. It is the wine of a mitzvah
and therefore it raises them to a state of sobriety, elation and
holiness.

Another difference between the people of Israel and others
is that it is normal for a person, deep in sorrow, to drink
in order to dispel his gloom. It is true that for the moment he
feels happy, but since the happiness is only the result of

drinking, it disappears as soon as the effect of the wine has worn off. But the people of Israel drink only after they have become happy through singing and praising God. Only then do they drink, and as the happiness comes first, it remains even when the effect of the wine is no more.

3. Red Wine

This mitzvah is best fulfilled by using red wine since this wine is usually of a superior type. It also reminds us of the blood of the circumcision and the blood of the Pesach offering. The Israelites were commanded in Egypt, 'Let every male be circumcised and then let him come near to offer it' (the Pesach lamb). Later on we read, 'And all the Children of Israel did exactly as God commanded Moshe and Aharon.' Thus the blood of the circumcision and the blood of the sacrifice were closely connected.

On this night of Seder we remember the deeds of our ancestors and drink red wine to remind us of this blood.

Red wine also reminds of the blood which the Israelites in Egypt sprinkled on the doorposts of their houses when God passed over them and spared them from the deadly plague — may God even now shield us and deliver us from all who lie in wait to destroy us.

It also reminds us of the blood of the little children of the Israelites whom Pharaoh slaughtered day after day. He would bathe in their blood in order to heal himself of leprosy.

O, be not silent to this blood ! Even on this day of our freedom, more than three thousand years later, we remember this dreadful deed. For the eternal people cannot forget the blood of its tender children, and there is no forgiveness for those who are intent on destroying them.

4. The Mitzvah of the Four Cups Requires No Blessing

We might have expected that there would be a blessing '... Who has sanctified us with His commandments and commanded us to drink the four cups,' just as we have similar blessings for the other mitzvot of the night. The reason for this omission is that we do not drink all these at one time and there is the possibility that something may occur during the Seder which will prevent us from drinking all of them. In such circumstances the blessing will have been said in vain.

We could hardly say the expression '... to drink the four cups' when we only drink one, namely the wine for kidush. Having drunk this, we could not preface the drinking of the second cup with a blessing which says '... to drink three cups' for there is no such mitzvah. For these reasons we say no blessing at all for the mitzvah of the four cups of wine.

5. A Blessing for Each of the Four Cups

Sephardim and Ashkenazim differ as to whether one says the blessing '... Who creates the fruit of the vine' for each separate cup. The former say the blessing only on the kidush cup, and on the third cup which follows the blessing after food. The second cup is considered an extension of the first and the third and fourth are closely connected with each other. Ashkenazim follow the ruling of Rav Moshe Isserles by repeating the blessing for each of the four cups, since each one constitutes a separate mitzvah.

6. The Fifth Cup

After drinking the fourth cup which follows Halel, it is the custom to fill an additional goblet, larger than the others. This is then surrounded by the other goblets to emphasize its special status and is known as the 'Cup of Eliyahu.'

It was a dispute of the *Tana'im* which prompted the inclusion of the fifth cup. Rabi Tarfon said that everyone must drink five cups to symbolize the four different words used to describe the redemption and the additional word 'I will bring...' Although Rabi Tarfon's opinion was not accepted, nevertheless our Sages ruled that we should pour out a fifth cup, but not drink of it, as there is an element of doubt. When Eliyahu the Prophet comes and clarifies all our doubts he will explain this one to us as well. This cup of wine therefore bears his name — The Cup of Eliyahu.

The Sages of former generations have taught us that this cup which symbolizes the word 'I will bring' indicates the final redemption — to be announced by Eliyahu the Prophet — which will follow the destruction of *Gog* and *Magog*.

This Seder night is also known as the 'Night of Watching' and as the Hebrew word for 'Watching,' *shimurim*, appears in the plural form, it is interpreted as referring both to the redemption from Egypt in the past, and to the future redemption which we pray will come to pass in our own days. As this future redemption will be heralded by Eliyahu, we associated his name with this night.

Maharal of Prague suggests that before reciting the passage 'Pour out Thy wrath' as we open the door for Eliyahu, it is fitting to say the following, 'May the Merciful One send Eliyahu the Prophet — who is remembered for good — to herald glad tidings, salvation and comfort, as it is said 'Behold I send to you Eliyahu the Prophet before the arrival of the great and awful judgment day of God. He will restore the hearts of the fathers to the children and the hearts of the children to their fathers ... '

7. The Three Matzot

The three matzot which are placed on the Seder dish, one on top of the other, are given special names to distinguish them: Cohen, Levi and Israel.

'Cohen' is applied to the uppermost one because the cohen takes precedence in all matters. The middle one is known as 'Levi' because the Levite is next in rank below the cohen. The third one is called Israel.

The middle matzah, 'Levi' is divided in two at the beginning of the Seder. The smaller part is left in its place and eaten afterwards together with the top one, 'Cohen,' for the mitzvah of eating matzah. The larger piece is hidden away to be eaten as afikoman at the end of the meal. The lower one, 'Israel,' is eaten for korech.

On Shabat and Yom Tov we say the blessing for bread over two loaves or matzot. Why then, on this night, do we require three?

Matzah is known as 'the bread of poverty.' A poor man, fearful lest he will have no more, guards his bread carefully. He does not eat it all at once but divides it, laying part aside for the morrow. The honor given to the festival and to Shabat (for often the two coincide) demands that we use two whole matzot over which we recite the blessing '...Who brings forth bread from the land' before beginning the meal. For the blessing, '...Who has commanded us to eat matzot,' we use only a piece of a whole one to symbolize 'the bread of poverty.' Therefore we prepare three and divide the middle one. When we say the first of these two blessings we hold all three matzot, thus including the two whole ones, but when we say the second of them, we put down the lowest one and hold only the top one and a section of the middle one.

There are many other reasons for having three matzot on the table. They remind us of our three forefathers. Avraham, Itzchak and Ya'akov. Although we were slaves, we have a noble ancestry, none more noble than ours, and even in our servitude in Egypt, we guarded well the nobility of that ancestry.

The three matzot symbolize the three measures of fine flour which Avraham asked Sarah to bake when the angels visited them. 'Hasten (a reminder of the haste with which the Israelites left Egypt), knead three measures of fine flour and bake cakes of matzah.' (Bereishit 18). The day on which this took place was Erev Pesach.

This is a reminder of the first Pesach Sacrifices that were brought by the firstborn in Egypt. This, their first holy task, initiated them as cohanim. Whoever begins to serve as a cohen must bring three kinds of loaves (Vayikra 8).

Some people make these three matzot very large, using one tenth of an *ephah* of flour. They say that these correspond to the three cakes of matzah which were offered up as a *trumah* to God whenever a thanksgiving offering (*Korban Todah*) was brought. 'There are four occasions on which a thanksgiving offering must be brought : After coming safely through a sea journey, after coming unscathed through the wilderness, after recovery from an illness and after release from prison' (Brachot 54). Since we were released from imprisonment in Egypt and all these miracles were performed for us — we were brought safely through the sea and the wilderness and all our ailments were cured — we make three matzot of one tenth of an ephah of flour to remind us of the matzot of this same quantity that were brought together with the thanksgiving offering (Todah).

Matzah itself is the bread of poverty. In olden days the offering of the very poorest person consisted of one tenth of an ephah so it is appropriate to use this amount of flour in the 'bread of poverty' on our Seder table.

The Gaon of Vilna had a different practice. He followed the custom of the 'Rishonim' who ruled that only two matzot were required. One is divided and one left whole and the two blessings are said. On the subject of eating matzah, he also said that it was a mitzvah to eat matzah all the seven days of Pesach, according to the verse, 'Seven days you shall eat matzot' (Shmot 12). When our Sages said that it is not obligatory to eat matzot all seven days, but only on the first night, they were simply stressing the great importance of the mitzvah on that night; in comparison with this, eating matzah during the rest of Pesach seems like a voluntary act. But whoever eats matzah during the seven days of Pesach is without doubt, fulfilling a mitzvah.

8. H a s t e

The very matzah itself contains undertones of the theme of the Hagadah, which are slavery and redemption. The essential nature of the matzah is that it was made in great haste and contains no ingredients other than flour and water — two contrasting elements.

Before Israel's redemption, the people were subjected to cruel taskmasters who made them work incessantly. Even by night they were allowed no respite from their toil. Before dawn the taskmasters would already be urging them on to their daily labor. They would be driven forth from their houses to start their wearisome work before their dough had properly risen. They made their bread in haste when they were slaves and also ate it in haste.

When the power that enslaved them was crushed and the Egyptians sent them away in haste, again there was no time for their dough to rise before the Supreme King of Kings, the Holy One Blessed be He, revealed Himself to them. 'And they baked the dough which they brought out from Egypt into cakes of matzah for it had not risen, for they were expelled from Egypt and could not tarry, and they did not even make provisions for themselves.' They made their bread in haste when they were redeemed and they ate it in haste, for the road beckoned them on. 'And the Children of Israel journeyed from Ra'amses...'

Therein lies the greatness of this people. They do not seek rest for themselves but look rather for where their duties lie. They do not weep when they are afflicted, nor do they despair for they realize that their redemption cannot be far off. They willingly accept the hardships of slavery, knowing that the redemption is near at hand. While eating the bread of slavery they feel the taste of freedom.

And when life goes smoothly they do not become proud. They recall their past slavery and how God brought them out and commanded them '... so that your manservant and your maidservant may rest, as you do.' Now when they eat the bread of freedom, they taste the affliction and the exile.

When the command to eat matzot was given to them in

Egypt, it was associated with their imminent freedom. They were told to eat it together with the meat of the Pesach sacrifice. 'I will smite all the firstborn ... and I will pass over you.' But forty years after their redemption when Moshe, at God's command, repeated the commandments to them as they were about to take possession of the land — the most desirable of all lands — then he called the matzot 'the bread of poverty.' 'For seven days you shall eat matzot, the bread of poverty, for you came out of Egypt in haste — so that you may remember the day of your departure from Egypt all the days of your life !' (Dvarim 17).

When Israel went forth from Egypt, they did not merely throw off the yoke of slavery. They freed themselves from servitude to man and accepted the servitude of the Kingdom of Heaven. They became servants of God instead of servants of Pharaoh, and there is no higher form of freedom than this.

While they were in Egypt they wanted to be rid of their slavery as soon as possible and to become worthy of freedom. After they were redeemed they hastened to correct all the wrong that had been done during the twenty-six generations that preceded them, so that the world should not be deprived of its King, nor mankind of its Divine image.

'You have seen what I did to the Egyptians.' They were at ease in the world and their very ease brought about their downfall. But, 'You will be to me a kingdom of cohanim,' you will be the messengers of all the nations of the world, to serve God and to do His bidding. You are the ones who promised to keep My commandments even before you had heard them. You came out of Egypt in haste, and as a reward for this haste, your dough will never have time to rise, for you will always be called upon to do God's service. O praise, the servants of God !

Women also have to eat of the two matzot over which the two blessings are said.

9. Maror and Charoset

Men and women are equally obligated to eat some maror — the size of an olive — on Seder night for all were equally affected by the slavery. The name 'maror' — bitter herbs — is taken from the phrase, 'And they embittered their lives.'

Our Sages have enumerated five vegetables which are suitable for this mitzvah : Lettuce, endives, chervil, garden ivy and horse-radish. Of all of these, leaf lettuce is to be preferred, for, in the words of the Sages, 'it can be compared to the slavery in Egypt. At first the Egyptians beguiled the Israelites to work with their smooth talk, but later on they embittered their lives with hard work. At first, the lettuce seems almost sweet to the palate but later on its bitterness is noticeable.

The Hebrew word for leaf-lettuce is *chasah,* similar to the word chas which means 'to have pity,' for the Holy One, Blessed be He, took pity on us and redeemed us.

Our Sages have ordained that we dip the maror into the charoset so that it should not be too bitter, but we may not use so much that the bitter taste is entirely eliminated.

The charoset is a reminder of the apple tree under which the women of Israel gave birth to their young, concealing their pains so that they would not be detected by the Egyptians. 'Under the apple tree I roused you, there your mother brought you forth, there she that bore you brought you forth' (Song of Songs 8).

The affliction and subjugation of slavery caused the men to despair of being redeemed and they separated from their wives. 'Why should we beget children,' they said, 'for poverty and slavery ?' But the women who toiled at their side encouraged them to go on hoping and to fulfill the mitzvah. When the time came for them to give birth, they would go out to the fields without breathing a word about the pains of childbirth and there, under the apple tree, they would give birth. They chose the apple tree because only after it has produced fruit do the leaves grow and protect the fruit. 'We will do likewise, we will give birth to our children and then the Deliverer will come to save our children and redeem them.'

It was this virtuous act of theirs which sweetened the bitterness of our forefathers. We too dip our bitter herbs into charoset which is made of the apple.

There are other ingredients in the charoset, each of which is mentioned by King Shlomo in the song which depicts the love between Israel and their Father in Heaven. Israel is compared in Shir Hashirim (Song of Songs) to pomegranates, figs, dates and nuts. In each of these metaphors the Israelites were praised for their special behavior even while they were in a lowly state. Because of this exceptional behavior their bitterness was turned to sweetness and they were redeemed.

On this night the Holy One, Blessed be He, not only redeemed our forefathers, but also brought us out together with them, so that we partake of the sweet and the bitter together, just as they did.

We have already remarked that every separate facet of the Seder symbolizes a mixture of dishonor and praise, of slavery and redemption. The maror and the charoset are in this same category: a mixture of bitter and sweet. We mitigate the bitterness of the maror by dipping it in charoset, even as our forefathers in Egypt, in the midst of their slavery, used to lighten their sorrow by thinking of the redemption

The charoset itself is a reminder of the clay and the straw which the Israelites used for the making of bricks during their slavery.

Red wine is added to the charoset to remind us of blood — the blood of circumcision, the blood of the Pesach offering, and the blood of our young ones who were slaughtered in Egypt. This reminder impresses on us that everything which is bitter is not completely bitter, and everything sweet is not completely sweet. Servitude is not always slavery, neither is freedom the same as redemption.

Anyone who desires Pharaoh and Egypt, with all the defilement which they represent — for him the sweetness becomes bitter and his freedom turns into slavery. But one who relies on the Living God will find the reverse, his bitterness will become sweet and his servitude will turn to redemption.

We were slaves as long as we depended and admired Pharaoh in Egypt, but God brought us out, and only then did we become truly free. For if the Holy One, Blessed be He, had not brought our forefathers out of Egypt, then even if Pharaoh had freed us of his own accord, or if we had gained our freedom by our own efforts, then we and our children and our children's children would still be as if enslaved to Pharaoh in Egypt. It is only because God Himself — He and none other — redeemed us and made us His own special people that we have true freedom and redemption.

10. Karpas

Karpas is a green vegetable. Any type of green vegetable which is not bitter can be used. We eat this cooked or raw, whichever is the normal method of eating it, immediately after kidush. We wash our hands, but without the usual blessing, and then say the blessing appropriate to vegetables, '...Who creates the fruit of the ground.' In saying this we bear in mind that this blessing should also apply to the maror which will be eaten later in the evening. Less than the size of an olive is eaten so that no blessing need be said after it.

The simplest explanation of this karpas is that its very unusualness arouses the curiosity of the children. Another reason is to make it unnecessary to recite the aforementioned blessing before we eat the maror. The maror is eaten in memory of such a sad episode in our history that it is not fitting to honor it by reciting two blessings (the usual one for vegetables and the special one for maror).

A parallel idea can be found in the reading of the *tochechah* (Reproof Section), the chapter which warns us of the dire fate that will befall us if we fail to keep the Torah. We never share the reading of this chapter among several people. One person reads it through from the beginning to the end. Said the Holy One, Blessed be He, 'It is not seemly that My children should bless Me while they are being cursed.' Similarly we recite only one blessing for the maror and transfer the blessing for vegetables to the karpas.

The usual way of eating karpas is to dip it in vinegar or salt water. When the Beit Hamikdash was in existence, and for many years afterwards, it became the established practice for people to wash their hands, to the accompaniment of the usual blessing, before eating anything moist, since our Sages decreed that liquid became defiled through contact with unwashed hands. Washing the hands was therefore an important law and the blessing was said for it. Nowadays, however, we are not so concerned about ritual impurity and we wash our hands, with the blessing, only before eating bread.

On this night of Seder, however, we adopt those habits associated with ritual purity so that the change of action may induce the children to ask questions. There is a difference of opinion as to whether we should wash our hands before eating food dipped in liquid, but we try to give all our actions on this night special importance and to think of ourselves as the Cohen Gadol at his sacred service. Therefore we do wash our hands on this occasion, but without reciting the blessing.

Another reason for eating karpas is to show us how God had already planned our redemption even before our ancestors went down to Egypt. Maror causes discomfort to the stomach and karpas alleviates this pain, so we eat karpas first to remind us that God had already prepared the remedy before the suffering in Egypt began.

11. Korech

After eating the maror, the head of the household takes the third matzah ('Israel') and makes a sandwich of it with maror. This should contain matzah the size of an olive and the same quantity of maror (although not all our Sages agree that these amounts are necessary for korech). A sandwich like this is portioned out to each person at the table and it is this action which has the title 'korech.'

As the appropriate blessings have already been said for the matzah and the maror, no additional blessing is required for korech, but before eating it we recite the formula, found in every Hagadah: 'This is in memory of Hillel's practice in the Beit Hamikdash.' Hillel used to do this at the time when the Beit Hamikdash was standing; he would combine together matzah and maror and eat them jointly in order to fulfill the command, 'They shall eat it with matzah and maror.' (The Sephardim have a somewhat different formula).

Hillel the Elder explained that the phrase 'They shall eat it (The Pesach Lamb) with matzah and with maror' meant that these were to be eaten together at one and the same time. We eat this sandwich on Seder night to remind us of the time of the Sanctuary in accordance with Hillel's interpretation.

Some people dip the maror into charoset even for korech so that it should not taste strong, but others maintain that eating it together with matzah has the same effect and the addition of charoset is unnecessary.

12. The Bone and the Egg

When the Sanctuary was in existence, a table would be prepared after kidush with maror, an additional vegetable, matzah, charoset, the Pesach lamb and the meat of the chagigah offering of the fourteenth of Nisan. This latter had been slaughtered earlier to eat at the evening meal for the meat of the Pesach lamb is not the main food of the meal but is eaten only after one is already satisfied.

Because of our sins the Sanctuary has been destroyed and we have neither Pesach sacrifice nor festive chagigah offering. In place of these we put two cooked foods on the Seder dish, a roasted arm bone with meat on it and an egg. This latter is readily available and easy to cook. In olden days no festive offering was brought on the fourteenth of Nisan if Erev Pesach coincided with Shabat but if this happens nowadays we still have both of these on our Seder table.

Even if our Seder table lacks two essential mitzvot and we have to be satisfied with mere symbols of them, we are certain that He will save us. We know that He will redeem us again and rebuild for us His chosen House and there we will eat of the sacrifices and of the Pesach lamb as in olden days. Our redemption in the past was not due to our own strength, nor was it due to our righteousness that this privilege was granted to us. It was brought about only by the will of God, as hinted to us by the egg.

An egg has no opening, no 'mouth.' It symbolizes the hope that the mouths of our enemies and detractors should be closed. In each generation they have boasted that we will never be redeemed. They plot and plan against us saying, 'Let us cut them off from being a nation, so that the name of Israel will not longer be remembered.

In contrast to this we gather each year, even in conditions of servitude, and praise God for our past redemption. Each Jew sits like a king, sure in the knowledge that Israel will outlast all its enemies. On our Seder table there is an egg that has no mouth, — a symbol that the mouths of those who wish to destroy us should be silenced forever.

The roast bone and the egg are also reminders of Moshe and Aharon. Despite their share in the departure from Egypt, their names are not mentioned during the Seder, for this night belongs to God alone, 'I and none other, I and not a messenger.'

Rambam has given a rational explanation of the mitzvah of slaughtering the Pesach lamb and eating it. 'In order to implant in our hearts the true faith and to uproot the false ideas of Egypt, God commanded us to slaughter the Pesach lamb. This animal was an object of worship for the Egyptians and it was forbidden to kill it. It was for this very reason that we were commanded to kill the lamb and, openly, to sprinkle its blood on the doorposts. By this, we rid ourselves of their superstitions and showed that our attitude was the complete reverse of theirs. We demonstrated that what they considered the origin of anger and of plague was in effect, the cause of life and the means whereby we were delivered from death.'

This same argument applies to the meat and egg which appear on our Seder table, for it was part of the Egyptian religion not to eat these. Keter Shem Tov writes, 'It is my opinion that we were commanded to place the meat and the egg on the Seder table to show our complete disavowal of the worthless beliefs of the Egyptians. For during the times of Moshe, the Egyptians, like the Hindus today, refrained from eating anything that comes from a living creature, meat, fish, milk, blood, eggs.'

13. The Egg in Salt Water

After the matzah and the maror have been eaten, both separately and then together for korech, it is the custom to serve boiled eggs in salt water. Some people eat this immediately after kidush.

Darchey Moshe writes: 'In some places it is the custom to eat eggs during the meal as a sign of mourning, because the first night of Pesach always comes on the same day of the week as the night of the fast of the ninth of Av, so we are reminded of the destruction of the Beit Hamikdash to which we used to bring our Pesach sacrifice.'

The Gaon of Vilna supports this interpretation by quoting from Midrash Echah; 'He has filled me with bitterness,' — this refers to the first day of Pesach when we eat matzah with maror. 'He has made me drunk with wormwood' — the very thing with which he filled me on the first night of Pesach, has become wormwood for me on the ninth of Av.'

Rav Moshe Sofer has given another explanation for this custom; 'All other foods, the longer they are cooked the softer they become. The egg alone becomes harder the longer it boils. Israel is like this. The more the other nations subjugate us and afflict us, the harder we become and the more certain it becomes that we will not be subdued by them nor intermingle with them, for 'It is a people that dwells alone' and 'Even as they afflicted them so they spread and so they multiplied.'

The egg should be eaten with a spoon or a fork and not dipped into the salt water, for according to the phrase in the Hagadah 'we dip our food twice' and not three times.

Why do we eat the egg with salt water ? There are those who affirm that this reminds us of the overthrow of Sedom which occurred on the night of Pesach. The plain of Sedom which had formerly been fertile and rich was flooded with water and, as a result, the Dead Sea came into being. Lot's wife who looked behind her to see what was happening to the people of Sedom, turned into a pillar of salt.

Our Sages, of blessed memory, said; 'What did Lot's wife do on the night when the angels came to her husband ? She went to all her neighbors and said 'Give me some salt for we have guests,' for she wanted everyone to know that these strangers had come to punish them. She was therefore punished by being turned into a pillar of salt. Lot's wife was as wicked as all the people of the town and hated all visitors. Even though she was saved for a short time because of her husband's merit, she was not worthy of seeing the downfall of Sedom. The punishment that befell them, sulphur and brimstone, befell her too.

But we and our families enjoy having guests at our table. At the very beginning of the Seder we say, 'Whoever is hungry, let him come and eat.' We are not afraid of the punishment of salt that was meted out to the people of Sedom.

We rather eat of it to our heart's content, for the same thing which is used to punish the wicked is also used to reward the righteous.

14. Afikoman

When the meal is ended, but before the blessing for food is said, the afikoman is brought out from the place where it has been hidden. Everyone eats of it while leaning on the left side, at least the bulk of an olive. Some people eat even double this quantity. If the head of the household has not sufficient matzah to share out to each person, the others eat the required quantity from other matzah shemurah. No special blessing is said.

If the matzah that was specially hidden away for this purpose is lost, any other matzah shmurah may be used. The hiding of the matzah at the beginning of the Seder is not intended to reserve this particular matzah for use as the afikoman but only to arouse the curiosity of the children so that they should ask questions. In the answers to these questions, the story of the exodus is told.

We take great pains to ensure that we eat the afikoman before midnight because — as we shall explain — it is in memory of the Pesach lamb which could not be eaten after that time.

After eating the afikoman we pour out the wine for the third cup and then say the blessing after food. Neither food nor drink may be partaken of after this — apart from water — so that the taste of the matzah should remain in our mouths.

The eating of the afikoman is in memory of the Pesach sacrifice which was eaten at the very end of the meal. This meal included the meat of the chagigah offering and other foods, so that the meat of the Pesach lamb was eaten only when the diners were already full and they would not want to break the bones in order to get the last scraps of meat from it. This piece was always eaten with great joy and singing because of the importance of the mitzvah.

'We have eaten only a morsel, the bulk of an olive, but the song of praise which has accompanied it has penetrated the roof and reached up to heaven.'

Some people say that the afikoman is in memory of the matzah which was eaten together with the Pesach lamb. 'They shall eat it with matzah and with maror.' Because of this many people eat the bulk of two olives, one in memory of the Pesach lamb and one in memory of the matzah which is eaten with it.

Maharal said that we eat the bulk of two olives of afikoman because it is a mitzvah which is dearer to us than any other. The other mitzvot of this night require only one olive's bulk but we double the quantity for this to show our love of the mitzvah.

15. Customs Associated with the Afikoman

In the order of the Seder service as it appears in the ceremonial symbols the afikoman is referred to by the name *tzafun* — hidden, because it has been hidden away from the beginning of the meal until the time for eating it.

'Some people hide the afikoman under a pillow or cushion so that they may literally fulfill the verse 'How great is Your goodness which You have hidden away for those who fear You.'

Many are the customs that surround the eating of the afikoman. Some people take a stick in their hand and eat it in a great hurry, just as we read in the Torah, 'Thus you shall eat it, your loins girded, your shoes on your feet, your sticks in your hands, you shall eat it in haste for it is Pesach to God.'

Rabi Yeshayah Horwitz mentions that certain people used to kiss the matzah and the maror just as they kiss other sacred objects associated with mitzvot, a Torah Scroll, tefilin, etc.

There are some who set aside the larger section of the middle matzah for the afikoman and wrap it in a white cloth. This is placed on the right shoulder and then transferred to the left shoulder. It is passed round the table like this from one person to another. When it reaches the last one he quotes the verse 'Their kneading troughs tied up in their garments on their shoulders.' He then takes four paces and the rest of the company ask him, 'Where do you come from ?' 'From Egypt,' he answers. 'And where are you going to ?' 'To Jerusalem.' Then everyone choruses together, 'Next year in Jerusalem.'

Among Sephardi communities the matzah of afikoman is not hidden away but is tied on the shoulder of a child who goes out of the room and knocks at the door. 'Who are you ?' he is asked. 'An Israelite.' 'Where do you come from ?' 'From Egypt.' 'Where are you going to ?' 'To Jerusalem.' 'What are you carrying ?' 'Matzah.' Then the child enters the room, looks at the festive table and asks,' 'Why is this night different from all other nights ?' The matzah remains on his shoulder until it is time to eat it as afikoman.

In the Talmud we find the statement, 'Rabi Eliezer said, 'We snatch the matzah on the night of Pesach for the sake of the little ones that they should not sleep.' This is the origin of the custom for children to snatch the afikoman and surrender it only for a ransom.

However this is not the real meaning of the phrase. 'To snatch' in this setting means 'to hurry.' That is to say that we hurry to eat the matzah. It can also mean that we snatch the matzah away from the children lest they eat too much and fall asleep.

Some people keep a piece of the afikoman throughout the year until the next Pesach as a constant reminder of the great ideas inherent in the matzah.

16. The Order of the Hagadah

Rambam, in the laws concerning chametz and matzah,

writes as follows; 'It is a positive mitzvah of the Torah to tell of the miracles and wondrous deeds which were performed for our ancestors in Egypt on the eve of the fifteenth of Nisan. 'Remember this day on which you came out from Egypt.' 'You shall tell your son on that day...' Although it is the 'day' which is mentioned here, we put this command into practice at night, at the time when the Pesach lamb was eaten and when the matzah and the maror are present on the table.

'Even if a person has no son, or if he is a great scholar, it is his duty to relate the story of the exodus from Egypt and whoever does so at great length, is worthy of praise. It is a mitzvah to tell one's children even if they do not ask. 'You shall tell your son.' The singular is used, 'son' and not 'sons,' to teach us that a father must explain to each child individually according to his intelligence. If a child is young and simple the father should say, 'My son, all of us were once servants just like the servants you see here, and one night the Holy One, Blessed be He, brought us out and made us free.' If the son is older and more intelligent, then the father can tell him what happened to us in Egypt and the miracles which were done for us through Moshe.

'One should introduce variations into the evening's routine so that the children should become curious and ask questions. When they ask, 'Why is this night different from all other nights?' the father should answer them, 'This is what happened, this is what took place.' All manner of antics may be used to encourage the child to ask questions.

'If a man is childless, his wife asks him the questions. If he has no wife, the guests ask one another. Even if they are all wise, they ask 'Why is this night different from all other nights?' If a person celebrates Pesach alone, he asks himself the questions.

'We must begin telling the story of Pesach by mentioning the shameful aspect, but we end it by recounting the praiseworthy part. How is this done? At first we recall that our ancestors in bygone days, up to the times of Terach, went astray after nothingness and pursued the path of idolatry. Then we mention the true faith and we show how the Omnipresent brought us near to Him and set us apart from other nations to worship Him alone.

'We recall how we were slaves to Pharaoh in Egypt and all the evil that befell us there and we lead up to the miracles and wondrous deeds which were performed for us in the cause of our freedom.

'We explain at great length the paragraph beginning 'An Aramean wanted to destroy my father' and the longer one dwells on this paragraph, the more he is to be praised.'

The mitzvah of telling the story of the exodus from Egypt on this night has been carried out from the days when our ancestors departed from Egypt to our own times. However there was no fixed version of this tale when they wandered in the wilderness, when they entered their land under the leadership of Yehoshua or throughout the days of the first Beit Hamikdash. The 'Egyptian Halel' and several other Tehilim (Psalms), composed by the early prophets and by King David, were the only fixed part. The rest was left to the individual. Each person told the story in the light of his own understanding and according to the intelligence of his children. Even quotations from the Torah concerning the exodus were chosen at random by the narrator and explained according to his ability.

This state of affairs continued until the times of the Men of the Great Synod. They instituted fixed formulas for the blessings and for the prayers and also composed the narrative of the great events of Pesach. They called this narrative 'Hagadah' — a tale — from the phrase, 'You shall tell your son.'

After the destruction of the second Beit Hamikdash when we were exiled from our land, certain changes were inevitably introduced. It was no longer possible for a child to ask a question 'Why is it that on all other nights we may eat meat either roasted or stewed or boiled but on this night only roasted ?' Another question was substituted for this. 'Why is it that on all other nights we eat either sitting or leaning but on this night we may only lean?'

Similarly we could no longer point to the meat of the Pesach offering and say, 'What is the reason for this Pesach lamb which we eat ?' This has been amended to '...which our forefathers used to eat.' Some other variations also had to be introduced to fit in with the change of circumstance, such as the phrase, 'This is in memory of the practice of Hillel in the times of the Beit Hamikdash' and the words 'This year we are here, next year in the Land of Israel.'

Despite these small changes and the addition of some songs, the basic structure of the Hagadah and the formulas of the blessings it contains have remained virtually unaltered since the days of the Men of the Great Synod.

'BEGINNING WITH SHAME AND ENDING WITH PRAISE'

The Talmud tells us (Pesachim 116) that in order to fulfill the mitzvah of telling the story of Pesach as commanded in the Torah, we must 'begin with shame and end with praise,' that is to say, our narrative must begin by mentioning the shame that was our lot before we left Egypt, and it must end by recalling the praise to which we became entitled when we departed from there.

Rav and Shmuel appear to interpret this injunction differently. Rav says that we mention our digrace by saying that our ancestors used to worship idols, and the praise by saying that God brought us near to Him to serve Him. Shmuel is of the opinion that our disgrace is shown by saying that we were slaves to Pharaoh in Egypt, and our praise by the fact that God brought us out from there.

The basis for this idea of commencing the story of Pesach with our shame and ending it with the praiseworthy aspect, is to be found explicitly in the Torah itself. 'When your son asks you in time to come, saying 'What are these testimonies, and statutes and social regulations which God, our Lord has commanded you,' then you shall say to him, 'We were slaves to Pharaoh in Egypt and God brought us out from Egypt with a strong hand...' (Dvarim 6).

The duty of telling the story of Pesach is mentioned four times in the Torah; 1. and it shall be when your children will say to you, 'What is this service for you' (Shmot 12).

2. 'And you shall tell your child on that day saying...' (Shmot 13).

3' 'When your son asks you in time to come saying 'What is this ?...' (Shmot 13).

4. 'When your son will ask you in time to come...' (Dvarim 6).

According to the authors of the Hagadah, each of these verses refers to a different type of child, a wicked one, one who does not know how to ask, a simpleton and a wise one respectively.

Both the wicked son and the wise one are given replies which do indeed mention our disgrace first and then our praise. The child who does not yet know how to ask and the simpleton are told only the praiseworthy part, since they could not comprehend the whole tale.

The point of dispute between Rav and Shmuel is not which episode in history is truly symbolic of our shame, the idolatry or the slavery, but which type of child should be answered first. The Torah mentions the wicked son first whereas the Hagadah begins with the wise one. ('The Torah speaks of four sons, a wise one, a wicked one, a simpleton and one who does not know how to ask.') Both aspects of our shameful past, the idolatry and the slavery, are closely interlinked.

'We were slaves to Pharaoh in Egypt.' How did this come about ? Because 'our ancestors worshipped idols.' It was essential to purge them of this evil through the hardships of the exile before 'God brought us out from there.' The Holy One, Blessed be He, well knew that we would accept the Torah and because of this He drew us near to Him that we might serve Him.

THE STRUCTURE OF THE HAGADAH

The Hagadah, as we have it, enables us to fulfill a positive mitzvah of the Torah. If we examine its structure carefully, we marvel at the plan on which it is based. We see how all the mitzvot of the night are woven into it. We see how, stage by stage, it leads us on from simple explanations to deep profundities and mystical interpretations. We see its sanctity in every word and in every letter.

There are ten distinct facets to the Hagadah;

1. Actions and words which excite curiosity.
2. Questions.
3. Telling the wise son, and with him, the simpleton.
4. Praising God for all the four sons — for a promise for good tidings is implicit with each type of questioner referred to in the Torah.
5. The proof that the mitzvah of telling this story must take place on this night.
6. A lengthy reply to the wicked son.
7. Halel, divided into two sections.
8. The blessings at the end of Halel, the blessing for the redemption and for the song of praise.
9. The meal with all its special actions and mitzvot which form an integral part of the Hagadah.
10. The songs at the end, finishing with Shir Hashirim which is the holiest of all.

Thus the Hagadah begins with kidush (sanctification) and ends with Shir Hashirim which is *Kodesh Kodashim* (of the most sacred of all sacred things).

AN ELABORATION OF THESE TEN FACETS

1. The celebrant recites the usual kidush but does not follow it with a meal as is normal on other festivals. He washes his hands — but not in order to eat a meal. He dips

a vegetable into liquid and eats it before the meal, quite unlike the usual eating habits. He divides a matzah, hides half of it away, but does not eat it. He exposes the matzah to view and recites, 'This is the bread of poverty.' Everyone looks at it, expecting to eat it, but it is covered again without being tasted. A dish is arranged on the table containing maror and charoset into which the food will be dipped a second time. The couch for reclining is used throughout the evening and not only for kidush. The second glass of wine is poured out — and still no meal is eaten.

Every action arouses our curiosity.

2. The son questions his father, 'Why is this night different from all other nights?' It is immaterial whether the child asks of his own accord or whether he has been taught what to say because he cannot express these queries. Everyone at the table, adults and children, is full of curiosity and eagerly awaits the answers.

3. The father replies to his son as if he is indeed wise, for which father does not want his son to be wise? In his reply he carries out the mitzvah of the Torah, 'If your son will ask you, in time to come, ... You shall tell your son, 'We were slaves to Pharaoh in Egypt... and God brought us out from there...'

The mitzvah of telling the story of Pesach is not intended simply to inform a child who does not know. Even if we are all wise, understanding, experienced and knowledgeable in the Torah, it is still our duty to tell of the exodus from Egypt — even like those four old men of Beney Berak who, knowing all the Torah, did not find the night long enough to relate it and to discuss it. They had told this story repeatedly for sixty or seventy years and yet they joyfully discovered new meanings in telling it again. If their pupils had not interrupted them, they would not have known that the dawn had risen.

Our Sages tell us that even when the Messiah comes, this

story will continue to be told, for every redemption — from the first one to the ultimate one — finds its echo in the story of this redemption from Egypt, and the more one speaks of it, the more impressed he is with its magnitude.

4. But even if not all our children are wise and even if there be a simpleton or a wicked one among them, or one who is so far from us in his ideas that he cannot even ask a question, nevertheless we still thank God and bless Him four times over.

'Blessed is the Omnipresent,' God, who encompasses the whole world so that there is none beyond His ken, not even the wicked one. Because of this we thank Him and praise Him. 'Blessed is He' — even for the one who attaches himself to the wicked son, namely the one who has estranged himself to such an extent that he has ceased to question anything. 'Blessed is the One Who has given the Torah to His people Israel.' For this we have special cause to thank Him and to bless Him, for granting us the privilege of having a wise son who occupies himself with the Torah. 'Blessed is He' — even for the simpleton, for albeit he is not wise, yet he is innocent and follows those who perform the mitzvot.

For all these we must bless God.

The mention of each of these four types in the Torah brought good tidings to those who went out from Egypt — that they would enter the land and beget children.

Although the first type depicted is the wicked one, he is still our child. When the Torah speaks of educating children, it includes all types; when we sit together on this night and tell of the story of the exodus, our household is at peace. The power of this story is so great that it makes the wicked become wise and restores the innocence of the one who does not know what to ask, so that the father, together with his four sons, can unanimously sing songs of praise to God.

The mention of the four sons and their questions, quoted from the Torah, invokes brief answers. The wise son must be taught as the Torah commands. 'God has commanded us to do all these statutes' (of Pesach) right down to the last of the laws, 'We may not eat anything after the afikoman.'

The wicked one must be approached, in the first instance, with anger but afterwards an attempt must be made to befriend him by answering him at greater length than any of the other sons.

The simpleton must be given a brief explanation to enable him to understand.

The one who cannot ask questions must be shown the same anger which is displayed towards the wicked son, but gradually he will be brought near to the right path.

5. When we mention the son who 'does not know how to ask' and the verse which is to be addressed to him — ".. It is because of this that God did for me when I came forth out of Egypt' — we proceed with recalling that from this very verse our Sages have learned that the mitzvah of 'telling the sons' refers specifically to the night of Pesach, since 'because of *this*' is only befitting to say when matzah and maror are in front of the father to be pointed at.

On this night the father shall open his mouth and tell his tale to everyone sitting at his Seder-table, to all who see the matzah and maror lying in front of him, to all who see his face shining and listen to the song of this night. This is the moment to 'tell your son.' Then he will pay attention and listen, he will give ear and will understand.

6. Now is the time to direct your words to the most difficult of your sons, the wicked one, the one whom the Torah mentions first. You may tell him that he is doing nothing original in estranging himself from the service of God for our ancestors too were idol worshippers. But just as we have now come near to the service of God, so he too is destined to draw near to Him.

The wicked son asks, 'What does this service mean?' We

must reply to him in detail but he must pay great attention so that he understands what this service consists of.

'Our ancestors of old who were near to God, were the finest people in all the world, finer than all those who preceded them. But even they had to undergo, as it were, a refining process so that only the best remained. From all the many sons of Avraham, only Itzchak carried on the traditions of his father. The sons of Itzchak too were 'sifted' and Ya'akov alone remained.

'Now you my son, are of the descendants of Ya'akov. You are of noble stock. But even the sons of Ya'akov who were purged of all dross still required to be cleansed and purified before they were ready to undertake this service, this very service of which you say 'What does it mean.'

'And Ya'akov and his sons went down to Egypt.' When they went down there they did not know when they would return. They knew only that they had a great debt to discharge, but they were also given a great promise for the future.

'The Israelites who were redeemed explained, 'Blessed is the One Who keeps His promise to Israel,' but even before the redemption they said, 'Blessed be He,' for they knew that none but the Holy One, Blessed be He, could calculate when the slavery would come to an end. 'Blessed be He,' for every word that He uttered will surely come to pass.

'The Israelites in Egypt knew that just as God had fulfilled the promise made to Avraham, 'Your seed shall be strangers in a land which is not theirs and they shall serve them and they (the Egyptians) shall afflict them,' so He would also fulfill the second part of the promise, 'I will judge the nation which they will serve and afterwards they will go forth with great possessions.'

'It was their simple faith in this promise which helped our ancestors to endure the hardships which were their lot from the time of Lavan and Pharaoh down to the very last enemy. Now, my son, can you see how great were the tribulations that your ancestors endured, and yet they did not sink beneath their burdens, but rather rose above their slavery and their affliction. You too, were among those who were afflicted and persecuted. But you were not of those who died there, those who were unworthy of being redeemed. You were counted among those who were purged and purified.

'Then God began to show us how He kept His promise, how He judged the nation which had enslaved us, how He brought us forth from Egypt and how He smote the Egyptians at the Red Sea with two hundred and fifty plagues.

'And now, my son, you who were among those who were saved, consider how much cause we have to be grateful to the Omnipresent how many wonderful deeds He performed for us until He eventually built His chosen House where we might make atonement for our sins — and for your sins too, my son.

'You asked what this service means to us. We will not let you go without an answer. The other three sons have received a fitting reply, but the wicked one, the most difficult one, is still awaiting his. Raban Gamliel stated that whoever has not mentioned the Pesach lamb, the matzah and the maror has not fulfilled his duty. In explaining each of these we will fulfill our duty of replying to the wicked son.

'You asked what this service means to us and we answer you is the words of the Torah, 'You shall say that it is a Pesach offering to God because He passed over the houses of the Children of Israel in Egypt when He smote the Egyptians and delivered our houses' (Shmot 12).

Was this then the whole purpose of our being sent down to Egypt? You must know that there were many Israelite houses which were indistinguishable from the houses of the Egyptians, just as you, my son, have tried to make yourself indistinguishable from the non-Jews. Herein lay the great kindness which God did for us. He saved even that kind of house and passed over it, 'and the people bowed down in gratitude and worshipped.'

'It is because of you and those like you that we celebrate the Pesach, so sit down at the head of the table and let us celebrate it together with you.

'The Torah, in the same chapter, explains our use of the matzah. Before the dough of our ancestors had fermented, the Holy One, Blessed be He, revealed Himself to them and redeemed them. 'And they baked the dough which they had brought forth from Egypt into a matzah for it was not leavened, because they had been driven out from Egypt and could not tarry, and they did not even prepare provisions for themselves.'

'But surely it was only God Himself who could drive them out, and why could they not tarry? Could not He Who performed miracles and wondrous deeds for them allow them to tarry a little longer? No! If they had delayed even for a moment, those Israelites who speak as you speak and who act as you act would have sunk into the mire of Egypt and would have become unrecognizable from the Egyptians themselves.

'It was because of you, my son, that we were driven out, that we fled for our lives, so that you could live to see this day.

'Therefore, my son, this matzah and all the service connected with it is yours. It is a symbol of the miracle that was performed especially for you. Come then, and say a blessing for this matzah and we too will say the blessing with you.

'And this maror — what is its purpose ? It is because the Egyptians embittered the lives of our ancestors in Egypt, as we read in the Torah, 'And they made their lives bitter with hard work, with mortar, with brick and with all manner of work in the field.'

'Let us imagine a king who entrusts his child to a servant in his employ. Even if the servant received permission from his master to beat the child, would he dare to ill-treat it, knowing that his employer has always treated him well ?

'You may well ask how it came about that the Egyptians

301

who owed their very lives to Yosef dared to ill-treat the children. 'There arose a new king who did not know Yosef.' Our Sages have queried this. Why was he called a 'new king?' Was it not Pharaoh himself ? We are told that the Egyptians came to Pharaoh and said, 'Let us attack this people.' He answered them, 'How foolish you are. It is because of them that we are alive today. How can you suggest that we attack them ? Were it not for Yosef we would all be dead.' Whereupon they dethroned him for three months until he agreed that they might do with the Israelites as they wished.

'Our Rabis enlarged on this theme. They tell us that from this story we may learn that when Yosef died, the Israelites ceased to keep the covenant of circumcision. 'Let us become like the Egyptians' they said. As soon as they did this, God changed the love which the Egyptians had previously born for them to hatred.

'This is the meaning of the phrase 'who did not know Yosef.' Pharaoh beheld the generation that came after Yosef and could not recognize that they were his descendants. He therefore adopted a new attitude towards them — a new king with new decrees.

'Now you see, my son, all the dangers to which we were exposed, all the miracles and all the bitterness were caused by you. Be you the first, therefore, to celebrate the Seder. Recite a blessing for the matzah and thank God for delivering you from this bitterness, so that you may eat it today as a reminder and not as a reality.

'Therefore all of us, you and I and all your brothers and all your children, are in duty bound to give thanks to God, to the One Who did all these miracles for our ancestors and for us — and especially for you. Let us, in unison, exalt His name and utter praise to Him. 'Blessed are You, O God, Who has redeemed Israel.' Note that we did not say, '... Who has redeemed the righteous' or 'the wise' or 'the elders' or the 'innocent ones.' We say '... Who has redeemed Israel.' It is for the redemption of the whole people that we bless

God, for the redemption of every type of Jew, or all the four sons.'

7. The Halel, the songs of praise which they sang in Egypt and which the prophets of each generation sang, culminating in David, the sweet singer of Israel, were sung at every Pesach, year after year.

When the story of Pesach has been told and our hearts are full of gratitude to God for His great deeds and His great love of Israel, then the moment is ripe to sing the songs of praise, the songs that have been sung in every generation.

Normally we may not interrupt the recital of Halel, and especially not for a meal. Tonight, however, we break off in the middle for a feast. This feast, full of mitzvot, is by its very nature a praise of God, so the first part of Halel together with the meal and the second part are, in reality, one continuous hymn of praise, uninterrupted by any other theme.

8. This section of the Hagadah consists of two blessings. The first is for the redemption. It is said in the middle of Halel and marks the end of the story of Pesach. The second is said at the end of Halel and is known as the blessing for the song. It is as if we say 'We thank You for giving us a mouth with which to sing and a heart to understand so that we may sing Your praises.'

9. The meal and its many aspects, the matzah, the maror, korech, the egg and all the other mitzvot, right down to the afikoman and the blessing after food, all symbolize the story of the exodus from Egypt and the miracles which accompanied it.

10. This section was added by later generations. It consists of *piyutim* and ends with reciting the most sacred of all songs, *Shir Hashirim*. It is customary to say this as an expression of our intense love for the One Who exalted us and sanctified us and planted this love in our hearts.

THE HAGADAH IN ANY LANGUAGE

Since the chief purpose of the Hagadah is to acquaint our children with the story of Pesach and to spread abroad the miracles of the exodus from Egypt, the head of the household must explain the contents of the Hagadah so that all who are gathered at his table may understand.

He must especially bear in mind the women and young children who are not well-versed in Jewish learning. Outside of the Land of Israel where our sacred tongue is not so well known, the Shulchan Aruch permits the reading of the Hagadah and its explanations to be given in the vernacular so that everyone can understand and participate.

'It was my custom to say each verse of the Hagadah first in Hebrew and then in German so that all the members of my household should know of the departure from Egypt' (Yosef Ometz). Chatam Sofer of Pressburg likewise said the whole Hagadah both in Hebrew and in German.

Nisan SONGS AND ACCUSATION

CHAPTER TEN

SHIR HASHIRIM (Song of Songs)

It is our custom to read *Shir Hashirim* on the night of Pesach at the end of the Seder. In the Diaspora where the Seder is repeated on the second night of Pesach, the reading of this book is sometimes spread over the two nights, but it is more usual for the whole book to be completed on the first night.

In Ashkenazi communities Shir Hashirim is read publicly on *Shabat Chol Hamo'ed*, before the reading from the Torah. In some communities it is read from a scroll, hand-written on parchment, and the reader recites two blessings, '... Who has commanded us to read the Megilah' and *shehecheyanu*, but in many places it is read from a printed book without a blessing, each person reading it for himself.

Not only is there a mention of Pharaoh in this book but its contents are symbolic of the four different exiles and Israel's redemption from each (Machzor Vitry).

The Zohar tells us that Shir Hashirim embodies the entire Torah, the story of the exile in Egypt and the redemption of Israel from there, as well as from the other oppressors, so that by reading it we are enhancing the mitzvah of recounting the story of the exodus.

'I AM MY BELOVED'S AND MY BELOVED IS MINE'

Our sacred Scriptures tell us of the greatness of Shlomo who was wiser than all men — those who preceded him and those who follow him — even more than Eytan Ha'ezrachi (Avraham) and Heyman (Moshe) for 'he spoke three thousand proverbs and composed five thousand songs.'

The phrase 'Three thousand proverbs' refers to the Book of Mishley since each separate verse consists of two, three or even more ideas.

These three thousand proverbs were not the full extent of Shlomo's wisdom for he also composed five thousand songs. This statement refers to Shir Hashirim which is a parable of the deep love which Shlomo felt towards God and which expressed itself in a five-fold prophetic vision.

Shlomo himself is symbolic of the entire people of Israel in all generations unto the time of Messiah. From the day when God made a covenant with Moshe until the times when all the earth will be filled with the knowledge of God and 'the mountain of God's House will be established on the summit of all the mountains.' There are five periods in our history when the Jewish people are especially close to God, as He has said in the Torah, 'I will dwell in their midst.' In the intervals there are four periods when the nations of the world brought about a separation between Israel and God. But each separation was short-lived, for Israel again found the One it loved and cleaved to Him.

Five times Shlomo was granted the highest gift of prophecy and wisdom ever bestowed on man. He became closer to God than any other living being.

1. 'In Givon God appeared to Shlomo' (First Melachim 3).

2. 'And God gave to Shlomo wisdom and great understanding and a heart as great as the sand on the sea shore and the wisdom of Shlomo increased... and he was wiser than all men' (ibid. 5).

3. 'Then the word of God came to Shlomo saying, 'This house which you are building... I will dwell in the midst of the Children of Israel' (ibid. 6).

4. 'And Shlomo stood before the altar of God in the presence of all the assembly of Israel and he spread out his hands to Heaven, and said...' (ibid.). The phrase used is

Heaven and not merely *upward,* as if Shlomo held on to the Heavenly.

5. 'And God appeared unto Shlomo a second time as He had appeared to him at Givon' (ibid 9).

We find five parallel occasions on which Israel achieved the greatest possible nearness to God.

1. 'And the cloud covered the *Ohel Mo'ed* (Tent of the Meeting) and the Glory of God filled the Tabernacle' (Shmot 40). We see how God left — as it were — all His Heavenly company on high and made His dwelling place in the Tabernacle which the Children of Israel made in the wilderness.

2. 'And the cohanim were unable to serve because of the cloud, for the glory of God filled the House of God' (First Melachim 8). Here we see how He made for Himself a permanent place among the earth dwellers for four hundred and ten years.

3. The third occasion when God was especially close to His people was in the Beit Hamikdash built by Ezra — until the Greeks defiled it and the *Shechinah (Divine Presence)* departed from it.

4. The fourth occasion was when the Maccabees purified the House and the Divine Presence returned.

5. The fifth occasion will be when the third Beit Hamikdash is rebuilt — never to be destroyed again.

Five times does King Shlomo mention in Shir Hashirim this close relationship between God the lover, and Israel the beloved and each mention is parallel to one of those periods in history when Israel was near to God, until future redemption which is the closest relationship of all and will never be broken. 'Many waters cannot quench the love nor can the rivers wash it away ... for this love is as fierce as death.'

A PARABLE OF A LOVER AND HIS BELOVED

Shir Hashirim, differs from all the other Sacred Scriptures in that there is no mention of God's Name therein.

Shir Hashirim is written entirely in the form of a parable. Our Sages explain it as follows : Wherever the name Shlomo occurs in this book, it is sacred and refers to the Holy One, the One who is the embodiment of peace — *Shalom.*

They further said 'The entire world was never as worthy as the day on which Shir Hashirim was given to Israel. All the Writings are holy but Shir Hashirim is the holiest of all things holy.'

If a person is able to raise himself up from his lowliness, to separate himself from worldly matters and to sanctify himself by means of everything that is permitted to him so that he cleaves to God, he can be called 'holy.' The term 'holiest of all things holy' refers to someone who achieves an even higher standard than this. For him all worldly matters with which he is occupied become filled with sanctity. He eats and drinks and goes about his daily business. He does not stand aside from anything that is permissible. The Divine Presence rests on the deeds of such a man.

When a person achieves such a degree of sanctity he does not need to mention God's name explicitly. Like Shlomo himself, every action of his invokes God's presence.

The everyday affairs of this world are apt to separate a person from God, but if he is capable of investing such ordinary things with holiness, then they become more sacred than anything else and bring blessings to all who are in contact with them.

Our Sages teach us that Shir Hashirim is the most sacred of all the holy writings for it is based on the love between a lover and his beloved one. This love is stronger than all the emotions and is a metaphor for the infinite love between the people of Israel and the Holy One, Blessed is He.

SHIR HASHIRIM ON PESACH

Shir Hashirim shows how all earthly feelings that we experience are only to help us understand the only thing that really exists, that is, the love of God.

This is the meaning of the 'Song of Songs' — the song that is formed by all the various songs of the world, the great theme of the symphony that is composed of the music of each individual instrument and player.

Yet, not every person is capable to comprehend the allegoric meaning of this great song and not every hour lends itself to the full understanding of the metaphor in depth. When Man is immersed only in the parable, in the material world, he is not at all able to understand the higher message which the parable conveys. On Pesach however, the time of our Freedom, one can learn the Will of the Almighty from Nature and all the material world that surrounds him. The spiritual essence that exists in the material world is then revealed before us. Pharaoh and his army, horse and rider, the sea and its tempest, the earth and all of creation, all were subordinate to the will of God. By means of this revelation Israel attained redemption.

The metaphor of Shir Hashirim is especially relevant, therefore, on Pesach when we are all freed from the slavery of Egypt and the slavery to our evil inclination. At this time we are most apt to understand the Song of Love between God and His people; the Song of all Songs!' (Sefat Emet).

SOME COMMENTS OF THE ZOHAR ON SHIR HASHIRIM

'Rabi Yosi explained the introduction to the book, 'The Song of Songs which was written by Shlomo.' King Shlomo was inspired to write this book when the Beit Hamikdash was built and the whole world reached the pinnacle of perfection. Never was there such a moment of rejoicing for the Holy One, Blessed be He, since the world was created, as when the Beit Hamikdash was built.'

'This book is the quintessence of the Torah. If we would understand it properly, we would find in it the stories of the Creation, our revered forefathers, the exile and the exodus from Egypt, the song of triumph at the Red Sea, the ten commandments, the covenant which God made with Israel at Sinai, and the wanderings in the wilderness until they entered the land and built the Beit Hamikdash. It contains also an account of every period in history when Israel was exiled among the other nations. It tells us of the resurrection of the dead and of all that has been and all that will be until the end of days when there will be a perfect Shabat to God.'

'Because of the overwhelming importance of this book, our Sages have warned us against its misuse in picturesque metaphor: 'If anyone takes a verse from Shir Hashirim and makes it into a secular song, the Torah itself puts on sack-cloth and complains before the Holy One, Blessed be He, 'Your children are using me as a subject for jesting when they gather together for merrymaking.'

A NIGHT OF WATCHING

Twice in one verse the Torah refers to the night of Pesach as a 'night of watching.' 'It is a night of special guarding for God to bring them out from Egypt. This night remains to God a night of special watching for all the Children of Israel throughout all their generations' (Shmot 12).

Our Sages have interpreted this phrase, 'a night of watching,' in a variety of ways.

'A night of watching' — a night of anticipation and waiting — for God was watching and looking out for it, to fulfill His promise to take them out of the land of Egypt' (Rashi).

'A night of watching' — a night that is specially reserved for a double redemption, redemption for the nation and redemption, as it were, for God, The word 'watching' (shimu-rim) appears in Hebrew in the plural form, for we find that throughout the whole of the period that the Israelites were enslaved, it was as if the Divine Presence was enslaved with them. Similarly, whenever Israel went into exile, the Divine Presence, as it were, went into exile with them' (Yal-kut Shmot 210).

'A night of watching' — a night which is reserved for the

future redemption. Why is the word *shimurim* repeated in this verse? On this night God did great things for many righteous people, just as He had done for the Israelites in Egypt. On this night He delivered Chizkiah from Sancheriv and his army. On this night He delivered Chananyah and his companions from the fiery furnace. On this night He delivered Daniel from the den of lions. On this night the Messiah is destined to come. That is why the verse ends with the phrase: 'It is a night of watching for all the Children of Israel for all their generations.'

'A night of watching' — a night which is guarded from all harmful elements. It is for this reason that we do not recite the whole of the *Shma Israel* and the other prayers asking for God's protection that are normally said before retiring to sleep. Only the first paragraph of the portion of *Shema* is said, because on this night God especially guards His people from all harm' (Shulchan Aruch, Hilchot Pesach 481).

'Even though we drink four cups of wine and eat various things which normally might be harmful, on this night we are specially guarded againt any detrimental effects (Pesachim 99).

'It is reported of one of the great Sages that he would never lock the doors of his house. This has become the custom to leave the doors of our houses open so that when Eliyahu comes, we may go out to greet him without any delay for we know that on Pesach we are destined to be redeemed' (Ma'aseh Rokeach).

'One should certainly not lock one's door with bolts but in places where lawlessness abounds, one may not rely on a miracle' (Magen Avraham quoting Maharal).

'A night of watching' — that is a night of wakefulness — implying that people should not sleep but should give thanks to God and declare His mighty deeds when He brought us out of Egypt. We find a hint of this idea in the Hagadah in the story of the Sages who sat up all night telling the story of Pesach 'until it was time to say the morning prayers' (Ibn Ezra; Chizkuni).

FOUR NIGHTS

The Hebrew word for 'watching' *shimurim*, appears in the plural form and occurs twice in the same verse. Our Sages connect it with four other verses in the same chapter (Shmot 12), where the word 'night' is preceded by the definite article and therefore refers to a particular night (verses 8, 12, 29, 42).

Yonatan Ben Uziel and the Targum Yerushalmi explain that these refer to four special 'nights' in our history. The first 'night' was at the time of the creation when the 'earth was waste and void and there was darkness on the face of the abyss.' Darkness is always a synonym for 'night.' God dispelled this darkness and brought light into the world which He created.

The second 'night' began when God appeared to Avraham and made a covenant with him. This night lasted until his son, Itzchak, born to him in his old age, lay bound on the altar at God's command. As Itzchak gazed on the glorious light of heaven the lustre of his own eyes became dim, as the dimness of the night itself.

The third 'night' was when God appeared to the Egyptians at midnight, and slew all their first born, while He delivered the first born of the Israelites.

The fourth 'night' will come in the future when the time comes for the world to be redeemed. The power of the wicked will end and their might will be abolished. Moshe will go forth from the wilderness and the Messiah from above. They will call to one another from the clouds and the voice of God will be heard as they walk together. This is the night destined for redemption for all the Children of Israel and for all their generations.

THE MIRACLES IN EGYPT — A COLLECTION OF MIDRASHIM

Why were the Israelites enslaved by the Egyptians rather than by any other nation ? In those days the Egyptians ruled the world from one end to the other. No nation was so steeped in idolatry. No nation was so debased by immorality. Therefore Egypt was appointed as a snare for the Israelites, to see how they would resist this temptation.

'And the Egyptians made the Children of Israel work with rigor.' The Hebrew word 'rigor' (parech), with a slight variation, can be read as 'soft words' peh-rach. Rabi Elazar said : 'Pharaoh declared, 'Let us act wisely.' He gathered all the Israelites together and requested them to help him. He himself took a basket and a trowel and everyone who saw him, provided himself with these and began to make bricks. Throughout the day the Israelites eagerly worked with him as hard as they could. When darkness fell, Pharaoh appointed taskmasters over them, 'Count the number of bricks they have made,' he ordered them. When the total was reported he said to the Israelites, 'This is the amount of work you will do each day.'

'Every male that is born, you shall cast into the river.' Rav Chanan commented; 'What did the virtuous and modest women of Israel do when they heard this evil decree ? They took their infants and hid them in underground tunnels under their houses. The wicked Egyptians would bring their own children into the houses of the Israelites and prick them so that they would cry. When the Israelite babes heard other infants crying, they would cry with them. The Egyptians, having thus discovered the hiding place of the other children, would snatch them away and cast them into the Nile.

'Then the Holy One, Blessed be He, said to His ministering angels; 'Go down and see how the offspring of my beloved ones, Avraham, Itzchak and Ya'akov are being cast into the river.' The angels descended in dismay and rescued the children by placing them on rocks. Then the Holy One, Blessed be He, fed them as a mother would.

'Rav Avira explained: 'It was as a reward for the virtuous women of that generation that Israel was redeemed from Egypt. When the women went out to draw water, the Holy One, Blessed be He, provided them with fish in addition to the water. The women would cook the fish and heat the water and bring both to the field. There they would bathe the men, anoint them and feed them and the family life continued as usual. When the time came for them to give birth, they would do so in the fields under the apple trees. 'Under the apple tree I roused you. There your mother brought you forth. There she who bore you brought you forth' (Shir Hashirim).

'Then the Holy One, Blessed be He, would send an angel from heaven to wash the infants and tend them as a midwife. He would provide them with honey and with oil. 'And he fed him with honey from the rock and with oil from the flinty crag' (Dvarim 32).

'And God heard their cry.' Rabi Akiva said; 'Pharaoh's torturers would strangle the Israelites with the very bricks of the walls of their houses. The cries of the Israelites would be heard from the buildings and from the walls — and the Holy One, Blessed be He, heard these cries.

'And God called to him from the midst of the bush.' Rav Yosef said: 'Why did God speak to him from the midst of a bush? If a person thrusts his hand into a bush, he is not harmed because the thorns point downwards. If he wants to withdraw his hand however, the thorns will hurt him. Thus it was with the Israelites. When they went down to Egypt, they were welcomed. 'The land of Egypt is before you. Settle your father and your brothers in the best part of the land.' But when they wished to leave the land, the Egyptians held them back. 'I will not send out the Israelites.'

'And this stick you shall take in your hand.' This stick was the one created at twilight on the last day of the creation.

It was given to Adam in Gan Eden and he handed it to
Chanoch who handed it over to Shem. He, in turn gave
it to Avraham and from him it passed to Itzchak and then
to Ya'akov. Ya'akov took it down with him to Egypt and
entrusted it to his son Yosef. When Yosef died all his property passed into the possession of Pharaoh. Itro was one
of the sorcerers of Egypt and when he saw this stick with the
letters engraved on it, he coveted it until eventually he took
it and planted it in his garden.

'Until Moshe arrived in Midian no man had been able
to approach it, but when he entered the garden of Itro and
saw the stick and read the letters on it, he immediately took
it for himself with ease. Itro, seeing this, exclaimed: 'This
is the man who is destined to deliver Israel from Egypt,' and
he gave him his daughter, Ziporah, in marriage.

'Then Moshe and Aharon came and spoke to Pharaoh.'
Why were they not accompanied by the elders of the people ?
The Holy One, Blessed be He, had said to Moshe, 'You
shall come, you together with the elders of Israel to the
King of Egypt.' Our Rabis explained that the elders did
indeed start with them but gradually they stole away singly
and in pairs so that by the time they reached Pharaoh's
palace, not one remained as we read in the Torah, 'Then
Moshe and Aharon came ...' — by themselves, without the
elders.

'The Holy One, Blessed be He, rebuked them, 'If this
is your manner of behaving I will punish you accordingly!'
When Moshe and Aharon went with the elders up Mount
Sinai to receive the Torah, God sent the elders back, 'And
to the elders He said, you remain here.'

'And they said to Pharaoh, thus says God, the God of
Israel, 'Send out My people.' Rav Chiyah the son of Rav
Aba said: 'On that day Pharaoh was holding a celebration
and all the kings came from the east and from the west
to pay him homage. They brought him crowns which they
placed upon his head to show that he was chief of all the

317

kings. While this was taking place, Moshe and Aharon were standing at the entrance of Pharaoh's palace. The servants announced, 'Two old men are seeking entrance.' 'Let them enter,' said Pharaoh.

'There were four hundred doors to enter in order to reach the king's chamber. At every door lions, bears and other wild animals crouched. No human being could enter unless he fed these animals with meat. But when Moshe and Aharon came in they all gathered round them, licking their feet and accompanying them as far as Pharaoh.

'When they stood before Pharaoh and the kings beheld them, they were stricken with fear, for Moshe and Aharon looked like ministering angels, tall and stately as cedar trees. Their eyes sparkled like the stars of heaven, their flowing beards were white as snow and their faces shone like the sun. In their hand was the sapphire rod of God with His Ineffable Name engraved thereon, and when they spoke, it was like a fiery flame.

'When the kings beheld all this, they removed their own crowns and bowed down to them. Meanwhile Pharaoh gazed at them in amazement. Perhaps they too would place a crown on his head as the other kings had done — but they did not even inquire after his well-being. 'Who are you?' he said to them. 'We are messengers of the Holy One, Blessed be He.' 'What do you want?' 'Thus says the God of Israel, send away My people that they may serve Me!' 'Who is God,' exclaimed Pharaoh in anger, 'that I should listen to His voice to send away Israel. I shall not send them.' Then he said, 'Wait until I search through my book!' Entering his library he took out his register of gods and began to read, 'The gods of Moab, the gods of Amon, the gods of Zidon... I have consulted the records and can find no mention of His name!'

'Said Rabi Levi: 'This situation can be compared to the incident of a cohen who had a foolish servant. Once the cohen undertook a journey abroad and, after a time, the servant followed to seek his master. Entering the cemetery he began to call loudly to the passers-by : 'Have you seen my master here ?' 'Who is your master ?' they asked, 'He is so-and-so the cohen.' 'You stupid fellow, how can you look for a cohen in a cemetery ?'

'In the same way Moshe and Aharon answered Pharaoh. 'You fool. How can you look for the living among the dead ? All the gods listed in your records are lifeless but our God is a living God, King of the universe.' Then Pharaoh asked : 'Is He young or old ? What age is He ? How many cities has He captured? How many provinces has He conquered? How many years is it since He ascended His throne ?' They answered him, 'The power and might of our God fill the whole world. He is infinite. He existed before creation, and will exist after the end of the world and time itself. He created you and breathed into you the breath of life.' 'What kind of deeds does He do ?' 'He spread out the heavens and formed the earth. His voice douses out flames of fire. He breaks up mountains and shatters rocks. His bow is fire and His arrows are flames. His spear is a lighted torch and the clouds are His shield. His sword is the lightning. He forms the mountains and the hills. He brings down the rain and the dew. He covers the heavens with clouds. He makes the grass grow and the fruit flourish. He answers the cry of women in labor. He fashions the embryo in its mother's womb and brings it out into the light of the world. He deposes kings and enthrones them.'

'At this point Pharaoh interrupted them. 'You are speaking falsehoods. I am the master of the world. I created both myself and the Nile.' Then he summoned together all his wise men of Egypt and said to them, 'Have you ever heard of the name of the God of these men?' 'We have heard Him referred to as 'the son of the wise people' or 'the son of ancient kings.' Whereupon Pharaoh turned to Moshe and Aharon, 'I do not know who this God of yours is.'

'Go to your burdens.' Said Rabi Yehoshua Ben Levi,

'The tribe of Levi was exempt from hard labor. Pharaoh said to them, 'Because you are exempt from labor you say, 'Let us go... and sacrifice to our God;' go to your burdens.'

'Let heavier work be laid upon the men.' We learn that the Israelites possessed scrolls which they would read for their pleasure every Shabat. There they would read that God would redeem them as a reward for resting on the Shabat. But Pharaoh commanded 'Let heavier work be laid upon the people that they may labor and not dally around with vain matters' — they are not to amuse themselves nor to rest on the Shabat.'

'And the rod of Aharon swallowed their rods.' Rabi Elazar said, 'This was a miracle within another miracle. The rod turned back to its original form and swallowed the other rods. When Pharaoh saw this, he said, 'What will happen if Moshe says to the rod, 'Swallow up Pharaoh and his throne,' it would surely do so.'

'Rabi Yosi the son of Rabi Chanina said, 'A great miracle happened to the stick. Although it swallowed all the sticks which the others threw down — ten piles of them — it did not become any thicker.'

'The Holy One, Blessed be He, used the same tactics that earthly kings use when He inflicted the plagues on the Egyptians. If a country revolts against its ruler, what action does he take ? He sends legions to surround the area and first cuts off their water-supply. If they surrender, well and good, but if not he brings disgrace upon them. If they do not then surrender he shoots arrows against them. Then he brings foreign armies against them. If they still do not surrender he throws flames against them. Then he shoots at them with catapult stones. If they still persist in their rebellion he incites other nations to attack them. If they continue to revolt he imprisons them. If even this does not bring them to surrender, he slays the greatest among them.

'The Holy One, Blessed be He, did all of these. First He cut off their water-supply, 'And the water in their river changed to blood.' When they did not give in, He brought disgrace upon them through the frogs whose croaking was very difficult for them to bear. When they persisted He shot arrows against them — in the form of lice which penetrated the bodies of the Egyptians like arrows. Then He brought foreign armies against them in the form of the mixed multitude of wild beasts. After that He meted out punishment — in the form of the pestilence which slew their cattle. When they continued in their evil, He threw flames at them — in the form of boils which burnt their skin. Then He shot at them — in the form of the hail.

'Still they did not surrender, so He incited other 'nations' to attack them — the locusts. Then he imprisoned them by imposing thick darkness on them. When, even then, they refused to surrender, He slew the greatest of them — the first born.

'Why did God bring the plague of the blood first? Pharaoh and the Egyptians used to worship the Nile. Therefore the Holy One, Blessed be He, commanded Moshe, 'Go and smite their gods in their presence.' When a nation is punished, its gods are punished first.

'Over their rivers.' Wherever there was water, it turned to blood. '. . . and over every collection of water,' even water in a ladle became blood. Even the saliva that an Egyptian spat out became blood, for we read in the Torah, 'There was blood in the whole land of Egypt.'

'Rav Avin the Levite said, 'The Israelites became rich from the plague of blood. If an Israelite and an Egyptian lived together in the same house and shared a water tank, when the Israelite filled his cup he found water in it, but if the Egyptian filled his cup from that same tank, the water became blood.

'Then the Egyptian would say, 'give me some of your water' but as soon as it reached his hand, the water became blood. 'Come, let us drink together from the same vessel' suggested the Egyptian, but to the Israelite it was water and

321

to the Egyptian it was blood. Only when the Egyptian bought water from the Israelite with money, did it remain. By this means the Israelites became rich.'

'And the river will swarm with frogs and they will come up and will enter your houses . . . and into your ovens and kneading troughs.' When an Egyptian woman would knead the dough and light the oven, the frogs would get inside the dough and eat it. They would also get inside the ovens and become attached to the dough as it baked.

'Whenever a drop of water was to be found, even in a heap of earth, it became a frog. Chizkiyah said in the name of Rabi, 'If this is what happened then the rich people were not effected for their houses were made of marble and of mosaic. But the frogs would appeal to the marble, 'Make room for me so that I can carry out the will of my Creator.' Then the marble would split and the frog would enter through a crevice.'

'Take a full handful of soot from the furnace . . . ' Many great miracles were involved in the plague of lice. Moshe and Aharon each took a handful of soot from the furnace. Then Aharon transferred his handful to Moshe so that Moshe held both his own and his brother's. No-one can throw an arrow **upwards** for a distance of a hundred cubits, yet Moshe threw the soot of a furnace — a substance that has no real weight — as far as the heavens, right up to the Throne of Glory.

'Rabi Yochanan said, 'When the locusts came, the Egyptians rejoiced. 'We will gather them, cook them and fill our barrels with them.' The Holy One, Blessed be He, said, 'O you wicked people, does this punishment that I bring give you cause to rejoice?' Immediately God brought an exceedingly strong west wind which took up the locust . . . 'so that not one remained,' not even those that were preserved in pots and in barrels.'

'There was thick darkness.' Rav Avdimai said that that darkness was of unusually thick intensity. 'No man rose from his place for three days.' During those days, whoever was sitting was unable to stand, and whoever was standing was unable to sit and whoever was crouching was unable to stand upright.

'During these three days, the very cloud that darkened the skies of Egypt brought light to the Israelites to ask their neighbors for dishes of silver and dishes of gold. During the period of darkness the Israelites went into the houses of their Egyptian neighbors and saw what they had. When, afterwards, they asked them to lend them various dishes, the Egyptians would deny that they possessed these, but the Israelites would say, 'I know that you do possess these and, indeed, they are in such and such a place.' Then the Egyptians would say, 'If the Israelites wished to deal falsely with us, they would have taken these things during the period of darkness, without our being aware of it.'

'For all the Children of Israel there was light in their dwelling-places.' Note that the verse mentions 'their dwelling-places' and not 'in the land of Goshen' for wherever a Jew entered, the light entered with him and lit up all the corners and crevices.

'Why did the Holy One, Blessed be He, bring the plague of darkness ? There were some sinful people who did not want to leave their riches and go out of Egypt. Said the Holy One, Blessed be He, 'If I bring a plague on them so that they die, the Egyptians will say, 'The same things that happened to us happened to them.' God therefore brought the plague of darkness on Egypt for three days so that the Israelites who did not deserve to be redeemed would die and be buried without their enemies knowing of it.

'I will smite every firstborn . . .' As soon as the Egyptians heard these words, some of them became very frightened. They took their firstborn sons to the Israelites and begged them, 'Take my child to stay with you.' But at the stroke of midnight the Holy One, Blessed be He, slew all the Egyptian firstborn. Where an Egyptian firstborn was living in the house of an Israelite, God would slay the Egyptian while sparing the Israelite. When the Israelite awakened he found the Egyptian dead in his own house. The Israelites gave praise and said, 'At midnight I arise to give thanks to You for Your righteous judgements.'

'These are the two anointed ones who stand by the Master of all the world' (Zechariah 3). It was as if the Holy One, Blessed be He, were searching for someone worthy enough to justify Israel's redemption, until He found Moshe and Aharon. It may be compared to a king who wanted to marry a certain woman but people told him that she was very poor, all she possessed was two rings — but for the king this was enough. The Holy One, Blessed be He, said, 'Israel requires no greater merit for its redemption than Moshe and Aharon.'

'When they went out from Egypt, all the Israelites were circumcised, from the oldest to the youngest. They took the blood of the circumcision and the blood of the Pesach offering and sprinkled it upon the doorposts of their houses. When God passed over the houses to smite the Egyptians, He saw the blood and was filled with mercy for His people, '... and I saw you rolling in your blood.'

'There was not a house in which someone did not die.' The Egyptians had many wives and the firstborn of each died in this plague, whether they were sons or daughters. Only Batyah, the daughter of Pharaoh, was spared for she had a good advocate to plead for her — Moshe himself. (it was Batyah who had saved Moshe.)

'Even the firstborn of Egypt who happened to be in other places, far away from their land, they too died at midnight on that fateful night. The firstborn of other nations who chanced to be in Egypt at that time also died.

'God smote all the firstborn in the land of Egypt.' Rabi Shimon says, 'Great is the quality of peace. When a human king goes out to war, he goes with a mighty army but when he goes to make peace he goes alone. By contrast, when the Holy One, Blessed be He, as it were, goes out to bring peace,

He goes with a multitude, 'Thousands upon thousands serve Him.' But when He goes out to war, He goes alone, 'I trod the winepress alone, there is none with Me.' Likewise when He exacted retribution from the Egyptians, He did so alone — 'God smote all the firstborn,' God alone without the heavenly hosts that serve him.

'Rabi Yehudah said, 'All through that night the Israelites were eating and drinking and praising the Holy One, Blessed be He, while the Egyptians were bewailing the plague which had suddenly overtaken them. 'And there was a great cry throughout Egypt for there was not a house in which someone did not die.'

'There was a great cry throughout Egypt.' They saw their gods collapsing before their eyes. At that moment Pharaoh arose from his bed with a great cry and went with his princes to Moshe. With a loud cry, full of anguish, he called out, 'O Moshe, my friend, please, I beg you, pray to God for me. There will not be a man left alive in Egypt.' But Moshe said to him, 'I cannot go out for God has commanded us saying, 'No man shall go out from the entrance of his house until the morning.'

'On that night the Holy One, Blessed be He, performed many miracles for Israel. He slew the firstborn of the cattle and the firstborn of the captives. If a captive was asked, 'What would you prefer — that you should go free or that the Israelites should be redeemed?' He answered, 'We would rather stay here forever than that Israel should go out from Egypt.' God therefore punished them together with the Egyptians.

'From the firstborn of Pharaoh to the firstborn of the captive...' It may be compared to a king who made a feast for his son and killed his enemies. The king declared, 'Whoever is happy with me, let him share in the feasting celebration for my son. Whoever hates me, let him be killed together with my enemies.' The Holy One, Blessed be He, made a feast for Israel when He redeemed them. 'Whoever loves My son,' He declared, 'let him come and rejoice together with him.' The decent ones among the Egyptians came and celebrated the Pesach with the Israelites and went out with them '... and a mixed multitude of people went out with them,' but whoever did not want Israel to be redeemed, died together with the firstborn. 'He smote 'all' the firstborn in Egypt' (Tehilim 45). Everyone shouted, as is written 'There was a great cry throughout Egypt.' Everyone came to slay Pharaoh; at that time, 'Egypt was urging the people to hurry,' but they were declaring God's praises and saying Halel. Then Pharaoh called out to his warriors, 'Come let us call Moshe and Aharon,' but God said to them, 'You are not going to take My children out in the darkness of night! Let them go out publicly by daylight.'

'The Israelites were scattered throughout Egypt and 'They did according to the word of Moshe and they asked of the Egyptians vessels of silver and vessels of gold,' while Moshe himself was occupied with the bones of Yosef and with the vessels of the Mishkan which Ya'akov had prepared.

'Rav Yehudah said in the name of Shmuel, 'Yosef collected all the silver and the gold from Egypt, from Canaan and from all the other nations which came to Egypt, and when the Israelites went out of Egypt, they took it with them, '... and they emptied Egypt.'

'Rav Asi said that they made Egypt like a fortress in which there is no stock of food. Rabi Shimon Ben Lakish compared it to the bed of a sea in which there are no fish.

'This treasure existed in the Land of Israel until the time of Rechavam the son of Shlomo. Then Sheshak, the king of Egypt, made war against the Jews and took it from Rechavam. 'And he took the treasures of the house of God and the treasures of the king's house.' Then came Zerech, King of Ethiopia, and captured it from Sheshak. After that Asa, king of Yehudah, captured it from the king of Ethiopia and sent it to Hadadremon son of Tabermon.

'Then came the people of Amon and took it from him,

but Yehoshaphat, king of Yehudah, captured it from the Amonites. The treasure remained in the hands of the kings of Yehudah until the time of Achaz. Sancheriv captured it from Achaz but Chizkiyah recaptured it, and it was retained until the time of Tzidkiyah. Then the Babylonians came and took it from Tzidkiyah. The Persians captured it from the Babylonian and the Greeks from the Persians. Then the Romans looted it from the Greeks and there it still remains, in Rome.'

'Moshe took the bones of Yosef with him.' Our Sages tell us how greatly Moshe loved the mitzvot. While all Israel were very busy with the plunder, Moshe busied himself with mitzvot.

'How did Moshe know where Yosef was buried ? From the generation that had come down to Egypt with Ya'akov, only Serach the daughter of Asher was still living. Moshe went to inquire of her, 'Do you know where Yosef is buried ?' Serach informed him that the Egyptians had made a coffin of metal which they had sunk in the Nile so that its waters would be blessed. Furthermore the Egyptian magicians and soothsayers had told Pharaoh, 'If you do not want the Israelites ever to leave Egypt, hide the bones of Yosef, for this people will never go out of this country unless they find them.'

'Moshe went to the banks of the Nile and called aloud, 'Yosef, Yosef, God has sworn to Israel that He will one day redeem them. Now the time has come for that promise to be fulfilled. Give honor to the Lord, God of Israel. Do not delay the Divine Presence. Do not delay Israel and the clouds of glory. If you appear, we will be able to depart but if you refuse to show yourself, then we are absolved from the oath you made us swear.' As Moshe spoke these words, the coffin of Yosef began to rise from the depths of the Nile and floated to the surface.

'Rabi Natan was of the opinion that Yosef was buried in the sepulchre of the kings of Egypt. Moshe went and stood in that place, calling to him to come forth so that the promise made to the Israelites could be fulfilled. Then the ground trembled and the coffin of Yosef emerged.

'During all the years that Israel was in the wilderness the coffin of Yosef and the Holy Ark of God went together, (the Hebrew word for 'ark' and 'coffin' are identical). Passersby would ask, 'What are these two arks ?' 'One is for the dead and one is for the Divine Presence.' 'How comes it for these two to be together ?' They answered, 'The one buried here carried out all that the Other One commanded"

'The bones of Yosef.' This can be compared to robbers who entered a wine cellar and drank a bottle of wine. The owner noticed them and said, 'Enjoy the wine but replace the bottle.' The Holy One, Blessed be He, said to the tribes, 'You sold Yosef, now replace his bones in their rightful place.'

'And the Children of Israel journeyed from Ra'amses to Sukot' a distance of one hundred and thirty miles. There, seven clouds of glory assembled, one from each of the four directions of the compass. There was also one from above to protect them from the rain and the hail and to shield them from the burning heat, one from below so that the thorns would not harm them, and one went in front of them to level the valleys and the hills and to prepare a resting place for them. Six hundred thousand of them went on foot, only the children rode on horses.

'And a mixed multitude of people went up with them.' There were many heathens, to the number of two million and fourty hundred thousand, together with sheep and cattle.

'And they baked the dough which they brought from Egypt into cakes of matzot, since it had not risen, as they were expelled from Egypt and were unable to tarry, nor did they prepare provisions for themselves.' They would break off a piece of the dough which they had brought from Egypt and place it on their heads so that it baked in the heat of the sun. This parched bread had to suffice them until the fifteenth of Iyar for they had no other provisions. This demonstrates the greatness of Israel, for they did not ask Moshe, 'How can we go out into the wilderness without provisions ?' Our sacred writings explicitly state, 'Go and proclaim in the ears of the inhabitants of Jerusalem, saying, 'Thus says God, I remember the kindness of your youth, the love of you as a bride, how you went after Me in the wilderness in a land that was not sown.'

PERSECUTION OF JEWS — BLOOD LIBELS

Ever since Edom became a mighty nation in the world and swallowed up the kingdoms of Babylon, Persia and Greece, it outdid them in inflicting all manner of suffering upon Israel. It was Edom that destroyed the Beit Hamikdash, burned Jerusalem and the other cities of Yehudah and made so many of our people into prey for the vultures of the skies. Those that remained were exiled and scattered to the four corners of the world. From that time onwards we have had neither rest nor respite, and not a day has passed that did not bring anxiety and trouble in its wake.

The wicked descendants of Esav continued afflicting us with all kinds of sufferings, even more than the earlier generations had done, for this was a base kingdom, without honor and glory. Neither sword nor spear, neither bow nor arrow, sufficed as weapons for Edom-Rome, but they sharpened their teeth against us like beasts of prey and sought to destroy us with their mouths.

It was in the kingdom of Edom-Rome that the blood libel was first heard, a blood libel from a bloodthirsty nation, a nation descended from Esav. This nation, defiled beyond description with blood, imputed to us the vicious slander that we slaughtered their sons and daughters to use their blood for making our bread of poverty, the matzot for Pesach. During the long years of exile our people have shed rivers of blood because of this libel, for the Edomites wanted to turn our festivals into mourning.

Whenever Israel, overwhelmed by suffering, wanted to free

itself for a while from its heavy yoke and to celebrate the festival of its redemption, its heart would begin to tremble. What is this most abject of nations plotting against us ?

But our festival did not cease nor was its joy diluted. At the doors of our houses, on this night of watching, we placed watchmen to protect us against plotters and to frustrate their evil devices. And if those who plotted against us succeeded, we went to the stake and suffered all the torments of hell — and yet our festivals did not cease.

The 'Taz' in his comment on the Shulchan Aruch remarks (Hilchot Pesach 472), 'In our times we refrain from using red wine for the four cups because of the libelous slanders which we have endured on account of our sins,' but nevertheless our festivals did not cease nor was the mitzvah of the four cups abolished.

More than once God broke the fangs of the snarling dogs and delivered us from their hands, so that the slanderers departed shamefacedly. But many a time their teeth were broken only after they had 'consumed Ya'akov and laid waste his dwelling place' in many lands of the exile. The echoes of these slanders spread from land to land, reaching even the Arab world. Yes, the blood of Edom polluted every nation and the nations together tried to devour us in unison.

It was the festival of Pesach, and especially the Seder night, that Edom chose for its foul purpose. It was then that they gathered against us to consume our flesh and blood, both old and young, wise and foolish, princes and dukes — together with the common rabble. Only on rare occasions did an isolated voice dare to rise in protest against the atrocities that were being committed.

'Remember, God, what they have done to us and be not silent over our spilt blood.'

All the kingdoms of the world, kings and princes, dukes and priests, in Greece and Rome, in Britain and Italy, in France and Germany, in Russia and Poland, in Syria and

Egypt, and even in the Land of Israel, in Chevron, in Jerusalem and in every other district, nothing availed them, neither their sovereignty nor their power, neither their riches nor their might. Despite all these, they were slaves at heart and lowly of soul.

In vain were all their efforts directed against Israel. In vain they attempted to afflict and to impoverish, to crush and to humiliate and to bring them down to the dust. Israel remained free even in the midst of its slavery. Israel was proud and exalted even in its lowliness — and those who enslaved them and tormented them were consumed with envy.

Especially was this true at Pesach time and during the few days immediately before and after the festival. For from the moment that God brought them out from Egypt, they became truly free people to the very depths of their being. The enemy who tortured and oppressed them touched only their body — their soul was not affected.

Any individual Israelite who was sorely stricken had but to remind himself afresh of the episode of the exodus from Egypt and immediately all his present troubles were forgotten. He could sit at his Seder table like a veritable king, his face radiant with the joy of freedom and redemption, his whole being attuned to the glory of God.

But it was that selfsame moment in which Israel again experienced the sweet taste of freedom that excited the envy of kings and rulers who had never known for themselves the meaning of true freedom. For the sake of that very moment, Israel would often have to eat bitter herbs the whole year through, even while the taste of the freedom of Pesach still lingered.

In the kingdoms and dukedoms of those who envied Israel, jealousy was rife. Each kingdom eyed its neighbor suspiciously for as one kingdom rose, another inevitably fell. The liberty of one spelt the enslavement of another.

The freedom of one Israelite, however, did not adversely

affect the freedom of another in the slightest degree. The more Israelites who were free, the greater was the sum total of their freedom. Therefore Israel invites all to share in its freedom, every Israelite and every other nation who forswears the use of the sword. Freedom is the gift of all mankind and the soul of each living thing blessed God for this.

It is because we affirm, 'Let whoever is hungry come and eat' that we are considered guilty in the eyes of all the nations. It is because we believe that 'whoever is in need should come and celebrate the Pesach' that they hate us and envy us and devise slanders against us.

Since the origin of these libels was jealousy, even the wisest among them and the most enlightened ones were not exempt. On the contrary it was they who initiated this wickedness followed in the path they had marked out. For all wisdom which is not combined with freedom of the soul is more exposed to envy and to jealousy than are either ignorance or stupidity.

It was among the ancient wise men of Greece that this hideous libel was first uttered. As their fortunes declined when they were soundly beaten by the Hasmoneans, they fabricated this story. The Romans inherited it in the same way that they inherited the wealth of the nations they conquered, and they bequeathed it to those who came after them, wherever their kingdom extended.

Josephus in his book 'Contra Apionem' quotes the heathen as saying, 'Antiochus found within the Mikdash a man, reclining on a couch, with a table spread with dainties before him. He was eating sea-fish and birds. It is the custom among the Jews, each year at an appointed time, to seize a Greek, to feed him and fatten him, and then to bring him to the city and slay him there. Then he is offered as a sacrifice according to their custom with great pomp and ceremony. Then they throw the corpse into one of their wells.' Democrates, the philosopher, writes as follows: 'Once in seven years the Jews capture a heathen, offer him up as a sacrifice and cut his flesh in pieces.'

Even Socrates relates how 'the drunken Jews, on Purim, killed a heathen and hung him on a tree in place of Haman.'

As the fires of hatred spread throughout the world and the libels increased year by year in every country, historians wearied of recording each separate slander. These lies became the daily bread of Israel, wherever they lived.

To relate all that the chroniclers, both Jewish and non-Jewish, have written on this subject would be well-nigh impossible, but we will mention just a few of the better-known of these infamous blood-libels.

In the year 4904 (1144), Theolbald of Cambridge, a renegade Jew, testified that each year the Jews of Europe conspired to sacrifice a Christian child for their festival of Pesach. That year the lot had fallen to slay a child in the town of Norwich, Britain. The enemies of Israel who occupied leading positions in the church, eagerly seized on this 'evidence' and, finding a dead child, they beautified him. Henceforth he was known as St. William and this tale quickly spread throughout Europe.

Two years after this event, the second Crusade began and the crusaders, with the aid of this libel executed their evil designs on Israel.

Three years after the first blood libel in Norwich, in the year 4707, the body of a Christian was 'discovered' in Wurzburg, Germany. He had drowned in the river on the twenty second of Adar and the Jews of the locality were accused of his murder. After three days of indiscriminate slaughter in the town, the crusaders marched on other cities. A massacre of Jews took place on the twentieth of Nisan — during Chol Hamo'ed Pesach — and outbreaks of violence continued until Shavuot.

Another twenty four years passed and again the fires of hatred burned, this time in France where the Tosafists lived.

The city of Lyon was the target; the Jews were slaughtered like cattle, the entire community was wiped out because of this blood libel and the name of the Almighty was sanctified by their death.

Rabi Ephrayim son of Ya'akov of Bonn who recorded the events of that period, relates: 'At the command of the oppressor, Rabi Yechi'el son of Rabi David was arrested, together with Rabi Yekutiel, son of Rabi David, who were cohanim and pupils of our teacher Rabi Shmuel, and also Rabi Yehudah, son of Rabi Aharon. They bound them with ropes and set fire to some wood, but the ropes on their hands caught alight and snapped. Then the three men said to their tormentors, 'See, the fire has not harmed us, surely we should be set free.' But the wicked oppressors declared, 'As we live you shall not escape' and they smote them with the sword and cast them into the furnace, together with thirty one other Jews who were with them, and they died before God. As the flames soared higher, they lifted up their voices together and sang exultantly. Then the heathens said, 'We have heard your song but do not understand it. We have never before heard a song like this.' The song that the heathens heard on that fateful day was the prayer, 'It is our duty to praise the Master of all things' (alenu leshabe'ach).

In the year 4781 (1221), another blood libel was heard in the town of Erfurth of which a non-Jewish historian relates: 'When non-Jewish merchants visited the town and saw the Jews prospering in business, they were filled with envy and slandered them with having kidnapped one of us, slain him and eaten his blood. Then the enemy fell upon the community and burnt the Synagogue together with all who were praying in it.'

In the communal register of the town of Mainz we find the names of those who were murdered on account of the blood libel: 'Rabi Shem-Tov Halevi who killed himself in front of the Holy Ark, Madronna and Rachel her sister, both virgins, threw themselves into the fire...and Yosef, the younger Halevi, threw himself into the fire...Those who were accused were given the chance of 'purifying' themselves by converting, but these holy people scorned the words of those who incited them and, sanctifying God's name, they went to the stake.'

In the year 4995 (1235), in Fulda, Germany, the Crusaders murdered five Christian children at one time and brought witnesses to testify before the Emperor, Frederik II, that they had seen with their own eyes 'the Jews coming out of this house with flagons full of blood in their hands.' The whole city was in an uproar but when the bodies were brought before the Emperor, he investigated the matter and drove out the slanderers with the command that they were to bury the corpses immediately. Then he published a 'letter of acquittal' in which he declared that this blood libel was completely false. But this letter of acquittal became a weapon in the hands of our enemies who thirsted after Jewish blood, for they said, 'The Jews have surely bribed the Emperor,' and the troubles continued unceasingly, too numerous to record.

In the year 5024 (1264), in England, the blood libel was again revived during Pesach and much blood was spilt in many communities all over the country. In London alone, one thousand five hundred people were slaughtered. The rest of the Jews escaped with their lives to the fortresses but their houses and property were plundered and Jewish life became worthless. Eventually an expulsion order was promulgated against the Jews in the year 5051 (1291) with explicit instructions that they were never to return.

In the year 5027 the Jews of Forzheim in Baden were accused of having slaughtered a Christian girl and gathering up her blood. Three Rabbis of the town were arrested and subjected to inhuman tortures in order to exact a confession from them. When the Rabbis realized that they would no longer be able to withstand the tortures, they killed themselves' Their memory is perpetuated in the register of departed souls of the community of Mainz and two laments were composed in their memory and are included in the Selichot.

At the same period there were blood libels in the town of Sinzach on the Rhine, in Wiesenberg, Mainz, Munich and Bachrach. All these communities went up in flames. Many times the bishops tried to persuade the Jews to change their faith but each time these suggestions were repelled. Our saintly ancestors spurned all their efforts and slew their wives, their children and themselves, rather than fall into the hands of their oppressors.

The greatest havoc of this period was wrought in the city of Prague on the last day of Pesach in the year 5149 (1389). Many thousands of Jews were killed and despite the efforts made to induce them to convert, not a single one agreed and all went willingly to the stake.

Rabi Yosef Hacohen tells us in Emek Habacha, 'On the twenty second of Nisan the heathens of Prague surrounded the vineyard of God, the house of Israel, the entire people. Each man came with his axe and like hewers of wood they put forth their hands against them and smote them at the edge of the sword. They brought forth from their graves those who sleep in the dust, and they smashed their tombstones. There was none to deliver them on the day of God's wrath.'

The poet, Rabi Avigdor Kara also composed a special lament entitled, 'All the troubles which have befallen us' which is included in the minchah prayer for Yom Kipur in the community of Prague. 'Blood met blood in the month of Spring / on the last day of Pesach. the time appointed for redemption of the beloved one / The zealous ones hastened to say to each other / this is the Pesach sacrifice.'

Many were the stories told about the blood libels in the community of Prague during the days of Maharal, how he used his power and performed wonderous deeds in order to deliver the remnants of his people from destruction. Many were the popular legends that grew up concerning **Maharal** and how he fashioned the 'Golem' and saved his people by miraculous means, by virtue of the special wisdom that God granted him.

Rabi Kalonymus, 'Ba'al Hanes,' who is buried at the foot of the Mount Olives, near the grave of Zechariyah the prophet, was instrumental in saving miraculously the Jews of Jerusalem from the effects of a blood libel. The Ishmaelites had killed one of their own children and thrown him by night into the courtyard of the Synagogue in an attempt to destroy their enemies, the Jews. Although it was Shabat, Rabi Kalonymus wrote one of the Sacred Names of God on a piece of parchment and placed this on the forehead of the murdered child. Immediately the latter stood up and pointed an accusing finger at the true murderer. But Rabi Kalonymus passed judgment on himself for having desecrated the Shabat and commanded that after his death, whoever passed by his grave should throw a stone thereon. The people of Jerusalem carried out his wishes, and it became the custom that whoever passed there added a stone to the heap on his grave.

At the end of the Middle Ages, for many nations the period of the Renaissance, the blood libels spread to Turkey, Egypt, Syria and even to Chevron in the Land of Israel, for this bestial libel knew no boundaries. Although the enemies of the Jews in the Arab world copied the wickedness of the Christians in Europe, it was mainly among the latter that this slander took root and spread. It flourished especially in the period of the Renaissance, nurtured by the leaders of the Church.

One of the more terrible episodes concerns a Christian child named Simeon in Trieste. He was two or three years old when he disappeared from his home on the first day of Pesach. His body was eventually discovered in a stream that flowed near the Jewish quarter of the town. At the command of the Bishop, the leaders of the Jewish community were arrested and subjected to ghastly tortures until they 'confessed' that they had killed the child in order to eat his blood.

News of the murder spread quickly through all the towns of Italy and Germany, Jews were arrested, tortured and burnt at the stake. The Rav of Regensburg, one of the greatest scholars of his day, was saved only by a miracle.

If you chance to wander through these countries today and come across a monastry or church with the name St. Simeon, engraved above the entrance, you will know that it refers to that very child whom the church declared a 'saint.' His 'sainthood' was dearly bought — at the cost of his own blood and the blood of many, many Jews.

In Poland and Russia these vile deeds were perpetrated, not in secret places or in hidden corners, but with the full blaze of publicity, with the pomp and ceremony of kings and princes. Wretched Jews were dragged to the block after 'confessions' had been extorted from them by torture.

In the year 5358 (1598), the corpse of a small child, the son of a peasant, was discovered in a marsh near Lublin. Five Jews were arrested and forced to 'confess' that 'they had drunk wine mixed with blood sucked from the body of a child,' and that this blood had been mixed with the dough of the matzot.' The High Court of Lublin had found them guilty and a death-cell was erected in the courtyard of the Great Synagogue. The tortured victims were torn in pieces and the parts sent 'on show' throughout the four corners of the city. The child was declared a 'saint' and buried in the local cathedral.

During a blood libel that occurred on Pesach in the same year in the town of Sandomirz, the bishop of Cracow ordered the judges of the High Court in Lublin to conduct the inquiry with all the tortures of the Inquisition. His instructions were faithfully obeyed.

The cruel persecutions of Jews in Germany and in Italy resulted in a large-scale migration to Poland, but the hatred

followed them there. In 5356 two brothers, Rabi Moshe and
Rabi Yehudah, the sons of Rabi Yekutiel, were falsely
slandered and tortured until they 'confessed' their sins. They
paid for their 'crime' on the fourteenth and eighteenth of
Iyar respectively. Their martyrdom is recorded in the Selichot of the Lithuanian usage:

> 'They spoke falsely against me and libelously accused
> me,
> Their mouths uttered lies and they testified falsely,
> Moshe and Yehudah, the sons of Yekutiel, fell into
> their snare,
> For the sanctity of God's great and revered Name,
> they surrendered their lives,
> Both of them expired after severe torture when their
> honor was brought low,
> They bound them like animals and dragged them
> like dogs,
> They buried them among the rogues after crucifying
> them like thieves,
> They nailed them up with hands and legs spread out,
> They were consumed in fire so that their human
> image was destroyed.'

At the beginning of 5500 the blood libel was so widespread
throughout Poland that a great Polish writer, Kitowitz, remarked that 'Jewish matzah is invariably baked with Christian
blood.'

The boundless cruelty of the oppressors was seen even in
the way they treated their own people, for in order to fabri-
cate a blood libel it was necessary to produce a victim, and
this they did with utter callousness.

A Christian child was found dead near the town of Posen
in the year 5456 and the event is described in the communal
register. 'A pupil was murdered in the forest, a short distance
from us, and it was not known who killed him. Not only
had he been murdered but this murder had been carried

out in a most cruel manner, the like of which had never been known before. His eyes had been gouged out, his hands and legs cut off and his heart extracted.'

A shameful declaration exists from that period, made by Augustus II, king of Poland. 'The infidel Jews shed the blood of Christian children in order to make matzot, and one of their own has testified to this' — referring to a renegade who had become demented.

From then on, until recent times, there was hardly a town throughout the length and breadth of Russia, Poland, Lithuania and Galicia, and in all the neighbouring provinces too, in fact wherever Jews dwelt, that their Christian neighbours did not kindle the fires of hatred.

They trained their little children to fear the Jews, turning them into 'small foxes who damage the vineyard.' They impressed on them to beware, 'Look, the Jew is coming, he will kill you and drink your blood on Pesach.'

The priests encouraged the worshippers from the pulpit to stir up trouble among the Jews, but all this was as nothing compared with the dreadful deeds that took place under the evil Chmelnizki — may his name be blotted out — in the years 1648 and 1649, deeds which were repeated, times without number, until the days of Petlura and Heller.

Nothing availed against this wickedness, neither petitions nor letters of 'protection' obtained from some minor prince, nor even bribery. Our persecuted brethren even turned in their despair to some renegades, and here and there would be found one who would make an effort to silence the voice of slander.

Emissaries were even sent to the Pope in Rome to plead for his intervention, but the respite, when it came, was short-lived and obtained only after paying enormous bribes.

That the libel was completely false, everyone agreed. That it had been invented purposefully and fostered maliciously was known to all, but its falsity did not prevent our ancestors from being tortured with every possible cruelty known to

340

man. Entire families and communities were wiped out, leaving none to mourn their fate.

Over and above all these enemies were the ones in our own midst, as the prophet Yeshayahu had foretold, 'Those who would overthrow you and these who would destroy you, come from your midst.'

At that time a false-messiah arose, Ya'akov Frank. He, together with his followers, forsook the God of truth and, converting to Christianity, aligned themselves with our enemies. The church leaders were pleased to use them as weapons to blot out the remnants of our people and never were there harder times for the Jews in Europe. The Frankists themselves wrote spiteful letters to the Church leaders, 'All believers among the Jews, those who believe in the Talmud, consider it a sacred duty to slay a Christian, extract his blood and eat it with the matzot on the first of Pesach.' The symbols by which the order of the plagues is remembered was interpreted by the Frankists to imply that this hideous story was true.

The Church, which in those days enjoyed unlimited power, compelled the Jews to participate in a public debate with these Frankists. Although the Jews knew that the purpose of this debate was not to clarify the truth, but was merely a device to trap their leaders, they had no alternative. Two outstanding personalities of that period were sent to this public debate, Rabi Chaim Hacohen Rapaport and Rabi Yisrael Ba'al Shem-Tov. It is said of the former that on the appointed day he wore the garments of burial beneath his ordinary clothes, certain that he would not come back alive. But God helped them in their hour of need and they returned with great honor, causing a severe downfall to their enemeis.

It is told of Rabi Yechezkel Halevi Landau, the Rav of Prague, that once on the eve of the fourteenth of Nisan, he he was sitting alone in his room, deep in learning. His door was heavily bolted but from beyond came the noise of an unruly mob approaching his house. The rabble gathered outside in an attempt to break through.

At that crucial moment God enlightened the eyes of the holy man. Rabi Landau knew that this night was fated to be the occasion for the infamous blood libel. Looking around he found a flask of blood hidden in his bookshelves — placed there by the slanderers to give them an excuse for falling on their prey.

Realizing that there was no escape from this desperate situation, he quickly put the bottle to his lips and drained it to the last drop. Water, for ritual purposes, was at hand so he rinsed the bottle to remove all traces of blood and drank this too. All this he carried out with the utmost speed before opening the door to the angry crowd. They marched straight to the place where they had previously hidden the blood, ready to point the accusing finger. To their great amazement the flask was empty without even a trace of blood.

They retired shamefacedly saying that only God himself could have saved both this man and his community.

The libels were repeated in many places in the western world and in the Orient. The most famous were in Damascus in 5600 (1840), the Tissa-Esler affair in Hungary, and Hilzner in Poland. Each of these stirred up Jewry throughout the world.

The last was the most serious of all. During the years 5671 (1911) through 5673 (1913) all Jews under Russian rule were seized with terror because of the blood libel brought against Mendel Beilis. This was brought before a jury with the avowed intention of declaring to the world that the Jews ate human blood. The Russian government was even asked to consider ways and means of stopping religious murders being carried out by Jews.

World Jewry rose to the challenge and even found some support from a few honest and upright non-Jews who recoiled from these falsehoods. Russia's enemeis were preparing war against her, and this forced her plotting against the Jews. The evil Russian plan was foiled for the time being — and then the first World War broke out, bringing fresh disasters to the Jewish people. This was followed, twenty years later, by the second World War when Hitler, 'the chief slaughterer' rose against us.

'Arise, God, let not man prevail. Let the nations be judged in Your presence' (Tehilim 9).

'My heart was hot within me, while I was pondering, the fire burned. Then I spoke with my tongue' (ibid. 39).

'With no fault of mine, they run and prepare themselves. Arise to help me and see' (ibid. 59).

'Pour out Your fury on them and let Your fierce anger overtake them' (ibid. 69).

'Pour out Your wrath upon the nations which do not know You and upon the kingdoms which have not called upon Your name, for they have consumed Ya'akov and have laid waste his habitation' (ibid. 79).

'How long, O God will You hide Yourself for ever, will Your wrath burn like fire' (ibid. 89).

'O God, our God, You answer them. You are a God Who forgives and Who avenges their deeds' (ibid. 99).

'For they have opened the mouth of wickedness and deceit against me. They have spoken against me with the tongue of falsehood' (ibid. 109).

'How many are the days of Your servant ? When will You execute judgment against those who persecute me' (ibid. 119).

In these immortal words King David spoke for all Jews in every generation and in every place.

Nisan PESACH AND THE OMER

CHAPTER ELEVEN

THE FESTIVAL OF PESACH

'Why is the festival generally known as Pesach and not as it is termed in the Torah, the Festival of Matzot ? A verse in Shir Hashirim hints the answer to this question.

'I am my beloved's and my beloved is mine.' Israel's thoughts are directed entirely towards the Holy One, Blessed be He, just as the whole attention of the Holy One, Blessed be He, is centered on Israel. Thus God called this day the Festival of Matzot in praise of Israel who went after Him in the wilderness without waiting for their dough to rise and not asking where they were being led. Israel called this day the Festival of Pesach in praise of the Holy One, Blessed be He, and of His kindness towards us when He passed over the houses of the Children of Israel, sparing us while He smote the Egyptians' (Rabi Levi Itzchak of Berditchev).

PESACH AS AN INDICATOR OF THE OTHER FESTIVALS

Pesach is not only the first of the festivals of the year but it is an indicator of all the other festivals. It is from Pesach that we learn on which day of the week the other important occasions occur.

Let us write the first six letters of the Hebrew alphabet in a column. These will indicate the first six days of Pesach. By their side we write, in a parallel column, the last six letters in reverse order, i.e. the final letter first. The letters in this second column correspond to the various festivals and fasts of the year. In fact these letters are either the initial letters of the festival itself or of its most prominent feature.

From these two columns we can see at a glance on which day of the week each special occasion of the year occurs. E.g. Tisha b'Av, the fast commemorating the destruction of the Beit Hamikdash, begins with the last letter of the Hebrew alphabeth. This letter, in our columns stands by the side of the first letter, showing us that this fast always occurs on the same weekday as the first day of Pesach. Similarly, Shavuot which begins in Hebrew with the next-to-the-last letter of the alphabet always occurs on the same weekday as the second day of Pesach, and so on for each festival.

The first day of Pesach can only occur on a Sunday, Tuesday, Thursday or Shabat, and never on the other weekdays.

THE ORDER OF PRAYER

On Yom Tov itself, i.e. the first and seventh days of Pesach, (in the Diaspora the second and eighth days as well) we say the same prayers as on any other festival. For shacharit the prayers are the same until we reach the phrase 'Bless God Who is to be blessed' (Barchu). Then, if it is Shabat, we continue as on any other Shabat. If it is a weekday, we continue as on other weekdays. When we come to the 'amidah,' we say the special one for the three Regalim (pilgrim Festivals), with the phrase '... this Festival of Matzot, the season of our freedom.'

The amidah of musaf is the same for all the Regalim with only slight variations when we mention the different sacrifices that used to be offered on each occasion in the time of the Beit Hamikdash.

After shacharit on the first day (and in the Diaspora on the second day too), we say the complete Halel with the appropriate blessings. On the other days we omit parts of Tehilim, 115 and 116. The reason for these is that the Egyptians were drowned on the seventh day of Pesach. When the Israelites wanted to rejoice, God rebuked them, 'The work of My hands is drowning in the sea and you want to sing praise to Me!' In the Book of Mishley we are told, 'Do not rejoice at the downfall of your enemy.' Although the drowning of the Egyptians took place on the seventh day of Pesach, we omit these passages on Chol Hamo'ed too so that these days should not seem more important than Yom Tov itself.

On Chol Hamo'ed the prayers are the same as for weekdays, except that we add a paragraph to the amidah, 'Let our remembrance...' (ya'aleh veyavo). Then Halel is recited, omitting the said paragraphs. This is followed by the reading from the Torah and musaf which is the same as on Yom Tov.

On Shabat Chol Hamo'ed, shacharit is the same as on any other Shabat with addition of 'ya'aleh ve-yavo.' Musaf is the same as for every Yom Tov but Shabat is mentioned and that particular blessing ends with the phrase '...Who sanctifies the Shabat, Israel and the festivals.'

The prayer 'ya'aleh veyavo' is added to the amidah of morning, afternoon and evening prayers through-out Pesach. If someone forgot to add this, he may do so if he remembers before he reaches the end of the blessing. If he has already completed the blessing, he may add this paragraph before he says the blessing beginning with the words, 'We give thanks...' (mo-dim). If he has started saying modim before he remembers his omission, he reverts to the blessing beginning with the words, 'Accept...' (retzeh). If he remembers only when he steps backwards to say the last sentence of the amidah, then he must repeat the whole of the amidah. This also applies if he cannot remember whether or not he has said this additaonal prayer.

349

READING OF THE TORAH ON PESACH

The rules for reading the Torah on Pesach are the same as for other festivals. On the first and seventh days (in the Diaspora on the second and eighth days as well), five people are called to the reading of the Torah and a sixth person reads a passage about the relevant sacrifices (Bamidbar 28) from a second scroll.

On Chol Hamo'ed four people are called to read from the Torah. The first three read sections concerned with the festival itself and the fourth person reads about the sacrifices offered on those days. On the days of Yom Tov kadish is said after the fifth person has been called to the reading of the Torah and on Chol Hamo'ed after the fourth person.

On Shabat of Chol Hamo'ed seven people are called to read from the Torah as on every Shabat and an additional person reads the maftir from a second scroll.

The reading from the Torah deals with different aspects of the story of Pesach, the exodus from Egypt, the Pesach sacrifice and the festival itself. The section from Shmot 12, is read on the first day of Pesach because it contains the first mention of the festival in the Torah. On the second day of Pesach we read the section from Vayikra 22, because it mentions the counting of the Omer which began on that day. On the seventh day we read from Shmot 13, the episode of the crossing of the Red Sea which took place on that day. The reading for the other days follow the order in which the chapters appear in the Torah: Shmot 13 on the third day, Shmot 22 on the fourth day, Shmot 34 on the fifth day and Bamidbar 9 on the sixth day.

THE HAFTAROT

The Haftarah for the first day is taken from the Book of Yehoshua because it discusses the Pesach sacrifice which the Jews offered at Gilgal after they had crossed the Jordan into the Land of Israel. In the Diaspora where the second day of Pesach is also Yom Tov, the Haftarah is taken from the Book of Melachim and deals with the Pesach celebrated by King Yoshiyah.

The Haftarah for Shabat Chol Hamo'ed is taken from the Book of Yechezkel, Chapter 37. It speaks of the revival of the dry bones — a theme relevant to this period of the year for the revival of the dead is destined to take place in Nisan.

On the seventh day of Pesach the Haftarah is read from the Second Book of Shmu'el, Chapter 22, for, like the reading from the Torah on that day, this chapter is a song of praise and in addition, the exodus from Egypt is mentioned.

In the Diaspora, Chapter 10 of the Book of Yeshayahu forms the Haftarah for the eighth day of Pesach because it speaks of the destruction of Sancheriv which took place on Pesach.

On Shabat Chol Hamo'ed, in Ashkenazi communities, Shir Hashirim is read before the reading from the Torah. In the Land of Israel it is usual to read this from a proper scroll handwritten on parchment, with the appropriate blessings. If there is no Shabat during Chol Hamo'ed we read Shir Hashirim on the first day of Pesach. If the festival begins on a Sunday, Shir Hashirim is read on the last day of Pesach, Shabat.

Other rules concerning the festival, Chol Hamo'ed and Shabat Chol Hamo'ed which are the same as for the comparable days of Sukot can be found in Volume One (p. 193).

PESACH AS A DAY OF JUDGMENT

Our Sages tell us that on Pesach, God judges the world

to decide whether it is deserving of a good harvest. It is there-fore most fitting that our prayers on Pesach should include a plea for plenty and not for famine !

Three times the Torah mentions the word 'rejoicing' when it speaks of Sukot and once when speaking of Shavu'ot, but in connection with Pesach there is no express mention of this. However our Sages learn, by analogy, that it is equally important to rejoice on Pesach even though the word itself is not explicitly stated.

The reason for its omission is that the world is judged at four periods of the year: On Pesach for the grain harvest, on Shavu'ot for the fruit harvest, on Rosh Hashanah man-kind is judged and at Sukot the world is judged for water. But when the world is judged on Pesach for its grain harvest, the rest of the year with its other judgments still lies ahead and the rejoicing cannot, as yet, be wholehearted. As the year progresses and each judgment is fulfilled, the rejoicing increases.

Why is it that the judgment regarding the crops is made particularly on Pesach — the season of our redemption ? The ripening of the crops is comparable to man's freedom. The crops lie hidden in the ground, enchained, imprisoned, just as the Jews in their exile, until the ripening process releases them and gives them freedom. Pesach, when the Jews were granted their freedom from slavery, is an appropriate time for judging whether the seeds maturing in the ground are to be granted their freedom to benefit mankind.

THE PRAYER FOR DEW

On Pesach we stop saying the prayer for rain, because rain at the end of Nisan is a curse rather than a blessing. The harvest season is approaching and rain will cause the crops to spoil. We pray instead for dew. From the time of the Creation the first day of Pesach was destined for dew.

From the first day of Pesach to the eighth day of Sukot we omit from the second blessing of the amidah, the phrase

'Who causes the wind to blow and the rain to fall.' Some people substitute the phrase, '... Who brings down the dew' and others insert no additional words — each according to the local custom or to the custom of his ancestors.

During all this period we also omit the words '... and grant rain and dew' from the ninth blessing of the amidah. Sephardim have two different versions for this year: '...and grant dew and rain...' and from the first day of Chol Hamo'ed Pesach they pray for the blessing of dew but do not mention rain.

We continue to insert the phrase, 'Who causes the wind to blow and brings down the rain' during the ma'ariv prayer on the eve of Pesach, for not all people attend the Synagogue in the evening and it might not become generally known that these words should no longer be said. This would then give rise to a situation in which the harmony of the Jewish people would be disrupted by people reciting different prayers

We do not change the wording of the amidah during the shacharit service on the first morning of Pesach even though everyone comes to the Synagogue, because a person who did not attend on the previous evening might think that the changed version had been introduced the night before, in his absence. The following year, bearing this in mind, he might then omit the phrase, 'Who brings down rain' when he prays at home on the eve of Pesach. Once again Jewish unity might be disturbed by people using different versions of prayer.

The variation is therefore initiated during the musaf service when everyone present in the Synagogue was also present during shacharit. All are therefore fully aware that from now the changed version is in force and all offer up the same prayers to the Omnipresent.

Why do we begin to praise God for sending rain on the last day of Sukot and continue only until the first day of Pesach, even though rain is still beneficial to the crops

throughout Pesach itself? Our Sages tell us that rain spoils
the enjoyment of a festival so that when we pray for rain
on Sukot we ask God that it should not continue on Pesach
so that our full rejoicing on that holiday should not be
marred.

The congregation does not use the changed wording of
the amidah until it has heard it from the Chazan or from
someone else who announces it in the Synagogue. In some
congregations, the Chazan together with the worshippers, sing
the prayer for dew and the accompanying hymns before
musaf. It is usual for the Chazan to clothe himself in white
for musaf on the first day of Pesach. Clad in the same garments that he wears on Rosh Hashanah and on Yom Kipur,
he begs mercy for the crops which mankind so vitally needs.

If one remembers before reaching the end of the second
blessing of the amidah that he has included the words 'Who
brings down the rain,' he should repeat the whole of that
blessing — provided he has not yet said the words at the
end, 'Blessed are You' (Some say he must begin saying the
whole of the amidah again). If he has already mentioned
God's name, he should finish with the words 'Teach me Your
statutes' and then repeat the whole blessing. If he has finished
the blessing he must go back to the beginning of the amidah.

If he cannot remember whether or not he has said the
correct version, within thirty days after Pesach he must say
the whole of the amidah again, for he has not yet become
accustomed to the changed wording. After 30 days he can
be sure that he is saying the correct version. If he mentioned
rain, even though he immediately corrected himself and
said 'Who brings down the dew' he must repeat the blessing.

In the ninth blessing of the amidah, if he mistakenly mentioned the rain and even if he had not completed the blessing,
he reverts to the beginning of the blessing. Similarly if he
remembered his mistake before finishing the amidah, he
must repeat the whole of that prayer.

RULES FOR HAVDALAH

When Yom Tov ends, whether it is followed by Chol Hamo'ed or by a weekday, Havdalah must be said; the prayer 'atah chonantanu' (which mentions the holiness of Shabat and festivals over the weekdays and includes a petition for God's help during the new week), is added to the fourth blessing of the amidah evening prayer.

We use wine for havdalah but we begin with the blessing 'Who has created the fruit of the vine' and omit the verses which precede and follow this blessing as said at the end of Shabat. The blessing 'Who has created the lights of the fire' is included in havdalah only at the end of Shabat and Yom Kipur when the use of all fire is forbidden. The blessing 'Who has created kinds of balmy spices' is also said only at the end of Shabat because on Shabat each Jew is invested with an 'additional soul.' As it leaves him when night falls, he revives his spirits by smelling the spices. On Yom Tov this does not apply as no extra soul is granted.

If Yom Tov begins as Shabat ends, havdalah is said because the sanctity of the Shabat is greater than that of Yom Tov. In the amidah at the end of Shabat he says, ('atah chonantanu') and during kidush for Yom Tov, havdalah is said. However the last sentence of the latter is changed to read 'Who distinguishes between the holiness of Shabat and the holiness of Yom Tov instead of '... between the holy and non-holy.'

On such an occasion so many blessings are recited over one cup of wine that we have a simple set of symbols to enable us to remember the order which is; 1. Who creates the fruit of the vine, 2. Who sanctifies Israel and the appointed season, 3. Who creates the

355

*lights of the fire, 4. Who distinguishes between holy
and holy, and 5. Who has kept us alive . . .*

*Even though the Shabat is ending, we omit the
blessing on spices because the joy of the coming Yom
Tov has the same effect as the spices. If Yom Tov
is immediately followed by Shabat, no havdalah is
said since its sanctity is superceded by the holiness
of the Shabat.*

THE 'ADDITIONAL SOUL'

The statement above that on Shabat the Jew is granted
an additional soul can be understood in light of the following
explanation :

The additional soul that the Jew enjoys is given to him
from Above, because the Almighty has invested the Shabat,
which is the inheritance of all of Israel who observe the
Shabat. Possession of an additional soul, of a higher spiritual
quality, an additional soul, additional to the holiness that
they, themselves sanctify, is granted them as a gift from
Above. The soul, the spiritual quality of Yom Tov, is not
greater than themselves, since this added holiness is due
to them, as they fulfill God's command to sanctify and
appoint the various festivals.

THE COUNTING OF THE OMER

*'You shall count for yourself from the morrow
of the Shabat, from the day when you bring the
Omer for the offering, seven complete Sabbaths there
shall be, until the morrow of the seventh Shabat,
you shall count fifty days' (Vayikra 23).*

*We have been commanded to count seven weeks
from the time of bringing the Omer offering on the
sixteenth of Nisan, to the festival of Shavuot which
is fifty days afterwards. We commence counting on
the second night of Pesach (in the Diaspora this is
the second Seder night) and continue for forty-nine*

days. Our Sages interpret fifty days as meaning 'until the fiftieth day.'

It is a mitzvah for each individual to count the Omer for himself. 'You shall count for yourselves,' i.e. each individual for himself.

This mitzvah is still in force today, even though there is no Beit Hamikdash and no Omer offering. Some authorities maintain that today this mitzvah is kept as a Rabbinic law.

The correct time for counting the Omer is as night falls, for the Torah tells us, 'complete weeks' and the only way to ensure that this is fulfilled, is by commencing the counting at the beginning of the sixteenth of Nisan. As the first counting is made as night falls, we follow suit with the counting on each subsequent night.

We pray ma'ariv first and count the Omer immediately after the amidah. Praying ma'ariv is a mitzvah which is carried out every day of the year, and it therefore takes precedence over a mitzvah which is performed less often. A person who forgot to count the Omer at the right time may do so at any time through the night until daybreak, but if he still forgot he should do so during the following day without the appropriate blessing.

The blessing '... Who has sanctified us with His commandments and commanded us to count the Omer' is said first, followed by the actual counting, 'Today is the ... day of the Omer' (or 'in the Omer' according to local usage). When he reaches the seventh day he says, 'Today is the seventh day which is one week of the Omer.' He then continues with this formula, e. g. 'Today is the eighth day which is one week and one day' and so on, until the end of the Omer, numbering in weeks as well as in days. If he forgot to do this, counting only the days or only

the weeks, he must repeat the formula but without
the accompanying blessing.

When mentioning the number, whether of days or
of weeks, one must be very careful to use the precise
grammatical form, differentiating between masculine
and feminine, singular or plural. The blessing and
the counting are said standing because of the verse
in Bamidbar, 'from the time when the sickle is put
to the 'standing' corn.' However if he counted while
sitting, he has fulfilled the mitzvah and need not
repeat it.

After counting, it is usual to say 'May it be Your
will that the Beit Hamikdash be rebuilt speedily in
our days.' Having mentioned the Omer offering, we
pray that we may have the opportunity to bring this
offering to the Beit Hamikdash, according to all the
details specified in the Torah.

The Omer should be counted at the beginning of
the night, that is to say, as soon as the stars appear.
If he counted before this, at twilight, he does not
need to repeat it although it is proper to do so,
omitting the blessing this second time.

If one is asked what number of the Omer should
be counted next, he must be very careful with his
reply. If he himself has not yet counted he should
not mention the number itself, for by so doing he
will have counted the Omer without having said the
blessing. He should rather tell his questioner, 'Last
night we counted so and so many days of the Omer.'
One should be particularly careful about this on the
thirty third day of the Omer since this is a popular
holiday and people mention the day quite freely.

When saying the blessing a person should be quite
certain as to which number he intends to count,
although if he relies on overhearing someone else and
repeating it after him, he has fulfilled the mitzvah.

If he intended to say one number and, after the blessing, said a different one, or was reminded of the correct number, he does not need to repeat the blessing. If he said the blessing and counted, and then discovered that he had counted wrongly, provided he has not spoken of anything other then the Omer, he may say the correct number without repeating the blessing.

If he completely forgot to count one day, he counts the days for the remainder of the Omer period without saying the blessing. If, however, he cannot remember whether or not he has counted on any particular day, he may continue to count the rest of the Omer with the blessing.

Women are exempt from the mitzvah of counting the Omer. Generally speaking, if a woman does count, she does so without a blessing. However if a woman takes it upon herself to pray regularly, then she counts the Omer with the blessing.

It is customary to follow the counting of the Omer with the recital of Tehilim 67 which contains forty nine words corresponding to the days of the Omer.

It was the established custom in the Land of Israel and in Egypt for the 'chazan' to count after the people had done so for themselves so that they should not consider themselves exempt from counting since they had heard the chazan do so. However in order to prevent anyone in the congregation from making a mistake in the counting, it became the custom for the chazan to count first.

In the Diaspora where the Seder service is repeated on the second night of Pesach, it is the custom to begin the counting of the Omer at the conclusion of the second Seder.

It was a time-honored custom in many communities for pious men to read the chapter from the Torah concerning the Omer after the second Seder. This reading reminded us of the actual service of ancient days and compensated for the mere 'service-by-lips' (prayer) which has to suffice today. Among the Sephardim it is the custom to read this chapter before commencing the counting of the Omer on the night of the sixteenth of Nisan.

THE OMITTING OF 'SHEHECHEYANU'

There are many reasons for omitting the blessing *shehecheyanu* when we begin to count the Omer;

'The purpose of this mitzvah of counting the days is to prepare ourselves for the festival with which the counting ends — Shavu'ot — and when we reach it we say the blessing to thank God for having kept us alive to that day. This blessing therefore applies both to what preceded the festival and to this festival itself' (Ridbaz).

'The counting is only to ensure that the first fruits are brought at the correct time but has no intrinsic value. Furthermore if one forgot to count one day, then the mitzvah would be incomplete and the blessing would have been said in vain' (Abudraham).

'We say this blessing, *shehecheyanu* only for something over which we rejoice or from which we derive benefit, e.g. the Lulav which we rejoice over, the blowing of the Shofar which helps us to remember our Father in Heaven, the reading of the Megilah because the Merciful One had pity on us and saved us, or a *Pidyon Haben* (ransom of the firstborn) as thanksgiving for the safe delivery of a child. In our days however, the counting of the Omer is no cause for rejoicing. On the contrary we grieve over the loss of the House of God — may it be rebuilt speedily' (Rashba).

ON THE REASONS FOR THE MITZVOT

The fact that God has commanded us is sufficient reason for carrying out a mitzvah with enthusiasm. If our

Sages have indeed provided us with reasons it is because knowing the underlying idea — as far as our limited intelligence can comprehend this — is in itself a mitzvah, part of our service of God. For it is not only man's heart that must be wholly directed to God's service, but all his other faculties too, his intelligence and his understanding must join forces with his heart to serve God.

Where our Sages have given no reason for a particular mitzvah, then we recognize that this, like every other mitzvah, is a manifestation of the wisdom of the Creator and far beyond human understanding. To recognize this, is the greatest use to which we can put our intelligence.

We can understand this better by considering two different types of people, the town dweller and the peasant. The peasant lives isolated in the country, cut off from contact with society, knowing nothing of its wisdom or its ways. By his own reasoning he may work out a pattern of healthy living, but he is a victim of doubt. He is never sure that his actions are correct or that the reasoning behind them will produce the required result.

The town dweller, on the other hand, lives among people, learns from his fellowman and benefits from the accumulated wisdom of society. Without fully comprehending all that he does, he is confident that by performing the actions of the learned people around him, his life will be well-ordered and healthy.

Our Sages have given 'reason' for the mitzvot, also for the benefit of such people who are motivated to act only if they see so called 'logic' in the prescribed deeds. Once these people are made to perform mitzvot through showing them the external logic, they may later reach the domain of wholesome faith.

REASONS FOR COUNTING THE OMER

'When Moshe told Israel in Egypt, 'You shall serve God,' they asked him, 'When will that service take place?' 'At the end of fifty days,' he told them. Then, each person counted the days leading up to this greater event' (Rabenu Nisim). Today we cannot carry out the service in the Beit Hamikdash, we cannot bring the Omer during Pesach nor the first fruits on Shavuot. Our only way of performing the service of God is by taking upon ourselves the yoke of the Torah. So we prepare ourselves for this as our ancestors did in the wilderness. They too could not bring the Omer offering, nor could they bring the first fruits for they never entered the Land of Israel. They could only look forward to accepting God's Torah. We too, look forward to this and, like them, count the days leading up to that event.

'We can compare this to a prince who discovered a man who had been thrown bound, into a pit. The prince told him, 'I will bring you out of this pit and after a time, I will give you my daughter in marriage.' The man rejoiced greatly as he considered his good fortune. 'Not only has the prince brought me out of this pit but he also wants to let me marry his daughter.' The prince was as good as his word. After freeing him, he clothed him in fine garments and gave him presents of silver and gold. When the former prisoner saw how the prince fulfilled part of his promise, he began to count the days until the whole promise would come true' (Sefer Minhagim).

'The heavens and the earth were created for the sake of the Torah. Israel exists only in order to keep the Torah and was redeemed from Egypt only that it might accept the Torah and fulfill its mitzvot. This aspect was far more important to the Children of Israel than the freedom from slavery. We have therefore been commanded to count the days from the second day of Pesach to the day on which the Torah was given, in order to emphasize our great yearning for this important day — even as a slave laboring in the burning sun yearns for the shade and counts the hours until that moment arrives.

If a person counts the days leading to a fixed goal, it is

an indication of his longing to reach that goal. It is noteworthy that we count the days that have passed rather than
the days that still lie ahead, because the pain at the thought
of the days of waiting and counting is greater than the joy
of the thought of the days that have already passed' (Sefer
Hachinuch).

The additional reasons are found in the Abudraham:

'... Since each individual was busy with the work of the
fields and the people were widely scattered, it was important
to count the days leading to the next pilgrim festival to
ensure that none would forget.'

'The period between Pesach and Shavuot is a time of
general anxiety concerning the crops and the harvest. We
read in Tractate Rosh Hashanah 'Why does the Torah
command us to bring an Omer on Pesach ? So that the crops
of the field may be blessed...' The Holy One, Blessed be
He, therefore commanded us to count these days so that
we should remember that the fate of the world is in balance
and that we should return to God with a complete heart,
to entreat Him to have mercy on us and on all His creatures
and on the land, that the harvest may grow as required.'

SEVEN QUALITIES

Our Sages who delved into the deeper meanings of the
Torah, meanings that are hidden from ordinary understanding, have associated this period of seven weeks with seven
attributes which are personified by our great ancestors. These
characteristics are essential to the continued existence of
the world and help mankind to rise from its lowly state,
as the days which elapsed from the time of the exodus
to the giving of the Torah enabled the Children of Israel
to rise from being makers of bricks and garments of straw
for Pharaoh to become a people, specially chosen by God,
a nation of cohanim, kings and princes, all devoted to His
service.

Avraham personifies the virtue of lovingkindness. Through

his selfless love of mankind, the whole world was brought nearer to God.

Itzchak personifies strength of character and from him the world learned to fear God. His whole being was devoted to the service of God and to the fear of Him. In this he neither faltered nor flagged. When he was bound on the altar, it was not his faith that was being tested but Avraham's.

Ya'akov was the personification of glory. All his actions, whether towards God or towards his parents, towards Esav or Lavan, whether they concern the struggle with the angel, his treatment of his children or his attitude to Pharaoh — all were perfect. If some of his actions seem strange and liable to criticism by ordinary people, the Torah itself declares that 'Ya'akov was a perfect man,' the likes of whom never existed. There are men who seem righteous in their nature and just in their actions, but are really corrupt. On the other hand Ya'akov's actions arouse surprise in us, yet God Himself considers him the epitome of glory and uprightness.

Moshe typifies eternity — the eternity of the Torah. All earthly possessions, those we give to others and those we accept from them, are of transient value. The Torah alone is of permanent worth. Both the giver and the taker are rewarded. Moshe gave his life for the Torah and thereby merited its quality of eternity and bestowed eternal merit on all generations.

Aharon's special characteristic was splendor. He loved peace and pursued peace, he loved mankind and brought them near to the Torah. Anyone who saw the splendor and sanctity of Aharon, how he absorbed the teachings of his younger brother and, free from all envy, rejoiced over his greatness, could not help but be influenced by him and his teachings.

Yosef typifies that virtue which lies at the foundation of all morality. The righteousness of Yosef's life was such that he rose to the greatest possible heights of sanctity. This quality of fundamental morality was of such vital importance that, despite the violence and other evils prevalent among the generation of the flood, the people would not have been destroyed had they not, in addition, violated this essential aspect of society.

King David typifies sovereignty. It was not David's wisdom or strength that brought him to kingship, nor did he achieve it simply by inheritance. His kingdom was granted him by the King of Kings. God took him from the sheepfolds, from tending the flocks of lambs — to tend the flock of Israel. God chose him for this task for He knew that even were he to rise to the greatest heights, in his own eyes he would always be a humble servant. David was of lowly origin, yet all the kings, from east and west, came to do him homage. He taught the world that God is the Supreme King. He taught mankind to sing songs of praise to the Master of the Universe. He rejoiced in the greatness of others even as he rejoiced in his own greatness, for he recognized that such greatness was a symbol of the Magnitude of God. He took his greatness and the greatness of all those around him, and returned it with praise to the One to whom all greatness belongs.

'And David blessed God in the sight of all the assembly and he said, 'Blessed are You, O God. . . Yours is the greatness and the strength, the glory, the eternity and the splendor. . . . Yours is the sovereignty and You are uplifted above all . . . for who am I and what is my people that we should be able to offer willingly . . . for all comes from You and from Your own hand we have given to You . . . for sovereignty belongs to God and He rules over the nations.'

Each of these seven qualities is closely intertwined with the others and all are inter-dependent. None exists in isolation. Kindness without strength of character becomes soft-heartedness. Glory without kindness leads to sin. None of these qualities is complete if kindness is lacking. Each characteristic has a light of its own which it sheds on the others even while it absorbs their light, but the quality of loving kindness is greater than all of them.

Our Sages have designated the seven weeks of counting as an opportunity for correcting the various defects of character by stressing these seven special qualities.

The first week is devoted entirely to kindness. On the first day of that week, the emphasis is laid on the epitome of kindness. On each subsequent day of the week, the stress is placed on a different quality combined with kindness. During the second week the stress shifts to strength of character with which each of the other characteristics is interwoven in turn on consecutive days. This pattern is repeated throughout the seven weeks.

When the Children of Israel came out of Egypt, they counted forty nine days until they reached Chorev and stood at the foot of the mountain to receive the Torah. Throughout this period they gradually improved, adding each virtue in turn and combining it with the one previously acquired, until, on the last day, they achieved complete sovereignty and the whole world became, in their eyes, a Kingdom of Heaven and they themselves became a kingdom of cohanim and a holy nation, sanctified for ever by the Torah.

If it should chance that the lustre of these lofty virtues becomes tarnished, that tarnish is but temporary and can be removed by earnest endeavor. The purity that Israel acquired at that time can not be removed in its entirety. If an erring Jew should wish to return to that state of purity achieved when the Torah was given, he can do so more easily during these days of counting the Omer, that especially lend themselves to purification from the time of the giving of the Torah, and for all time.

HIDDEN MEANINGS

'When the Children of Israel were in Egypt, they became defiled by all manner of impurity until they sank to the forty-ninth degree of spiritual uncleanliness. The Holy One, Blessed be He, brought them out from slavery and invested them with forty nine degrees of purity. This was not part of the original promise made to Avraham. The fact that the exodus from Egypt is mentioned fifty times in the Torah demonstrates for us the great kindness that the Holy One, Blessed be He, showed to Israel.

'When we count the forty-nine days of the Omer from the second night of the festival, it reminds us that each day marks a step away from the defilement of Egypt and a step towards spiritual purity. At the end of this period the Israelites were worthy of receiving the Torah' (Zohar Chadash).

'The days of counting the Omer are mentioned in the Torah along with the other festivals to teach us that these days are akin to the festivals — like an extended Chol Hamo'ed, preceded by Pesach and followed by Shavuot' (Sefat Emet).

'At this time of the year, between Pesach and Shavuot, all the crops of the earth ripen to provide man with his material needs for the whole year. In the same way man's soul is given its sustenance at this time for the coming year.

'A Jew who keeps all the mitzvot connected with bringing the Omer on Pesach and Lechem Hapanim on Shavuot has already been judged favorably and it is as if he is exempt from being judged on Rosh Hashanah' (Sefat Emet).

BASING THE COUNTING ON THE OMER

It is written in Sefer Hachinuch:

'Should you ask why we begin counting 'from the morrow of the Shabat' and not from the first day of Pesach, the answer is that the first day of that festival is entirely devoted to the memory of the great miracle of the departure from Egypt. This was a sign of the renewal of the world and of God's constant care for mankind. We cannot intermingle any other joy with this nor make mention of any other event. For this reason, the counting commences on the second day of Pesach, but when recording the number of each day, out of a sense of respect for the holiness of the mitzvah of counting we do not say, 'Today is so many days from the second day of Pesach' but we reckon from the special sacrifice of that day, namely the Omer. The offering of the Omer is a symbol of our faith in Divine providence and in God's desire to grant life to mankind and to renew, each year, the crops whereby man lives.'

A further explanation can be given by delving into the hidden meanings of the various terms:

The Torah has two words to describe a day of rest, 'Shabat' and 'Shabaton.' Pesach unlike the other festivals, is never referred to as 'Shabaton,' and even the title 'Shabat' is used only when we are told of the mitzvah of counting the days from the bringing of the Omer offering. 'You shall count for yourselves from the morrow of the Shabat from the day when you bring the Omer for the wave offering, seven complete Sabbaths, until the morrow of the seventh Shabat, you shall count fifty days and you shall offer up a new meal offering to God' (Vayikra 23).

This verse of the Torah is the source of the mitzvah of bringing this offering. The cohen took the Omer of barley in his hand and waved it in the four directions of the compass and also upwards and downwards. We find no other wave offering which consisted of flour, except for the meal offering of the unfaithful woman.

The Torah also tells us that the Omer was an offering made on behalf of the public. It uses the phrase 'for your will' which is not used in connection with any other public offering. All these changes in phraseology surely imply some special meaning.

Israel went out from Egypt on the fifteenth of Nisan. If God had not brought them out on that day, if He had tarried but a little longer, the Israelites would have been irretrievably lost. When God did bring them out, He immediately raised them from the lowest depths to the loftiest heights, from the most profane state to the greatest sanctity of Shabat. The difference between the word 'Shabat' and the word 'Shabaton' is that the former is sanctified by God, whereas the latter derives its sanctity from Israel.

On that first Pesach, Israel was powerless to sanctify the Shabat. God did so on their behalf, bestowing the holiness of the Shabat on the festival. On that 'Shabat,' the fifteenth of Nisan, the first day of Pesach, the Children of Israel achieved not only physical freedom. They were spiritually exalted to great heights. But this spiritual elevation did not come to them because they deserved it; it was rather a special privilege granted by the Most High.

Only on the morrow of that day did they become aware of this. On that day the Holy One, Blessed be He, said to them, 'I exalted you yesterday only that you might appreciate the great heights which you must try to achieve by your own will and your own efforts. Today you begin this task. You will count fifty days and during this period you will endeavor to elevate yourselves by degrees, until you reach the level at which you stood yesterday. If you do this, you can remain on that level for all eternity. Bring your offering of your own will, without inspiration from Above.

'Do not be distressed if the offering of your first produce is mean and small, barely one Omer of barley flour for the entire nation. Let it come of your own volition from the goodness of a true heart. Bring Me no more than this for you are not yet ready to offer large sacrifices, and if you do bring a greater one it will be rejected. This small offering that you bring to Me willingly, is sufficient for Me to bestow on you an abundance of good from every corner of the world, from the heavens above and from the earth beneath.

'Just begin to ascend and count each stage as you progress upwards. But as you count your progress do not look to the ultimate goal, for you cannot as yet appreciate it. Look behind you to the Omer, to your very first offering, and count from there so that you can measure your progress. Then your hearts will be uplifted as you walk in God's ways and you will be ready, at the end of fifty days, to reach undreamed of heights.

'At that moment you will offer to Me a 'new meal offering.' It will be truly new in your eyes for you neither knew nor imagined that it was possible for man to reach such a state in which the best of everything he possesses is dedicated to God.

'Then every individual and every group will bring to Me the best of its first ripe fruits in order to please Me, for therein lies My pleasure — that you should be Holy men to Me — men, and not angels!'

THE MITZVAH OF THE OMER

Rabi Yehudah said in the name of Rabi Akiva, Why has the Torah commanded us to bring an Omer offering on Pesach ? Pesach is the season when the crops ripen, and so God said to bring an Omer on Pesach so that the produce of the field may be blessed' (Tr. Rosh Hashanah 16).

Rambam (Hilchot Tmidin, Chapter 1) explains this mitzvah as follows : 'On the second day of Pesach, in addition to the usual Musaf sacrifice, a lamb is offered up together with an Omer for a wave offering. The Omer is a meal offering brought on behalf of the public. Since this Omer offering must be brought at a specific time, it overrides both Shabat and the state of impurity. (If the majority of those involved in bringing this offering or the majority of cohanim entering Jerusalem at the time of the offering, or the vessels used for the offering, are ritually unclean because of contact with a dead body, the offering is still brought at the specified time).

'This meal offering is brought only in the Land of Israel. It is a mitzvah to bring it from the nearest place to Jerusalem but it can also be brought from any place in the Land.

'It must be reaped at night, i. e. on the night of the

sixteenth of Nisan, whether this be Shabat or weekday. It must consist of standing grain, but if none is available, it can be brought from sheaves. It should be brought from the moist crop, but if this cannot be done, it may be brought from the dry crops. It was the custom to bring the Omer from the fields in the south for the crops ripened there earlier.

'One year a person would plough half his fields and sow the other half. In the following year he would rotate and plough the part he had sown and sow the part he had ploughed and from that he would bring the Omer. The Omer was brought from barley according to the tradition handed down to Moshe from Sinai.

'The representatives of the Beit Din would go out to the fields on the eve of Pesach and bind some of the barley stalks without detaching them from the ground so that it would be easier to cut them at the right time. All the neighboring villagers would assemble so that the cutting could take place with great ceremony.

'Three *se'ah* (measurements) of barley would be cut by three men using three sickles and carrying three boxes. This quantity is equal to about ten Omer.

'When it became dark on the eve of the sixteenth of Nisan, the reaper would say to the bystanders, 'Has the sun set?' 'Yes' they would reply. This question and the subsequent ones, together with the answers would be repeated three times.

'Is this the sickle?' 'Yes.'

'Is this the box?' 'Yes.'

'If it were Shabat the reaper would also inquire 'Is it Shabat today?' and receive an affirmative reply. Then he would ask, 'Shall I reap?' 'Yes' would come the answer.

'The thrice-repeated questions and answers were because of those Jews who had strayed from the congregation of Israel during the period of the second Beit Hamikdash and had misinterpreted the phrase, 'from the morrow of the Shabat' to mean the first day of the week. According to our

371

tradition the word 'Shabat' in this context means Yom Tov
and this is how it was understood by the prophets and by
the Sanhedrin in each generation, all of whom carried out
this ceremony on the sixteenth of Nisan, whether this occurred
on a Shabat or on a weekday.

'The Torah tells us, 'You shall not eat bread or parched
corn or fresh corn until this very day' i. e. the day on which
the Omer is brought. In the Book of Yehoshua (Chapter
five) we read, 'And they ate of the produce of the land
from the morrow of the 'Pesach,' matzot and parched corn.'
This is the first and indeed, only occasion in the entire
Torah on which the festival of the fifteenth of Nisan is
referred to as 'Pesach.' Since the main feature of the festival
was the eating of the Pesach offering on the night of the
fifteenth, the phrase 'on the morrow of the Pesach' can only
refer to the sixteenth of Nisan when the Omer was brought.
Those misguided people who maintained that the Omer should
be brought on the morrow of the Shabat which falls during
the Pesach week are clearly in error.

'After the barley had been cut, it was placed in the boxes
and brought to the courtyard of the Beit Hamikdash where
it was beaten. Then it was winnowed and sifted and passed
through fire in a sieve in such a way that the fire touched
every grain. When it had been parched in this manner it was
spread out in the courtyard for the wind to blow through
it. Then it was put into a coarse mill and ground. Of the
three se'ah of barley, a tenth part was taken. (An Omer is
the equivalent of one tenth of three se'ah). This quantity
was sieved thirteen times.'

EXPLANATIONS OF THE SAGES ON THE OMER

'You shall bring the Omer.' Rabi Yanai said: When a man
buys some meat in the market place, he has to take great
pains and exert much effort to cook it properly. The Holy
One, Blessed be He, however, makes the wind blow, brings
the clouds, makes plants flourish and ripens the fruit —

all this while people sleep in their beds — and the only reward we give Him is a mere Omer barley' (Vayikra Raba 28).

The Holy One, Blessed be He, said to Moshe, 'Go and tell the Children of Israel,' When I used to provide you with Manna, I gave every single one of you an omer ('An omer per person' — Shmot 16). Now when you bring Me this offering, all I demand is one Omer from all of you. Not only this, but I ask you to give it to Me merely of barley' (ibid.).

'He will wave the Omer before God.' How is this done ? Rabi Chama Ben Rabi Ukva said in the name of Rabi Yosi Ben Rabi Chanina : The cohen waves it in each direction in honor of the One to Whom the whole world belongs. He then raises it and lowers it in honor of Him to Whom the highest and the lowest creations are subject.

'Rabi Simon Ben Rabi Yehoshua said : He waves it in each direction in order to prevent harsh winds. He raises it and lowers it in order to prevent harmful dew' (ibid.).

'Rabi Yochanan said : Let not the mitzvah of the Omer appear insignificant to you. It was because of this mitzvah that Avraham was privileged to inherit the Land of Canaan, 'I will give to you and to your seed after you the land in which you have dwelt, all the land of Cannan ... so that you may keep my covenant.' Which covenant does this refer to ? To the mitzvah of the Omer. 'When you come to the land which I give you (the land of which I said 'I will give it to you and to your children') you will bring ... ' Your coming there is conditional upon your bringing this Omer.

'This mitzvah helped the Israelites in the days of Gideon. It helped them in the days of Chizkiyah. It helped them in the days of Yechezkel and it helped them in the days of Haman. Rabi Levi said : When Mordechai saw Haman coming towards him on his horse, he said, 'This wicked man is surely bent on killing me.' Turning to his pupils who were sitting learning in front of him, he said, 'Get up and flee lest you

be harmed.' They refused saying, 'Whether we live or die,
we will not forsake you.' Whereupon Mordechai wrapped
himself in his talit and beseeched the Holy One, Blessed
be He, while his pupils continued to learn. Haman inquired
of them, 'What are you studying ?' 'We are learning about
the Omer which the Israelites used to offer up in the Beit
Hamikdash on this day.' 'What does this Omer consist of ?'
he asked them, 'Is it silver or gold ?' 'It is an Omer of barley,'
they replied. He continued to query them, 'What is its value,
Ten Kantars ?' 'Far more' they answered, 'Ten Dinars.' Then
he said to them, 'Arise, for your ten Dinars have more power
than my ten thousand talents of silver' (ibid.).

LAWS OF THE NEW CROPS

The Torah commands us;'You shall eat no bread nor parched
grain nor fresh grain on this self same day until you bring the
offering of your God' (Vayikra 23).

We were warned not to eat of the new crop until the
sixteenth of Nisan, viz, the day when the Omer was brought
when the Beit Hamikdash was in existence. Until this Omer
had been offered up, it was forbidden to eat any of the
five types of grain: wheat, barley, spelt, rye and oats. Nowadays one may not eat of the new crops until nightfall of
the seventeenth of Nisan.

Not only is it forbidden to eat of the new crops before that
time, it is also forbidden to eat anything made of these new
crops, whether food or drink. Crops which are planted after
the sixteenth of Nisan may not be eaten until after the Omer
of the following year. This rule applies whether the crops
have been harvested before that date or not.

Grain sown before Pesach which has taken before the
sixteenth of Nisan may be eaten immediately after that day,
even though it was not fully grown before then.

In the Diaspora where the first two days of Pesach are
celebrated as Yom Tov it has become customary to forbid

the eating of the new crops until the seventeenth of Nisan has passed.

THE SIXTEENTH OF NISAN

In the Diaspora this day is kept as a festival and all the mitzvot of the festival apply to it with one exception — the prayer for dew is said only on the first day of Pesach. There is also a certain leniency on that day regarding burying the dead and treating a patient who is not dangerously ill. An egg laid on the first day of Pesach may be eaten on the second day.

In the Land of Israel the sixteenth of Nisan is the first day of Chol Hamo'ed. It is customary to celebrate it with more than the usual rejoicing, also in memory of the feast which Esther made on that day, for salvation was wrought for our people and Haman was hung.

This day was the first in the period of the counting and marked the first stage in the process of the purification of the Israelites from the defilement in Egypt.

Other episodes concerning purification took place on this day, e.g. during the time of Chizkiyah, the task of purifying the first Beit Hamikdash after it had been defiled by the abominations introduced by Achaz. On this day also the Hasmoneans completed their task of purifying the Beit Hamikdash from the defilement of the Greeks and the Helenists.

According to Rav Ya'akov Emden, Levi son of Ya'akov was born and died on this day.

In the year in which the Children of Israel left Egypt, the fifteenth of Nisan fell on Thursday and on that day they journeyed from Ra'amses and reached Sukot. On the morrow, the sixteenth of Nisan which was a Friday, they travelled from Sukot to Eytam at the edge of the wilderness and there they encamped until after Shabat.

CHOL HAMO'ED

The verse which says, 'You shall keep the Festival of Matzot for seven days' teaches us that it is forbidden to work during the intermediate days of the festival. Our Sages derive the prohibition of work during Chol Hamo'ed from this verse, but most of our great authorities maintain that it was the Rabanim who forbade work during this period and this verse lends support to their claim. Some of the earlier authorities also maintain that, according to the Torah, all work not connected with the festivals and whose avoidance does not cause great loss, may not be done on Chol Hamo'ed. One should therefore guard the sanctity of Chol Hamo'ed and refrain from doing anything except work which is specifically permitted (See Vol. 1 p. 194).

One should honor the occasion by wearing special clothes and eating festive meals twice a day. Maharil would wear his Shabat clothes on Chol Hamo'ed but on Yom Tov itself he would wear even better clothes for there is an additional mitzvah of rejoicing on the festivals. He would eat bread at every meal taken during Chol Hamo'ed so that it should be a festive meal. This is especially important during Chol Hamo'ed of Pesach for, according to the Gaon of Vilna, it is also a mitzvah to eat matzah on every day during pesach.

It is usual to cover the table with a cloth on Chol Hamo'ed as on Shabat. Some say that one should have two whole loaves (or matzot) available for each meal on Chol Hamo'ed, just as on Yom Tov and some also light candles.

We do not say the Thanksgiving Song (Tehilim 100) throughout Pesach for the thanksgiving sacrifice was not offered in the Beit Hamikdash at that time because of the unleavened bread which always accompanied it.

Although, in many respects, Chol Hamo'ed is considered like Yom Tov, we do not add to the blessing after meals the phrase, 'May the Merciful One cause us to inherit a day which is entirely good,' the phrase which is included on Yom Tov itself.

TEFILIN ON CHOL HAMO'ED

According to the Shulchan Aruch (Orach Chayim, 31) it is forbidden to put on *tefilin* on Chol Hamo'ed. This is the practice among the Sephardim and also among Ashkenazim who follow Sephardi customs, and among all communities in the Land of Israel. There are however some Ashkenazim outside of the Land of Israel who do wear tefilin during Chol Hamo'ed, and in doing so they follow the rulings of Rav Asher Ben Yechiel and his son, Rav Ya'akov Ben Asher, Maharil did likewise, basing his actions, as they did, on a statement in the Jerusalem Talmud, Mo'ed Katan, Chap. 3.

ON THE SANCTITY OF CHOL HAMO'ED

The days of Chol Hamo'ed are entirely sacred and God's presence rests on them. The name, Chol Hamo'ed, (the non-holy days of the festival) is merely a relative term. The intermediate days are not holy in relation to the first and seventh days of the festival, but in relation to the other days they are holy.

According to the Talmud in Tractate Pesachim and in Makot, a grave punishment awaits one who trifles with the sanctity of these days. Rav Sheshet said, 'Whoever belittles the festivals is as one who indulges in idolatory.' Rashi explains the word 'festivals' in this context as referring to Chol Hamo'ed. One who performs work that is forbidden during these days, or refrains from investing these days with sanctity by eating and drinking more than on ordinary weekdays, is said to belittle Chol Hamo'ed.

Every Jew must be careful to honor the days of Chol Hamo'ed, to hallow them with joy and gladness, and with feasting as on Yom Tov, so that he should not be drawn towards idol worship — Heaven forfend — for idolatory is a denial of the entire Torah.

The Talmud tells us that one who belittles the appointed seasons, (i. e. Chol Hamo'ed) — even though he possesses learning and good deeds — has no share in the world-to-come. One should therefore be extremely anxious not to trifle with the significance of God's appointed seasons.

On entering the house, one should loudly proclaim to all the family the same greeting used on Yom Tov, 'Mo'adim lesimchah,' for this is part of the honor due to the occasion. To use the same greeting as on weekdays would be to 'belittle' Chol Hamo'ed.

It is proper to light candles on every evening during Chol Hamo'ed as on Yom Tov, and indeed this custom is practised in many western lands.

'We have already learned of the reward which is meted out to those who invite poor learned people to their table during festivals. This applies in even greater measure to Chol Hamo'ed and whoever does so is assured that God will always provide him with abundant means for helping the poor' (Yesod Veshoresh Ha'avodah).

Nisan THE SEVENTH DAY OF PESACH AND THE END OF THE MONTH

THE SEVENTH DAY OF PESACH ❖ A BRIEF ACCOUNT OF THE EVENTS OF THE SEVEN DAYS OF PESACH ❖ THE ORDER OF THE NIGHT OF PESACH ❖ THE DIVISION OF THE RED SEA ❖ SOME MIDRASHIM AND EXPLANATIONS OF OUR SAGES CONCERNING THE RED SEA ❖ THE LAST DAY OF PESACH ❖ ISRU CHAG ❖ PIRKEY AVOT ❖ THE ORIGIN OF THIS CUSTOM ❖ AVOT ❖ DISTRESS AND MOURNING DURING THE OMER PERIOD ❖ THE PUPILS OF RABI AKIVA ❖ LAWS AND CUSTOMS CONCERNING THE OMER PERIOD ❖ THE KEY TO SUSTENANCE.

CHAPTER TWELVE

The seventh day of Pesach is not a festival in its own right as is the case with the eighth day of Sukot. It is but the final day of Pesach and we do not, therefore, say the blessing *shehecheyanu* when reciting *kidush*.

On this day many miracles were performed for our ancestors at the Red Sea and, because of this, the Torah commanded that 'the seventh day shall be a holy assembly for you, no work shall be done on that day.'

In most places where the Torah commands us to observe the first day of Pesach as a festival, we are reminded of the exodus from Egypt, but when we are told to hallow the seventh day of Pesach, there is no mention at all of the miracle which took place on that day, the miracle of the Red Sea. Similarly when the Torah tells us of the miracle itself in Shmot, Chapter 14, there is no mention of the day on which it took place nor of the festival which commemorates it.

We have already remarked on the fact that Israel has no celebration to mark the downfall of its enemies. It celebrates only its own redemption from those enemies. The Holy One, Blessed be He, does not rejoice over the destruction of the wicked nor does Israel indulge in such rejoicing. The seventh day of Pesach was designated as a festival for Israel before they knew that on this day the Egyptians would drown. Even after that event the Torah conceals from us the link between the sanctity of this festival and the episode of the Red Sea.

The main cause for Israel's joy on this day is the song which Moshe and the Children of Israel sang under Divine inspiration. This song of theirs merited a place in the Torah for all time and God Himself, together with His heavenly company, hearkened to it.

The date of the dividing of the Red Sea — namely the seventh day of Pesach — was not written in the Torah for the reason already given. However we know this to be so from our traditions and since it was allowed to convey the Oral Law to writing, we learn it from written sources too.

A BRIEF ACCOUNT OF THE EVENTS OF THE SEVEN DAYS OF PESACH

According to the Mechilta the order of events from the first to the seventh day of Pesach, was as follows;

Whenever Moshe spoke to Pharaoh, all he asked was that the Israelites should be allowed to go on a three days' journey into the wilderness in order to offer sacrifices to God. By this means, Israel would become men freed by God rather than slaves freed by Pharaoh. When they left Egypt, Pharaoh knew that they would not return and that God who had performed such miracles for them in Egypt, would feed and sustain them even in the wilderness.

Despite this knowledge, he pondered in his heart, 'They did not ask for more than three days so I still have a hold over them.' He therefore sent swift couriers with them to bring back word as to how they were faring and the Israelites did not hinder them from accompanying them.

On the morning of the fifteenth of Nisan, a Thursday, the Children of Israel left Egypt and journeyed from Ra'amses to Sukot, arriving there on the same day. There the Holy One, Blessed be He, encompassed them with seven clouds of glory.

On the following day, Friday the sixteenth of Nisan, they journeyed from Sukot and encamped at Eytam at the edge of the wilderness. On Shabat, the seventeenth of Nisan, the Israelites stayed in their places and did not travel. On Sunday, the eighteenth of Nisan, the Israelites began to put their things in order and to prepare their animals for journeying. Pharaoh's messengers said to them, 'Your three days journey is ended. It is time for you to return to Egypt.' But the Israelites answered them, 'It was not by permission of Pharaoh that we left Egypt. It was God's uplifted hand that brought us out.' The couriers replied, 'Whether you are willing or not is immaterial. You must fulfill the royal decree.' Whereupon the Israelites rose against them. Some of them were beaten, some were slain and some were wounded. Those who were left made their way back to Pharaoh and reported to him.

By the time these messengers went away it was noonday on the eighteenth of Nisan and Moshe said to them, 'Go backwards towards Egypt so that Pharaoh should not think you are fleeing. Let him overtake you near to his own land and if he wishes to protest, let him come and do so.' Moshe then blew the trumpet to signal them and they withdrew to Pi-Hachiroth, a journey of a day and a half.

As soon as the blast of the trumpet was heard, the weakhearted ones began to tear their hair and rend their clothes, for they were convinced that Moshe was taking them back to Egypt. But Moshe calmed them, 'God Himself has told me that you are free men. Your apparent retreat is merely to mislead Pharaoh.'

It took a day and a half for the couriers to reach Pharaoh so that it was Monday night, the nineteenth of Nisan, before they came and informed him that the people had fled. On Tuesday, the twentieth of Nisan, Pharaoh harnessed his chariot and, taking his people with him, pursued the Israelites. He reached them at the end of that day as they were encamping by the sea near Pi-Hachiroth.

On the seventh night of Pesach, i. e. Wednesday, the eve of the twenty first of Nisan, the Israelites went into the sea and emerged at daybreak on Thursday. When they saw how God's great hand had worked against the Egyptians, Moshe and the Children of Israel sang a song of triumph to Him.

On this day, the twenty first of Nisan, eighty one years previously, Moshe had been cast into the river by royal decree. Rabi Chanina bar Papa said that this event took place on the twenty first of Nisan. The ministering angels said to the Holy One, Blessed be He, 'O Master of the world, shall the one who, on this very day, is destined to sing the song by the Red Sea, be smitten on this day?'

One year before this, on this same day, Moshe had gone to Egypt from Midian entrusted with the mission of bringing out the Israelites. On the fifteenth of Nisan, the Holy One, Blessed be He, had appeared to him from the midst of the burning bush and for seven days had urged him to accept this task. These seven days later became the seven days of Pesach.

THE ORDER OF THE SEVENTH NIGHT OF PESACH

It was an ancient custom for pious Jews to remain awake throughout the seventh night of Pesach — or at least for most of that night — and to busy themselves with the study of the Torah. They would learn extracts from our sacred writings, the Written Law and the Oral Law and end with the sections from the Zohar that deal with the seventh day of Pesach. These excerpts have been collected in a book which is entitled, 'Tikun.'

The word means 'correction' or 'improvement.' Although the great miracles that were performed for the Israelites at the Red Sea found expression in the song that was given a permanent place in the Torah, this redemption was not wrought for them because they had originally deserved it but because they corrected their faults and improved themselves. This they did firstly, by believing in God and in Moshe, His servant, with unquestioning faith, and secondly, by their willingness to accept His Torah.

The anniversary of those miracles at the Red Sea is a fitting time to improve one's soul by deepening one's faith in God and in His Torah. Whoever wishes to purify himself is helped to do so by God and this is especially true of this seventh night of Pesach.

THE DIVISION OF THE RED SEA

Our Sages, of Blessed memory, tell us that at first Moshe did not tell the people the reason for their apparent retreat. It was only because of a few faint-hearted ones among them who were tearing their hair and rending their garments, that Moshe revealed his plan to them and assured them that they were indeed free — free for ever.

Hearing of the few who were fainthearted, we learn that the majority had such faith that when they heard that they were to withdraw, they accepted the decision lovingly, despite the passing thought that they might be returning to Egypt.

Why did God ask them to retreat? When the Israelites came out from Egypt, they had no special merits of their own which made them deserve to be redeemed. They were brought out only because of God's promise to Avraham. But God wanted them to deserve the redemption themselves. When they were three days journey from Egypt, secure under the Divine Presence and sheltered by the clouds of glory, their faith in God was strengthened. Then God spoke to them, 'Let them return' so that He might test their faith. Would they be prepared to revert to the slavery of Egypt? Anyone who was ready to do so because of his belief in God deserved to be redeemed on his own account.

Those whose faith was strong, lovingly accepted God's command and in so doing, imitated Avraham, of whom it was said, 'And he believed in God.' Because of this the promise made to Avraham was fulfilled through them.

It is as if the exodus from Egypt were repeated a second time. The first time it came about because of the promise made to Avraham and the second time because they themselves deserved it. (According to Pri Tzadik).

'And God caused a strong east wind to blow over the sea all that night.' If God wanted to divide the sea, could He not have achieved this easily ? By one single utterance He could have transformed the sea into dry land. Why did He bring this strong east wind ?

'God wanted the Israelites to be imbued with implicit faith that the entire creation depended on His word. The wilderness and the inhabited places, the sea and the wind, the clouds and the fire — all are the work of God's hands and subject to His direction. There is no aspect of nature that exists outside of His control. Once this firm belief was deeply rooted in the minds of the people, they were privileged to share in a miracle in which the laws of nature were over-ruled.

'It may be compared to an incident in which Rabi Chanina Ben Dosa said; 'May the One Who by His word makes oil burn, also cause vinegar to burn at His command.' Now why did Rabi Chanina mention the flamable property of oil ? He could simply have prayed that the vinegar would ignite. But this episode teaches us that only when a person recognizes that the laws of nature operate solely at the command of God, does he become worthy of having a miracle performed for him that violates the laws of nature' (Pri Tzadik).

'When the Divine Presence was revealed to the Israelites in Egypt and at the Red Sea, it was like a bridegroom meeting his bride before their wedding, the wedding that was to take place on Shavuot' (Rabi Bunim of Pashischa).

'He led them in the depths of the sea as in the wilderness.' The sea and the wilderness are alike in that both are un-inhabited. The Israelites learned from this that they could find a dwelling place anywhere in the world. The world exists because of righteous people and by their efforts, the desolation of both the sea and the wilderness can be overcome' (Sefat Emet).

'Then Moshe and the Children of Israel sang.' Although the verb in this phrase is always translated in the past tense, 'and they sang,' the Hebrew grammatical form is in the future 'and they will sing.' The Torah wanted to tell us that the Israelites had always longed to sing praises to God, that the very essence of the Children of Israel was to proclaim to the world the existence of the Creator.

'During the years of exile and slavery they were unable to utter songs of praise, nor were they able to testify to God's presence — until the Holy One, Blessed be He, helped them by His wondrous deeds. When they saw their erstwhile enslavers dead and realized that their redemption was complete, the song burst forth from their lips of its own accord' (Sefat Emet).

'I will glorify Him.' The root of this word in Hebrew is similar to that meaning 'to dwell.' The Israelites implied that they would make a dwelling place for God in their midst and that they, in turn, would dwell in God's presence.

'Rabi Shimon said; When the Israelites stood by the sea and sang God's praises, the Holy One, Blessed be He, revealed Himself to the heavenly company, so that the Israelites should know their King Who had wrought for them all these great miracles and mighty deeds. By this they were inspired to greater heights than all the prophets. We know that this did indeed happen when we see how every individual Israelite sang exactly the same words at exactly the same time, all in perfect harmony and yet each singing as if he, under Divine inspiration, were the only one doing so.

'Even the embryos in their mother's wombs sang the same song, for the vision they beheld was greater than that seen by Yechezkel the Prophet. It was as if they had beheld God Himself. And when their song came to an end, their souls were enraptured and they were overwhelmed with longing to see yet more. Because of this great longing they were unable to continue their journey.

'Then Moshe said to the Holy One, Blessed be He, 'Because of their great longing to gaze upon Your Presence, Your Children do not want to depart from this place.' Whereupon God concealed His glory from them, but although Moshe requested them to move many times, they were still unwilling, until God indicated to them that His glory dwelt in the wilderness. Then Moshe made them journey — as we read in the Torah, 'And Moshe made the Children of Israel journey from the Red Sea and they went out to the wilderness of Shur.' The word 'Shur,' in Hebrew, means to look, that is to say, that the Children of Israel went out to the wilderness because they wanted to look at the glory of their Holy King' (Zohar).

Further comments on the Song of the Sea can be found in Vol. I. p. 344.

SOME MIDRASHIM AND EXPLANATIONS OF OUR SAGES CONCERNING THE RED SEA

'And it was when Pharaoh sent out the people.' The Hebrew word 'and it was' can be translated as 'Ah, woe,' an exclamation of distress. It was Pharaoh who bewailed thus. Rabi Shimon Bar Yochai explained; We may compare it to one who lost a great treasure in a dung heap. Being loath to exert himself to look for it, he merely poked at the surface with a small stick. Then along came someone else, full of energy, who dug down and found the buried treasure. When the loser saw how the finder built himself a fine palace and walked abroad with a retinue of servants, he bemoaned his fate, 'Ah, woe is to me, what I have lost !'

'When the Israelites were in Egypt, laboring with clay and bricks, they were despised by the Egyptians, but when they later saw them encamping by the Red Sea, with their ensigns flying like a royal parade, they began to lament, 'Ah, what have we sent away from Egypt!'

'Some say that it was Moshe who uttered this lament of woe. It may be compared to one who accompanied a princess as she went to her wedding canopy, but foreseeing that he would not be able to take her to the house of her groom, he began to cry. When people asked the reason for this, he said, 'I am crying because I have worked so hard to bring her thus far, but I cannot come to the wedding canopy with her.'

'Moshe answered in the same way. 'I cry because I toiled to bring the Israelites out of Egypt but I cannot go into the land with them.'

'And God did not lead them by way of the land of the Philistines.' Why was this ? The tribe of Efrayim erred in calculating the time of the redemption and went out earlier. As a result 300,000 of them had been killed. They had reckoned the years of slavery from the time when God had made the covenant with Avraham, (Bereishit, 15) instead of from the birth of Itzchak. Because they anticipated the redemption by thirty years, thirty times ten thousand of them were slain by the Philistines. Their bones were scattered along the route, piled up in heaps for thirty years, until the rest of their brethren went out from Egypt.

'The Holy One, Blessed be He, said, 'If the Israelites see the bones of the tribe of Efrayim scattered by the wayside, they will take fright and want to return to Egypt.'

'It may be compared to a king who, while abroad, married a woman and wanted to return home with her. Before he reached his country however, the woman died. After burying her, he married her sister but decided to bring her to his country by a different route so that she should not be dismayed at seeing her sister's grave.

'There is further reason for God not bringing them to the Land of Israel by the straight route. As soon as the Canaanites heard that the Israelites were entering the land, they burned crops, chopped down trees, destroyed buildings and stopped up wells. Then the Holy One, Blessed be He, said; 'I did not promise Avraham their ancestor, that I would bring them into a waste land but into a land full of plenty. I will therefore make them wander in the wilderness for forty years until the Canaanites make good what they have destroyed.

'And the heart of Pharaoh and of his servants were turned towards the people and they said, 'What is this we have done, that we have let Israel go from serving us?' The Torah tells us, in this verse, that the departure of the Israelites from Egypt, spelt the death blow of the kingdom of Egypt. The Egyptians said, 'From now on, all the nations of the world will belittle us for they will say, 'If these who were in their power were allowed to leave their country, what purpose is there in our sending to distant lands to bring slaves for ourselves from those places?'

'And the heart of Pharaoh and of his servants was turned.' In the past, 'the servants of Pharaoh said to him, how long will this people be a snare for us?' but now they said, 'What is this we have done that we have let Israel go from serving us?'

'They said, 'If we had been smitten but had not sent them away, it would have been worth our while. If we had not been smitten but had simply sent them away, they would not have taken our wealth and it would have been worthwhile. But now, we have been smitten by the plagues, we have let them go that they no longer serve us and, in addition, they have deprived us of our wealth.'

'It is like one who ordered his servant to buy some fish for him in the market place, but when the fish was brought home it was found to be putrid. The master then commanded the servant. 'Choose your punishment. Either you eat the fish or you receive one hundred strokes of the whip or you give me a hundred coins.' The servant chose to eat the fish but no sooner had he begun to do so than he said, 'I cannot carry on, let me rather be smitten.' When he had already received sixty strokes, he said, 'I cannot bear any more. I will give you the hundred coins.'

'Thus it was with Egypt. They were smitten by the plagues, they sent the Israelites away and their wealth was taken away from them.'

'And the Children of Israel went out with an uplifted hand.' The Torah teaches us by this that when the Egyptians were pursuing the Israelites, the former were reviling and blaspheming them, while the Israelites were exalting, glorifying, praising and singing to the One Who is Master of all wars.

Rabbi Ishmael compared the exodus from Egypt to a dove which had fled from a bird of prey and was about to take refuge in a cleft of a rock, but it found that a snake had nested there. If the dove entered the cleft it would surely be bitten by the snake whereas if it retracted its step it would be caught by the bird of prey. How did it solve this dilemma? It began to make a noise and to beat its wings so that the owner of the dove-cot came to its rescue.

'This is how the Israelites acted in their dilemma. They could not go forward into the sea because it had not yet been split asunder, nor could they go backwards for Pharaoh was fast approaching. What did they do? 'They were greatly afraid... and the Children of Israel cried to God.' Immediately, 'God saved them on that day.'

'When they saw Pharaoh approaching, an evil thought entered their heads prompting them to grumble against Moshe. 'And Moshe said to the people, 'Do not fear.' We can see the greatness of Moshe, how he encouraged them and pacified all those thousands and tens of thousands.

'Stand firm and see the salvation of God.' 'When will that be?' they asked him. 'Tomorrow.' 'O Moshe,' the Israelites said to him, 'We have no strength to last out.' Then Moshe prayed and God showed them groups of ministering angels standing ready to help them. 'And God said to Moshe, 'Why do you cry to Me?'

'Then Avraham, Itzchak and Ya'akov came and stood before the Holy One, Blessed be He, as He revealed Himself at the sea. 'In the presence of their fathers He did wonders in the land of Egypt, in the fields of Tzoan.' The heads of the twelve tribes too came and stood behind God's chariot.

'Then God said to Moshe, 'My servants, and My faithful ones have risen from their graves and are pleading before Me for their children who are exposed to danger, while you stand and multiply your prayers. Why do you cry to Me ?'

'And the angel of God journeyed ... and came between the camp of Egypt and the camp of Israel and there was a cloud and there was darkness and it lit up the night.' The cloud was for Israel and the darkness was for Egypt. The Egyptians who were enveloped in darkness saw the Israelites in the light and threw arrows and stones at them, but the cloud and the angel shielded them.

'And I lifted you on eagles' wings and brought you to Myself.' How does the eagle differ from all the other birds? All other birds carry their young between their legs because they fear other birds who fly above them. The eagle alone, carries its young on its back for it fears only the arrows of man. 'It is better, says the eagle, 'that the arrow harms me rather than my children.'

'Said Moshe to the Holy One, Blessed be He, 'The enemy is behind them and the sea is in front of them. In which direction should they go ?' What did God do ? He sent the great angel, Michael, who made himself into a wall of fire between the Israelites and the Egyptians, so that the latter were unable to pursue the Children of Israel.

Meanwhile the angels on High, seeing the plight of the Egyptians, sang no songs of praise to their Maker on that night.

'Then Moshe enquired, 'O, Master of the world, what shall I do ?' 'Take the stick which I gave you, go to the sea on My behalf and say to it, 'I am sent on behalf of the One who created the world. Make way for My children that they may pass through you.' Moshe immediately performed God's bidding, but the sea answered, 'I will not do as you have said for you are a mere mortal, and furthermore, I, the sea, was created on the third day whereas you, a human being, were not created until the sixth day.'

'When Moshe told these words to God, He said to him, 'What happens to a servant who refuses to carry out his master's instructions ?' 'He is whipped' replied Moshe. Then God commanded him, 'Raise up the stick, stretch out your hand over the sea and cleave it.' Immediately, Moshe stretched out his hand over the sea and divided it. The Israelites however feared to enter the sea until Nachshon Ben Aminadav jumped in first. Then all the Israelites followed him into the sea and 'the water was a wall for them on their right and on their left.'

'And the Children of Israel came into the midst of the sea on dry land.' The words appear to contradict themselves. If it was the sea, then how was it dry land ? If it was dry land then why does the verse state, 'in the midst of the sea ?' We learn from this apparent discrepancy that the sea was not divided until they entered it and the water reached up as far as their noses. Then it became dry land for them.

'Rav Nehorai explained; An Israelite woman would be passing through the Red Sea with an infant in her arms. When the child cried she would reach out and take an apple or a pomegranate from the sea and give it to him, for the verse tells us, 'And he led them through the depths of the sea as in the wilderness.' Just as they lacked nothing in the wilderness, so they lacked nothing in the depths of the sea.

'When the Holy One, Blessed be He, was about to drown the Egyptians, Uza, the guardian angel of Egypt, prostrated himself before Him and pleaded, 'O Master of the World, You created Your world with the quality of mercy. Why do You want to drown Your children?' God immediately assembled all the heavenly company and asked them to arbitrate. When the angel Michael saw how the angels of the various nations were defending the Egyptians, he hinted to the angel Gavriel who flew to Egypt and extracted from a building a brick in which an Israelite baby had been immured... Standing before the Holy One, Blessed be He, he exclaimed, 'O Master of the World, This is how the Egyptians treated Your children.' Immediately God applied the quality of justice and drowned them.

393

'Then the ministering angels wanted to sing praises before God but they were silenced; 'The works of My hands are drowning in the sea and you want to sing praises to Me.'

'When the waters of the Red Sea were divided, all the waters of the world were divided even the water in pits, in holes and in caves were divided.

'Rabi Yosi Haglili commented; When the Israelites emerged from the sea, the whole nation was bent on singing God's praises. How did they achieve this? When they beheld the Divine Presence, even the infant on its mother's knees raised its head. The baby at its mother's breast ceased to feed and together they sang, 'This is my God and I will glorify Him.'

'From the day when the Holy One, Blessed be He, created the world until the moment that the sea was divided for Israel, no human being had ever sung God's praises. Now when the Israelites stood by the sea they burst into song. Then God said, 'It is for this moment that I have been waiting.' When the angels too, began to praise God, He said to them, 'No, let My children sing first.' 'At that moment all the glory of Heaven was revealed to the Children of Israel. Even a servant-maid saw what was denied to Yeshayahu, Yechezkel and the other prophets. Each one pointed with his finger and exclaimed, 'This is my God and I will glorify Him.'

'It was not Israel alone that sang God's praises but all the nations of the world joined in exalting Him. As soon as it became known that Pharaoh and his army had perished in the sea and that the kingdom of Egypt was no more, and that judgment had been executed against the idols which they had worshipped, all the other nations forswore their false gods and loudly proclaimed in unison, 'Who is like You among the gods, O Lord!'

'By means of this song, Israel's destiny was revealed to them. Moshe said to the Israelites, 'My brothers, you must know that merely by wisdom, by understanding or by strength man cannot conquer a single city. It is only the might of the Holy One, Blessed be He, that renders this possible.' Then, turning towards God, he prayed, 'O Master of the world, when the Amalekites come to fight against Israel, 'let fear and dread befall them.' Moshe also sought God's mercy for them for the time when they would enter the land with Yehoshua and for the time of the coming of the Messiah and for the Beit Hamikdash. Then the ministering angels exclaimed, 'The Lord reigns unto Eternity.'

'And Moshe made the Children of Israel journey from the Red Sea' — against their will. When Pharaoh and the entire population pursued the Israelites after they had left Egypt, all the horses were adorned with precious stones. After they were drowned in the sea, the jewels floated to the surface and were cast onto the shore. The Israelites eagerly collected these from the water's edge and when Moshe observed that they were unwilling to move, he said to them, 'Do you imagine that the sea will yield treasures like this every day?' and he made them travel against their will.'

THE LAST DAY OF PESACH

Jews in the Diaspora observe one day extra for each festival. Our Rabis and Sages have invested this additional day with the same sanctity that belongs to the other days of Yom Tov. All *dinim* applicable to a festival apply with equal force to the extra day celebrated in the Diaspora. (Only Rosh Hashanah has an extra day both in the Land of Israel and in the Diaspora). This means that when Jews in the Land of Israel are observing 'Isru Chag' (i. e. the day following each of the three pilgrim festivals), the Jews in the Diaspora are celebrating the last day of Pesach.

It is customary to be a little more lenient in certain matters on this eighth day of Pesach in the Diaspora — not in matters of law for we have already pointed out that the laws of the first day of Yom Tov apply equally to the extra day kept in the Diaspora. There are three exceptions; burial of the dead, treatment of sick persons and eggs laid on Yom Tov. In all other respects all days of Yom Tov are equal.

The leniency on the eighth day in the Diaspora applies only to those aspects of the laws of Pesach which some people observe with greater stringency. For example, people who, throughout Pesach, do not eat matzah that has been soaked in water, do partake of this on the eighth day. Also many people who do not eat in other people's houses on Pesach and do not lend or borrow dishes, do these things on the eighth day of Pesach.

The last day of Pesach demonstrates the unity of the Jewish people. By taking a more lenient view of the laws on this day, people can eat together and have no scruples about eating in each other's houses, thus emphasizing the idea inherent in the eating of the matzah, namely the unity of the Jewish people.

As a finale to all that has been written about Yom Tov, we quote some passages from the Sidur of Rabi Ya'akov Emden, based on Rambam.

'A person should eat, drink and rejoice on a festival, but not to such an extent that he turns to levity, for the evil inclination can more easily tempt a person who overindulges in food and wine. Laughter and levity are not synonymous with rejoicing but rather with folly and stupidity. We have not been commanded to be stupid and foolish but to serve our Maker with rejoicing.

'It is the duty of the Beit Din to appoint officers on the festivals, to patrol the parks, orchards, river banks and wherever people congregate for purposes other than learning, in order to warn them against promiscuity, gluttony and mixed dancing, for these have nothing to do with true rejoicing. Their sole purpose is to stir up hatred between Israel and their Father in heaven. On the contrary, all should strive to be holy, to be beloved of God and to be acceptable to Him.

'Each person should visit his Rav on Yom Tov. He should consider such a visit as if he were in the presence of God and the Rav were an angel in God's service.'

We remember the dead in our prayers on the seventh day of Pesach, and in the Diaspora on the eighth day. (See Vol. 1, p. 197).

ISRU CHAG

Rabi Moshe Isserles writes (Orach Chayim 429) : 'It is customary to eat and drink more on Isru Chag, i. e. the day following each of the three pilgrim festivals. Beit Yosef, quoting from the Jerusalem Talmud, says that this day is called 'the child of the festival.'

Everyone should endeavor to retain the flavor of the festival by honoring the day following it with festive meals. Happy is he who can carry this out, who can arrange a feast for his friends and acquaintances at which songs and praises to God are sung at the table. Nowadays this table represents the altar of God and it is as if one had built an altar and brought a sacrifice thereon. God reckons it as if one had offered up a burnt-offering to atone for any sins committed during the festival. In doing this, we would be following the practice of Job who, when his children held a feast, was apprehesive, 'perhaps my children have sinned in error,' and he brought a sin offering on their behalf. (See Vol. 1. p. 222 for further information on the subject of Isru Chag).

THE READING OF PIRKEY AVOT

It is an ancient custom, going back to the days of our Sages of blessed memory, to read *Pirkey Avot* (the chapters of Tractate Avot in the Mishnah) on each Shabat during the summer months. One chapter is read each week after *minchah*. In most communities we begin on the first Shabat after Pesach and finish on the Shabat before Rosh Hashanah.

The complete book is finished for the first time on the Shabat before Shavuot and on the following Shabat we revert to the first chapter again. We begin reading the book for the third time on the Shabat when we read the portion of *Pinchas* and for the fourth time when we read the portion *Shoftim.*

As there are less than six weeks between this Shabat and Rosh Hashanah, we read two chapters on each of the last two weeks to complete the book on the last Shabat before that festival.

In Sephardi communities it is the custom to read the book through only once, a chapter a week from the Shabat after Pesach to the Shabat before Shavuot.

The origin of this custom of reading Pirkey Avot on Shabat after minchah is to be found in the writings of Rav Saadiah Gaon and Rav Sar-Shalom Gaon and is based on the sayings of our Sages of blessed memory.

They said that this reading was ordained in honor of Moshe who died on Shabat at minchah time. 'If a scholar dies all study ceases.' This means that no public learning takes place at such a time, but so that learning should not cease completely it was ordained that these chapters should be read, read but not learned.

Before minchah regular study may take place in public but after that, each person learns alone or at the most, in pairs. Only Pirkey Avot is said together.

As a reminder of the death of Moshe, it is also customary that from minchah onwards on Shabat, people do not greet one another with the normal Shabat greeting. Should a person be thus greeted, he returns the salutation in a low voice.

Rav Sar-Shalom Gaon quotes from the Jerusalem Talmud; 'Rav Yoshiyah said, 'Remember the Torah of My servant Moshe.' Even though Moshe received the Torah from God and gave it to the people, he himself must be remembered.' We find further in the Jerusalem Talmud, 'Said Rabi Zera, 'And the days of weeping in mourning for Moshe were ended,'

i. e. the days of weeping in mourning for him were ended, but his memory never faded and in his memory the houses of study were idle.'

Great scholars in the generations following the Geonim have given additional reasons for saying Pirkey Avot.

'It is because the ordinary people gather together for the reading from the Torah at minchah time on Shabat, we teach them the great virtues which are contained in that book' (Machzor Vitry).

'It is a widespread custom to say Pirkey Avot on Shabat, between Minchah and Maariv for the sake of idlers, that they may be brought nearer to the Torah.' (Rabi Meir of Rottenberg).

According to the Sephardi custom this book is read only on the Sabbaths between Pesach and Shavuot. Abudraham says that the reason for this is the fact that these are the days leading up to the giving of the Torah (i. e. this book helps us to improve ourselves so that we are worthy of the Torah).

According to Rabenu Yonah, the Torah abides only among those who have rid themselves of bad qualities and acquired good virtues.

Ohev Israel writes that just as the Children of Israel sanctified themselves between Pesach and Shavuot for the giving of the Torah, so we prepare ourselves to receive the Torah by improving our characters through studying Torah on Shabat.

Midrash Shmuel writes that people are more prone to illness in summer than in winter, so while we heal our souls by study, our bodies too are guarded against sickness.

Pirkey Avot actually contains only five chapters, but an additional one, entitled 'The acquisition of the Torah' was added to it. This chapter is most appropriate for reading on the Shabat nearest to Shavuot when the Torah was given. Even those who are accustomed to read Pirkey Avot throughout the summer months agree that the reading during these six weeks is the most important.

The author of Tikun Issachar writes that when the first day of Pesach falls on Shabat, then in the Land of Israel there are seven Sabbaths between Pesach and Shavuot. (The last day of Pesach in the Diaspora will be 'Isru Chag' in the Land of Israel). When this happens the first chapter of Tractate Derech Eretz Zuta should be read on this seventh Shabbath for its content is similar to that of Pirkey Avot. When we read this on the eve of Shavuot, we remember that 'derech eretz (good manners), precede the Torah.'

Some say that even in the Diaspora when the last day of Pesach occurs on Shabat we should commence reading Pirkey Avot then, and read the afore-mentioned chapter on the eve of Shavuot.

There are some who maintain that Moshe died, not on Shabat at minchah time, but at dusk on Erev Shabat, for we are told that immediately before his death, Moshe wrote a Sefer Torah for each of the tribes, and this he could not have done on Shabat. The two opinions as to exactly when Moshe died can be reconciled as follows: Moshe did indeed die on Erev Shabat at dusk, but because of the sanctity of the Shabat, the Israelites did not allow themselves to think of this tragic event. However when the sun began to set as Shabat drew to its close, they called to mind the calamity that had befallen them. It seemed to them as if Moshe had that very moment passed away. So, ever afterwards the death of Moshe is remembered as if it had taken place towards the end of Shabat.

AVOT

Tractate Avot is part of the Mishnah and belongs to the Seder Nezikin. It comes in between Tractate Avodah Zarah and Tractate Horayot. Why is it placed in this volume of the Mishnah which instructs judges in the statutes and judgements of Israel? 'It is because none are so in need of the ethics propounded in Pirkey Avot as the judges. If ordinary people do not behave in an ethical way, they harm none but themselves, whereas a judge who behaves unethically harms other people in addition to himself (From the introduction of Rambam to *Seder Zera'im*).

The title 'Avot' — fathers — derives from the fact that its contents — ethical behaviour and good manners — have been handed down to us by our fathers and are an integral part of the Torah. They were given to Moshe on Sinai and, like other Laws of the Torah, have come down to us by tradition.

As the teachings expounded in this book are the most important of all the teachings of our Sages of blessed memory, they may be said to be the 'fathers' of all such dicta. All other ethical teachings are derived from these.

Some of the moral lessons in this book are of such a high ethical standing that many a person will feel that it is useless even to attempt to reach such a goal. On the other hand, some of the teachings are so much part of our lives that anyone who disobeys them is obviously an outright sinner. In fact, no Jew would dream of doing so and we might well ask, 'Why were these teachings included in this book ? We would in any case practice them.'

The book itself answers both of these objections. Each chapter is prefaced with a quotation from Tractate Sanhedrin, 'All Israel have a share for the world-to-come.' and ends with a quotation from Tractate Makot, 'The Holy One, Blessed be He, wanted to make Israel worthy. He therefore gave them Torah and many Mitzvot.'

All Israel, that is every single Jew, even the most insignificant, has a share by which he is bound for ever to the world-to-come. Let no Jew say, 'This thing is too lofty, beyond my reach. Only the holiest and purest can attain it. It is not of this world but of the world-to-come.' On the contrary, each individual has within him an unbreakable bond with the world-to-come.

Also let no Jew say, 'What have I to do with the words of the Sages. I know those things by myself and carry them out already.' The Torah contains many laws of this nature, laws which people keep even if they had not been written down. But it was a special act of kindness on the part of the Holy One, Blessed be He, that He commanded us to do these obvious things by His decree. Thus it comes about that not only are we doing something which we want to do, but we are rewarded for fulfilling God's decree.

The teachings of Pirkey Avot are of this nature. Even if they appear simple and obvious, whoever practices them is carrying out the Torah that was given on Sinai and he is rewarded for so doing.

'All Israel has a portion for the world-to-come.' Note that the phrase is worded 'for the world-to-come' and not 'in the world-to-come.' Rabbi Chayim of Volozhin explains that the latter phrase would mean that this place is there already, and every Israelite has a portion in it whether he deserves it or not. But in truth, the meaning is that every one possesses a portion in himself which is *for* the-world-to-come. All Israel has the ability to merit it by deeds.

DISTRESS AND MOURNING AT THE PERIOD OF THE COUNTING CF THE OMER

Irmeyahu the prophet, in reproving Israel said, 'They do not say in their hearts, 'Let us now fear our God who gives the rain, *Yoreh* and *Malkosh* (the former rain and the latter rain) in its due season, Who keeps for us the appointed weeks of the harvest.' Your iniquities have turned away these things and your sins have withheld the good from you.'

The One Who gives the rain, the early rain and the late rain, also has the power to withhold it. Should we not therefore fear Him and refrain from angering Him ? Even after He has saturated the ground with the early rain, and the late rain has fallen on the fields that are full of straw and stubble, as long as the seven weeks of harvest between Pesach and Shavuot have not passed, the world still stands in need of God Who 'keeps the appointed weeks of the harvest' against harmful winds and dews, against blasting and mildew. Should we not fear Him and abstain from provoking Him?

This is especially true of the weeks between Pesach and Shavuot. During these seven weeks, man's livelihood for the whole year hangs in the balance. Will he be blessed with plenty during the ensuing year, or — God forbid — cursed with famine? If Israel deserves good, then God opens for them the storehouses of life and blessing to satisfy their needs for the entire year. But if — Heaven forfend — Israel is not deserving of God's bounty, then the fear of punishment hangs heavily over them at this period.

Because of this we count the days from the time of bringing the Omer, that is from the time of the harvest to the time of the first ripe fruits, that we may note how many of them pass without bringing trouble in their wake. As we count we pray that all these days may pass in peace so that wheat harvest may be safely gathered in to provide abundance for the whole year ahead.

'Why is it that we do not find a single mention of rejoicing in connection with the festival of Pesach? The outcome of the harvest is decided on Pesach and man does not know whether his crops will fail or succeed' (Yalkut Emor).

In Vayikra Raba we read; 'They shall be seven perfect Sabbaths.' When can they be said to be perfect? When Israel carries out the wishes of the Omnipresent.'

These fifty days are a period of continuous judgment and therefore there is continuous anxiety that they should pass smoothly. It is especially important at this time that people should behave properly towards each other and not trifle with one another's honour.

The Holy One, Blessed be He, said, 'I treat you as if you were members of the royal family. You sleep peacefully in your beds while I guard your possessions and provide you with food for the whole year — only that you should be

403

friendly to one another. But you do not behave like this. I will send famine amongst you instead of abundance. Instead of enjoying peace you will be devoured by fiery bolts and many of you will perish of pestilence. Because you did not honour the living, you will have to honour the dead. Is it not better that you show respect for the living, even as I do for you, so that your days be full of goodness and blessing.'

TRAGEDIES WHICH BEFELL DURING THIS PERIOD

Never was there a generation so rich in Torah, in wisdom and in good deeds as that of Rabi Akiva, but see how it was punished because the people did not treat each other with respect. 'Rabi Akiva had twelve thousand pairs of pupils, spread out all over the country from Gevat to Antipatros and all died during a short space of time between Pesach and Shavuot, because they did not treat each other with respect.' (Tr. Yevamot 62).

In later centuries many tragedies befell the Jewish people in Germany at this time of the year. In the year 4856 (1096) many communities were destroyed, adults and children were massacred and the leading scholars were burnt alive as martyrs.

These tragedies were repeated in an even larger scale during the days of Bogdan Chmielnicki — may his name be blotted out — in the years 5408 and 5409 (1648 and 1649). They began with a vicious blood libel and culminated in the shedding of rivers of Jewish blood. These tragic events occurred mainly at this time of the year and although we were sated with troubles, too numerous to record, we remember each one of them. We beseech God's mercy that we may never experience such tragedies again and that we may see our blood avenged, as a reward for improving ourselves and returning to God with all our hearts.

Then the memory of distress and mourning will no longer dominate this period of the year but it will become, instead, a period of gladness and rejoicing and we will enjoy an abundance of all the good things of life. But until that time when we achieve eternal salvation, we cling to our memories of days gone by — days full of tragedies, one following fast on the heels of another.

The author of 'Turey Zahav' expressly mentions the disasters of the year 4856 (1096), during the Crusades in Germany, as a reason for observing the days of the Omer as a period of semi-mourning. This thought finds expression in special hymns which are recited on each Sabbath between Pesach and Shavuot.

Rabenu Yerucham and Ba'al Haturim quote Rav Hai Gaon as their authority for forbidding any work to be done after sunset during the Omer period. 'Between Pesach and Shavuot it is the custom to abstain from work from sunset to sunrise as a sign of mourning for the pupils of Rabi Akiva who died at that time of the year and who were buried at sunset. Since work was forbidden while a burial was taking place, it was usual to arrange the funeral at night time so that people should not be prevented from following their usual livelihood during working hours. 'If a scholar dies, all work is stopped and everyone accompanies him to his final resting-place.'

LAWS AND CUSTOMS CONCERNING THE OMER PERIOD

As a sign of mourning for the twenty four thousand pupils of Rabi Akiva who died at this time of the year, it is customary to observe certain practices, not to celebrate weddings and to let one's hair grow. But one should not miss an opportunity that occurs for saying the blessing 'Shehecheyanu.'

In general, people let their hair grow for thirty three days of the Omer period, but there are different ways of carrying this out. The Sephardim observe these signs of mourning until the thirty fourth day of the Omer. From then on a person may have his hair cut. This is only allowed on the thirty third day if this is Erev Shabat. If the thirty third day

405

occurs on a Sunday, it is not permitted on the previous Friday.

Among Ashkenazim there are various customs regarding the observance of these signs of mourning. Some permit hair to be cut until Rosh Chodesh Iyar. They then abstain until the thirty third day of the Omer, on which day it is permitted, and resume the prohibition until Erev Shavuot. By this means they will have observed this sign of mourning for thirty-three days.

Others observe this half mourning up to the thirty third day only, each person following the custom of his ancestors.

On the thirty third day of the Omer these signs of mourning are abandoned. Tachanun is not said in the morning, nor at minchah on the previous day. Should this day fall on a Sunday, Ashkenazim permit the hair to be cut on the previous Friday.

We have mentioned the custom of abstaining from work from dusk to dawn during the Omer period. Some suggest that it is because of the phraseology of the Torah when describing this Mitzvah 'Seven complete Sabbaths' where the use of the word 'Sabbath' implies a cessation from work.

Some say that this custom applies only to women. This is especially so among Sephardim who say that it is in memory of the righteous women of the generation of Rabi Akiva and his pupils who ceased their work to honor those who died in the plague and busied themseves with their burial.

Although weddings may not take place during the Omer period, it is permitted to arrange a match and to celebrate an engagement, but without too much rejoicing.

Some people undertake to study Tractate Shevuot during this time of the year, because it contains forty nine pages, corresponding to the days of the Omer, and because the name is similar to the festival which marks the end of the Omer — Shavuot.

In writing to friends at this time of the year, it is customary to write the day of the Omer at the head of the letter so that the mitzvah of counting may be constantly to the fore of one's mind.

There are some who remember the tragedies which took place at this time of the year and head their letters with a short prayer after writing the date ; 'In the merit of counting the Omer, may God, the Guardian, shield us from evil decrees.'

THE KEY TO SUSTENANCE

On the Shabat following Pesach when we announce the coming month of Iyar some people have the practice of making the *chalah* in the form of a key and sprinkling it with sesame seeds. This is to remind us of the Manna which began to fall in the month of Iyar and also symbolizes that the key to our livelihood is in God's hands. We pray that God will open for us His store of treasures and pour abundance on us.

GLOSSARY AND INDEX

409

226, 227, 230, 234, 237, 238, 256, 275, 276, 309, 318, 363, 368.

Cohen Gadol — the High Priest 107, 239, 283.

Contra Apionem 332.

Counting of the Omer, see Omer.

Cracow 338.

Crusaders 335.

Cup of Eliyahu 274, 275.

Damascus 342.

Dan, the Tribe of 44.

Daniel 77, 85.

Darchey Moshe 286.

Dedication of the Mishkan 111, 135, 136, 142.

Darius 142.

David, King of Israel 71, 91, 211, 212, 237, 292, 303, 343, 365.

Day of Nikanor, see Nikanor.

Dead Sea 287.

Democrates 332.

Derech Eretz Zuta — a tractate in the Talmudical appendixes 400.

Diaspora 188, 191, 242, 252, 307, 348, 350, 351, 356, 359, 374, 375, 395, 400.

Din pl. Dinim — Halachah law 32, 33, 395.

Divine Presence, see Shechinah.

Dvarim — the Book of Deuteronomy 16, 25, 31, 90, 119, 279, 294, 316

Dvarim Raba, see Midrash Raba.

Edom 36, 37, 45, 329, 330.

Efravim — the Tribe of Ephraim 389.

Egg — of the Seder 248, 249, 251, 255, 264, 284, 287, 303.

Eglah Arufah — 'the-heifer-of-the-broken-neck' prescribed in case of an unsolved murder 102.

Egypt, Egyptian 12-14, 16, 17, 24, 31, 33, 34, 36, 39, 41, 44, 46, 58, 69, 70, 106, 112, 119-121, 123, 125, 126, 128, 129, 149-151, 153, 155, 158-160, 193-195, 197, 204, 206, 212, 222, 223, 230, 233, 235, 250, 253, 254, 257, 259, 260, 261, 265-271, 273, 275, 278-286, 288, 290-304, 307, 311-315, 317, 319, 321-328, 331-337, 347, 359, 361, 362, 367, 368, 375, 381-385, 389-395.

El Erech Apaim — a prayer mentioning the thirteen Divine Attributes 204.

Elazar, Rabi 315, 320.

Eliezer, Rabi 67, 160, 210, 290.

Eliezer Hamodo'i, Rabi 68.

Elifaz 33, 38.

Elim 41, 42.

Eliyahu — Elijah the Prophet, see also Cup of Eliyahu 68, 104, 154, 248, 275.

Emek Habacha 336.

Emor — a portion in the Book of Leviticus 403.

England 335.

Erev Pesach — the day before Passover 129, 130, 156, 166, 169, 171, 181, 182, Ch. 8, 251, 252.

Erev Shabat — Friday, the day before the Sabbath 55, 59, 85, 207, 252, 405, 406.

Erev Shavuot — the day before the festival of Pentecost 406.

Eruv Chatzerot — an act of legal 'mixing' to enable transferring from one 'private domain' to another on Sabbath 204, 239-242.

Eruv Tavshilin — an act of 'mixing' the cooked food prepared for a festival and the